THE
BONA FIDE LEGEND
OF

COOL PAPA BELL

THE BONA FIDE LEGEND OF

COOL

PAPA

SPEED, GRACE, AND THE NEGRO LEAGUES

BELL

LONNIE WHEELER

Abrams Press, New York

Library of Congress Control Number: 2020932374

ISBN: 978-1-4197-5048-9
eISBN: 978-1-64700-111-7

Printed and bound in the United States
1 3 5 7 9 10 8 6 4 2

Abrams books are available at special discounts when purchased in quantity for
premiums and promotions as well as fundraising or educational use.
Special editions can also be created to specification. For details, contact
specialsales@abramsbooks.com or the address below.

Abrams Press® is a registered trademark of Harry N. Abrams, Inc.

ABRAMS The Art of Books
195 Broadway, New York, NY 10007
abramsbooks.com

CONTENTS

AUTHOR'S NOTE

For a while there, it seemed like Cool Papa Bell was the man who would ease me into fiction. He deserved a biography—cried out for one, in fact—but there were good reasons why one had never been completed, starting with a shortage of the raw materials ordinarily used to reconstruct a life. Bell's image derived largely from an oral heritage, inspired by eyeballs and exaggeration, which provided much in the way of theme and tone but precious few snapshots. Without some of the traditional mines to tap—immediate family, old buddies, correspondence, comprehensive records, or attentive reporting— fundamental aspects of his circumstances, routines, interactions, and even his Hall of Fame career simply wouldn't make it to the surface. One capable researcher spent ten years in pursuit of an appropriate monograph, only to be turned away by the chasms and complications.

The solution, I figured, was fiction by dots. The tale of Cool Papa could be told with as much legitimacy as might be mustered, and the gaps painted over with poetic plausibility. A virtual biography, if you will: the Cool Papa Bell of the imagination.

It has been ten years since I first broached this notion with the literary agent on whom I've been depending for decades. He replied by suggesting alternatives, including a conventional biography. Having already reconnoitered that terrain, I packed up my notes and moved on. But after a few other projects and periodic reminders of the gentleman outfielder's irresistible nobility—matched, of course, with the earthy allure of the Negro Leagues—I came crawling back to Papa, determined this time to give stubbornness a chance.

The research proliferated but didn't betray the genre. Waffling, I even batted out a couple of chapters in what was to pass as Bell's narrative voice, testing the conceit on my chief adviser and more casual consultants. They responded with coughs and nudges.

Ultimately, all the nudging turned me face-to-face with this conclusion: For a proper portrait of Cool Papa, the place for imagination was not in *my* mind but the reader's. Fiction it *mustn't* be. Rather, let the absent material play its part. The abiding myth, after all—the player so fast he once stole two bases on a pitchout, so instantaneous he could flip off the light switch and be under the covers before it got dark—is the essence of Bell's gossamer legacy. May that myth be documented where possible and cherished where not.

The essence of Bell, meanwhile, is not the urban legend of his outlandish speed but the epic nature of his unfailing grace, to which fabrication could not do justice. The sharecropper's son, though never far removed from Mississippi poverty or anywhere close to his professional due, became, through it all, an angel of equality and a generous man of enchanting virtue.

"He was the most beautiful ballplayer," reflected Willie Wells, the Hall of Fame shortstop.

"I'd have to say that Cool Papa was the cleanest, most decent man I ever saw," declared "Double Duty" Radcliffe, the famous catcher-pitcher.

"He was the most gentle man I knew from the Negro Leagues," attested Buck O'Neil, the Negro League icon.

"If everybody was like Cool," summed up Judy Johnson, the Hall of Fame third baseman, "this would be a better world."

Bell's ancient ballplayer pals are of course long gone by now, but their voices blend in a rather poignant portrayal, do they not? Without a word of fiction.

LOOKING OVER JORDAN

A S FAST AS HE WAS, THERE WERE PLENTY OF times when it didn't feel that way to Cool Papa Bell; not after his various parts reported in. His knees kept up a steady complaint. His legs in general were so customarily tattered that he taped sponges around the messiest spots to keep the blood and gunk from soaking into his uniform pants. His feet were so chronically sore that he concocted and even sold his own salve, 'Cool Papa' Bell's Foot Ease: "Directions: — Apply on corns for three nights . . . Remove with knife . . ."

But there was nothing slowing him down that day in Mexico City. Looking back on it years later, Cool Papa recalled the heady sensation of being all over the outfield the entire afternoon. It was an unusually big outfield, and a big outfield, to him, was like open road underneath a roaring convertible—better, even, since he had never learned to drive. So it might have been the exhilarating sprawl of grass that put the extra voltage in the Mississippian's step that day. For that matter, it very well could have been the stimulating company of Jimmie Foxx, Rogers Hornsby, and Heinie Manush on the other side. And quite possibly, given his keen sensibilities, the discernible quickening may even have issued from the winds of change that he'd perceived throughout the spring and summer of 1936 and that now, in October, in Mexico, in that heavenly outfield at 7,400 feet, in the presence of all those lightly complexioned Hall of Famers in waiting, were finally at his back.

The Pittsburgh Crawfords, for whom Cool Papa graced center field, began the eventful year as the big cheeses and reigning champions of the Negro Leagues, the latter title having been acquired even as Satchel Paige, their ace and leading attraction, was AWOL in Bismarck, North Dakota, for double the salary and a Buick sedan. The Crawfords had swaggered onto the scene in 1931, owned and assembled by Gus Greenlee, the numbers, bootleg, and entertainment king of the city's Hill District. Bell signed on in 1933, joining Paige, Josh Gibson, Oscar Charleston, and Judy Johnson on a monumental roster considered the greatest in Negro League annals, at the least.

But it wasn't their eminence alone that made the Crawfords, by 1936, the epitome of black baseball. It was an organic synthesis of Paige's theater, Gibson's might, Bell's almost unimaginable speed, Greenlee's signature accommodations, and, most of all, the vigorous sub-society that the Hill District represented. Its epicenter was the Crawford Grill, Greenlee's headquarters, restaurant, jazz club, and vice depot, where Bill "Bojangles" Robinson served as best man for Paige's wedding to a house waitress, the Mills Brothers wore Crawfords uniforms and tossed a ball around in the back alley, Lena Horne sang with Duke Ellington's band while her father ran the numbers operation upstairs, and professional ballplayers kept lookout at the side door for cops and trouble (a duty that Bell declined).

"With Cool Papa Bell flying around the base paths, Josh Gibson drawing accolades as the black Babe Ruth, and Satchel Paige intentionally loading the bases, telling his fielders to sit down, and then striking out the side, Pittsburgh spearheaded the rejuvenation of black baseball during the 1930s," wrote Donn Rogosin in *Invisible Men: Life in Baseball's Negro Leagues*. "Pittsburgh became to black baseball what

The Crawford Grill, heart of the Hill District, 1401 Wylie Avenue, Pittsburgh

Harlem had been to black literature and the arts during the 1920s, the catalyst of a renaissance."

The prosperity of the Grill spawned a sporting analogue on Bedford Avenue, a stylish, boisterous, 7,500-seat ballpark constructed expressly for the Crawfords. At Greenlee Field, where a man could be ejected for taking off his shirt, the amphitheater was bisected by a linear view capturing three of the most magical players in baseball history—Gibson, Paige, Bell—from backstop to fence. When Cool Papa, turned out in no ordinary suit and tie, left the park on foot after three hits, a couple of steals, a ridiculous catch, and another Crawfords victory, ladies gawked and children followed.

It was not a sustainable situation, however, for the simple reason that the Crawfords were, indeed, the epitome of black baseball both on the field and beyond. Unlike so-called organized ball, the Negro Leagues were not administered by buttoned-down, business-schooled, legally advised, advantageously positioned captains of industry. Black-ball owners reflected the markets and customs of neither Wall Street nor Main Street, their bundles made from the commerce of their isolated, underserved communities—overwhelmingly, the same unauthorized trades in which Greenlee trafficked. Business models, such as they were, tended to drift with political climates and police pressure.

It happened that, in 1936, racketeering was under siege around the country. Alex Pompez, the popular owner of the New York Cubans, was sought for his ties to Bronx mob boss Dutch Schultz and fled to Mexico. Greenlee's troubles involved an insider tipping off local authorities when the day's illicit monies were being tallied, an untimely turn of events with his governmental associates on the outs. Their cash flow crimped, the Crawfords' payroll sputtered and their team bus was seized. Hedging his bets, Greenlee redirected some of his attention toward a more manageable asset, light-heavyweight boxing champion John Henry Lewis.

With the ground shifting throughout the Negro National League (now in its second iteration), the '36 season never really found its footing. The Chicago American Giants, the most venerable of the black teams—having been started in 1911 by Negro League patriarch Rube Foster—dropped their affiliation and set out as an independent club. Newark and Brooklyn merged, and the New York Black Yankees joined the unsteady confederation on the fly. The schedule was a shamble. By the East-West All-Star Game in late August—Cool Papa went three for three with a double—the regular season had all but gone to seed.

Breaking from custom, there was no championship playoff in 1936. Instead, the half-season winners, the Crawfords and Washington Elite Giants, pooled their talent and signed up for the prestigious *Denver Post* annual tournament.

The Denver affair was only two years removed from its first all-black entry. Competing against the best white teams this side of the major leagues, with an overwhelming roster that included Bell, Gibson, Paige, Buck Leonard, and Wild Bill Wright, the Negro Leaguers ran the table, seven straight games, blowing out most of their unfortunate opponents—the team from Borger, Texas, had plastic batting helmets made specially for standing in against Paige—and whipping an oil company outfit from Enid, Oklahoma, for the title. The roughnecks had never seen their likes.

The loaded team's veteran manager, Candy Jim Taylor, who directed the St. Louis Stars and Homestead Grays to Negro League championships, declared that the Denver club was the best he'd ever been associated with. Lacking that basis for comparison, Leonard Cahn, a scribe for the sponsoring newspaper, described the magnificent African Americans more loosely as "the cream in your coffee, the icing on your cake, the champagne in your cocktail. They're *class*."

Under the national spotlight, Bell's salient speed drew unprecedented attention. "Cool Papa Bell," reported the *Denver Post*, "made a hit with the fans. He is a streak of lightning going down to first base. Twice he beat out infield hits on balls fielded perfectly." Cool Papa was such a sensation that, to show him off, the festivities included an orchestrated dash around the bases in which he was timed and credited with tying the world record (which he ultimately broke). For winning the tournament's stolen-base crown—it seemed that the only thing stopping him from swiping bases was his propensity to hit triples—he was awarded a fielder's glove and a token of journalistic hyperbole. Wrote C. L. Parsons, the *Post* sports editor, "All these years I've been looking for a player who could steal first base. I've found my man; his name is Cool Papa Bell."

As it happened, the Denver tournament ran concurrent with the Berlin Olympics, where Jesse Owens harried Hitler with four gold medals, and Cool Papa could find a common theme in the two developments. Suddenly the concept of black athletes competing against and even getting the best of white ones seemed a little less unthinkable.

Just two months earlier, rising heavyweight contender Joe Louis had been knocked out at Yankee Stadium by Germany's Max Schmeling, prompting the Third Reich propaganda machine to stamp the fight as a triumph for Hitlerism; *Das Schwarze Korps* called it "a question of prestige for our race." For Bell, the racial hierarchy promoted by the Nazi Party hit close to home, championing the kind of stratified culture he'd long abided in his watchful way, from Deep South segregation to donkey baseball exhibitions (clownish games in which all

The Negro League all-stars who swept to the title of the 1936 *Denver Post* Tournament were hailed as the greatest team to ever grace that prominent annual affair. Among the luminaries were Satchel Paige (front row, third from left), Ray Brown (front row, center), Josh Gibson (front row, second from right), Buck Leonard (middle row, second from left), Cool Papa (middle row, center), manager Candy Jim Taylor (middle row, far right), and Wild Bill Wright (back row, second from right).

but the pitcher, catcher, and batter played astraddle stubborn farm animals) that he discreetly eschewed.

The subsequent weeks, though, were paradigm changers.

For the first decade of his career, beyond the age of thirty, the great center fielder hadn't dared to even dream about playing against or alongside white players at a championship level. There had been postseason exhibitions that exploited the color line and cross-race competition in the California Winter League, but those games proceeded on pretexts of novelty and mischief. Cool Papa took delight in outplaying and even drubbing the big-league teams but never let it show and was never deceived by any implications of doors opening. He might line up against Paul Waner and Dizzy Dean for amusement and extra cash, but never for keeps. The guardians of the game would make certain of that, even as its chief protector, Commissioner Kenesaw Mountain Landis—a former federal judge appointed by Theodore Roosevelt—disavowed any prohibition of black players.

Owens, however, set flags to waving that summer, and stirred so considerable a baseball personage as Horace Stoneham, president of the New York Giants, to proclaim that "in ten years, Negroes will be playing in white organized baseball." As grand as that sounded, the prospect of ten years didn't do a lot for Bell, who would be well into his forties by then. He contented himself with a polar view of the same landscape, assessing for the time being that the moldering of the Negro Leagues might not be altogether lamentable. For all the double standards he'd played through over the years, all the prevailing backwardness he'd tacitly acknowledged, he'd never given up on his idealism: If blackball was unsustainable for economic reasons, so was the color line on moral grounds. Events of 1936 were testifying credibly on behalf of that conviction. Between the Negro and major leagues there was, for the first time, gravitation, however faint.

Throughout the early '30s, newspapers that served black communities—chiefly *the Pittsburgh Courier* and *Chicago Defender*—had been stumping for big-league teams to take on Negro Leaguers. Communist journals pounded on the same theme. But after Owens's rush to glory in Berlin, coinciding as it did with the ringing triumph of the Negro All-Stars in Denver, mainstream voices chimed in conspicuously. "I see no reason why Negroes should not be admitted to major league baseball," wrote Dan Parker in the *New York Daily Mirror*. "If it weren't for them, where would America be in Hitler's Olympics? There is no place for racial discrimination in the American national game."

"Negroes belong in big league baseball competition," seconded Jimmy Powers of the *New York Daily News*. "They have the ability and it is only fair to them as Americans that they be given an equal chance. I believe big league ball would gain added sparkle if the great Negro stars were admitted."

In the meantime, the Crawfords hired Owens himself for a little added sparkle. As a gate attraction, he traveled with the club and ran exhibition races against various humans and horses. The players urged Cool Papa to challenge him, but Oscar Charleston, who managed the club in addition to playing first base—knowing that his proud switch-hitter was not likely to let Owens win—wouldn't allow it, wary of spoiling the spectacle. Finally, Charleston consented to the match race in Owens's hometown of Cleveland, but the gold medalist declined, claiming he hadn't brought his track shoes. Bell's teammates chided Owens for chickening out until Cool Papa prevailed upon them to knock it off because racing horses was humiliation enough for a national hero and Olympic champion.

With paychecks sporadic now, the Crawfords gradually dispersed to their respective homes and exhibition tours. In October, Bell hooked on with a contrived squad of Negro Leaguers who squared off in a series against a collection of major leaguers captained by Rogers Hornsby, a fading, forty-year-old luminary, and featuring Bob Feller of Van Meter, Iowa, the Cleveland Indians' seventeen-year-old pitching prodigy. The games were based in Des Moines to capitalize on the statewide celebration of Feller's rookie season, with a quick detour, by train, to Denver.

Bell set the tone at the very outset with a first-game, first-inning walk and steals of second base and third. He was then driven in by the great Charleston, who was something of a tone-setter himself, often utilizing his fists to that end. On this afternoon he applied them to the home plate umpire for reasons unreported and the ump answered in kind, occasioning field visits from about five hundred keenly interested fans, followed by the police. Thus was extra seriousness lent to the competition, which was won by the African Americans.

Feller and Paige faced off and equaled their billings in the second game. Satchel was familiar with Hornsby by reputation, of course, but not by sight, and requested of Cool Papa that he yell out from center field whenever the famous hitter stepped up. Bell would shout, "Here's Hornsby!" and Satch would strike him out. The scoring commenced only after the respective fireballers had retired for the day, and the Negro Leaguers would again have the better of it, as they subsequently did twice in Colorado and once more back in Des Moines—along the way, the Hornsbys pulled out a victory in Davenport, Iowa—before the series was prematurely ended on account of the autumn chill, or perhaps the mismatch.

But the mixed rivalry was not put summarily to rest. Hornsby and Earle Mack, assistant manager to his illustrious father, Connie, with the Philadelphia A's, had gathered a weightier group of big leaguers to play exhibitions in Mexico, and Gus Greenlee, in turn, marshaled the Crawfords, minus Paige—he no doubt had his own, better-paying gig—for a minority and much-needed share of the take. There were four eventual Hall of Famers on each side (Hornsby, Foxx, Manush, and pitcher Ted Lyons versus Bell, Charleston, Gibson, and Judy Johnson), but the Hornsby contingent was readier; when the Crawfords arrived in the capital city a day before the first game, they were surprised to learn that their high-profile opponents had been there for more than a week, acclimating to the altitude.

The Negro Leaguers were understandably out of sorts in the early innings and trailed 4–3 heading into the ninth, when they rallied for three runs. It was still 6–4 with two outs in the bottom half of the inning, with Manush on base and a two-two count on the rugged slugger Jimmie Foxx, who'd grown up on a Maryland farm and that season had powered a ball clean out of Comiskey Park. Foxx enjoyed the matchups against Negro Leaguers and once declined Lefty Grove's urgent appeal to come to his aid when Charleston charged the mound. "Hell, Lefty, I can't do that," old Double X told his pitcher. "He's my friend." When the Crawfords, or before that the St. Louis Stars, were in Philadelphia, Bell often made a point of finding a seat in the colored section to watch Foxx and the A's play.

From his much better vantage point in Mexico City, Cool Papa witnessed a two-two pitch so well-placed that most observers presumed it strike three. The umpire, however, was not one of them. Grateful for the full count, Foxx then proceeded to slam a game-tying home run into the brisk mountain air. Shortly thereafter, the ump declared it too dark to play on, and the tie stood. In vain, of course, Bell protested that the sun was still in the sky.

That night, after darkness had truly set in, Bell and Charleston were having dinner in an American-style restaurant when Foxx, who appreciated Mexico's racial indifference as much as his Crawford friends did, walked over, joined them, and acknowledged that the disputed pitch should have been called strike three, game over. "I owe you one," he said, and picked up the check.

It was a memorable gesture, given Foxx's coloring and stature, but the fact was that the likes of Bell and Charleston, baseball royalty to an adoring constituency, paid for very few meals in Mexico. After long summers in America's margins, Negro Leaguers found that the daily routines and extracurriculars played out very differently down there, as if stigmas of birth were checked at the border. Bell's best friend in baseball, the great shortstop Willie Wells, once told a journalist from a barber chair in Veracruz, "I am not faced with the racial problem in Mexico. . . . I've found freedom and democracy here, something I never found in the United States. I was branded a Negro in the States and had to act accordingly. Everything I did, including playing ball, was regulated by my color. Here in Mexico, I am a man. I can go as far in baseball as I am capable of going."

And yet, it was an American ballplayer who had just apologized to Bell and bought him dinner. It was an American athlete who had dominated the Olympics on the Führer's turf. American newspapers had called for the abolition of the color line, and it was, famously, an American founding principle, pronounced in the second paragraph of the Declaration of Independence, that declared all men created equal.

Who's to say if Cool Papa carried all of that, and the promise of 1936, onto the field the next time out, and the time after? The big-league side won the second game of the Mexican series, as Hornsby deposited a long fly into the French cemetery beyond the fence, and the third as well, when the ornery old Texan struck a ball to straight-away center with even greater impetus. But that was the day when the wind was at the back of the Crawfords' extraordinary center fielder, whichever direction he turned, and everything above the grass was his. Including Rogers Hornsby's best shot.

Afterwards, as the teams collected their equipment and milled about, Hornsby called out to Cool Papa.

"Come here, Lefty," said Rajah, his pique tempered by admiration. "That was the hardest ball I ever hit. How come you caught it?"

There's no record of Bell's reply. We do know, however, that Earle Mack—presumed to be his father's successor whenever Connie, seventy-three at the time, finally decided to hand over the A's—was thereabouts, and he, too, had something to say to the peerless player he'd been coveting since long before Mexico.

"If the door was open," Mack told Bell, compelled, at last, to confide his forbidden fancies, "you'd be the first guy I'd hire. I'd pay you seventy-five thousand a year. You'd be worth it in drawing power alone."

With that, the Crawfords, their heyday over, headed for the border, back to the land of reality.

CHAPTER ONE

JAMIE NICHOLS

G IVEN THE CHOICE BETWEEN EDUCATION AND baseball, James Nichols figured he'd just move to St. Louis and puzzle it out from there. He was something of a precocious youngster in both fields, said to be seventeen when he rolled out of Mississippi in 1920, although eighteen is more likely.

This is how it will have to be with his story. In the years after James—or Jay or J or J.T. (the *T* for Thomas) or Jamie or Jim or Jimmy, take your pick—rode the Illinois Central to where more people were and became the legendary ballplayer known as Cool Papa Bell, his age was generally calculated from May 1903. There are those, however, who believe that he was perhaps a year or two older, his birthdate having been moved up by his mother, Mary Nichols, so as to keep him out of World War I. For what it's worth, the U.S. Census of 1910, while not incontrovertible—but whose word we're uncertainly taking here—listed James as being born in 1902.

Education was the reason that Mary Nichols urged her son north to the city. The black schools in Oktibbeha County were one-room affairs open only from January to April. Instruction stopped at fifth grade and didn't bother much with reading and writing anyway, inasmuch as jobs requiring those skills were effectively unavailable to the students in question. James's mother, however, was never wholly committed to the status quo.

She was a stern, widowed woman with a considerable Native American legacy—the territory was largely Choctaw until the Treaty of Dancing Rabbit Creek was signed in 1830 and the tribe relocated to Oklahoma—who sharecropped a portion of her father's two hundred acres in the Oktoc community (variously known as Ebenezer) about three miles south of Starkville. Her father, King Hall, was a deacon at Ebenezer Baptist Church, and his farm was substantial enough to keep him on it when relatives opted for land in the Choctaw Nation. His produce, in fact, was favored by local customers. "My grandfather would load up a wagon and start up to Starkville," Bell recalled much later in an oral history interview with the Baseball Hall of Fame, "and people would wait for him and he would sell out before he got there and have to go back and get some more. If you buy a watermelon, he'll give you a cantaloupe for free. That's why they waited for him.

"He was considered a rich man, but he only had about four hundred and fifty dollars in the bank. He buried money," Cool Papa noted. "Indian people believed in burying money."

As fertile as the fields were, Mary Nichols would not plant her children's futures in them. She had kept James in school for two extra years, without a formal curriculum, so that he would receive credit for seven grades, and hoped that he wouldn't stop there, even if it meant leaving Mississippi. Mary impressed upon her innocently handsome, straight-backed son that, while a high school diploma would do him little good in the present, he ought not leave himself unprepared for a better day.

James was not unacquainted with institutional learning. Mississippi State University, situated in Starkville, was then in its formative stage as the Mississippi Agricultural and Mechanical College, which operated a creamery at its experimental station. Oktoc being the dairy capital of the South and James not being inclined toward picking and plowing, he made himself useful driving cows to the college barn for milking, helping them fill the buckets, then carrying the milk to the creamery. There, he caught the attention of a Professor Brown, who experimented with and taught a course in grading cotton and cross-breeding it with corn. Young Nichols was just into his teen years, a mannerly boy with an interest in practical things, and Professor Brown accommodated him with little tasks and a spare seat in the small class, of which the unobtrusive helper was happy to avail himself as long as the good instructor accompanied him through the door. If James sought to enter without his faculty escort, the collegians threw rocks at him.

Now and then the professor would head off to lunch or some such while the class was in progress and ask his de facto assistant to please take over for the next sixty minutes or so, helping the students with such particulars as pulling cotton from the gin and cutting the fringes off, after which he'd record the pertinent measurements. Hence, by a very generous interpretation—one in which it later tickled him to indulge—James, with only an unofficial seventh-grade education, was teaching college at the age of fourteen.

There was much to do at the experimental station, and in the country boy's estimation, every bit of it beat the corn and cotton patches. The juvenile wage at the station was fifty cents a day, but before long he was doing adult work and bringing home the two daily dollars that it fetched. He fed the wheat thresher so rapidly—seventy sacks in half an hour—that the grown men could scarcely keep up, and doubled as the resident elf, the only one skinny enough to be pushed under the machine by his feet in order to pick up a nut that came loose and screw it back onto the bolt. He liked the feeling of being capable. He also liked being out of the weather.

There was, however, a particular activity for which he'd eagerly be *in* the weather. One of his earliest and fondest baseball memories was made at a church picnic in the nearby community of Blackjack. Jamie was ten, barefooted, and befuddling the grown men on the other side with a knuckleball that his older sister, Bessie, had taught him using rag balls tied up with strings and weighted with cotton-seeds. When he came to bat, though, a large woman in attendance, fearful for the little fellow's safety, rushed up, set him on her shoulder, and hauled him off. Only after the others assured her that he wouldn't get hurt did she finally place him back at whatever was serving as home plate, whereupon he ripped the first pitch for a sharp single. James thought he'd never be happier until the game ended and a party of pretty girls came running his way with a massive piece of chocolate cake. At that moment he could envision baseball in his future.

As to what form that might assume, he had no notion. For black kids in Oktibbeha County, the closest thing to organized ball was community competition divided into three age groups. Representing Ebenezer, James played in the youngest class until a few of his older brothers, or half brothers, moved to St. Louis and he stepped up into the void.

We should, at this point, clarify the brother situation as best we can. Most of them, including Robert, Fred, and Sammie, were Bells and lived on a nearby farm with their father, Jonas Bell, and his wife, Patsie. Jonas Bell was also James's father from a liaison with Mary Nichols in the decade or more between the death of her first husband (she was sixteen when she was wed to Samuel Nichols, who was ill at the time and survived only a month more) and the marriage to her second. So Robert, Fred, and Sammie, reliable workers and enthusiastic ballplayers, were half brothers to James. But L.Q., often called Louis—also older than James, and another family member who knew his way around the bases—was James's full brother, and he, too, was raised in Ebenezer by Mary Nichols. Louis was the third-oldest and James the middle child of the seven who filled the little clapboard farmhouse their industrious mother rented.

For all the makings of awkwardness, it appears that the two households shared a close, cooperative coexistence, and brotherhood was not mitigated by any biological technicality. This is a testament to the character of the half brothers, because Mary Nichols would brook no bad actors in the company of those in her care. In that regard, James and other Nichols children considered her gratuitously mean for not allowing them near her brother, a charming thief, and in tacit protest they would conspire with the forbidden uncle to meet up furtively for rabbit hunting.

When Robert, Fred, Sammie, and L.Q. left for St. Louis, perhaps not all at once, James wished to go as well, but he wasn't yet old enough to secure a suitable job. Shortly thereafter, Robert and Sammie were sent to France with the 816th Pioneer Infantry, an outfit of black soldiers who got shot at a lot while they helped the engineers on the battlefields with things like building roads, bridges, and hospitals and digging trenches, latrines, and graves.

James, in the meantime, helped with whatever was asked of him at the experimental station—blending short staple cotton with long, or turning white corn blue, for example—and did a little experimenting of his own after hours, developing a slow, tantalizing curveball to supplement his knuckler. A men's team in an ambitious little burg called Artesia, several hills and a county over, recruited him in the hope of beating Starkville, which subsequently happened more than once.

The youngster's hitting, though, was less distinctive—a bit timid, actually. His priority was the avoidance of striking out, that skill having been magnified by an older cousin who was James's only link to professional baseball. Cousin Dave had a bum leg from a bullet wound, as Jamie understood it, and by whatever duty or happenstance rode the trains around the eastern half of the country. When the limping traveler returned to Oktibbeha County from a spring or summer sojourn, his wide-eyed disciples would spread out under a pecan tree for Sunday tales of the big cities and great players, such as Walter Johnson and Christy Mathewson, lustrous pitchers against whom no batter could touch the ball, and Ty Cobb and Honus Wagner, magical hitters who never struck out. James comprehended that his relative's shade-tree hyperbole didn't really compute—somewhere along the line Mathewson would have to pitch to Wagner, and what then?—but he resolved, nevertheless, to ward off strike three as a matter of principle. He comprehended, also, that these great ballplayers were universally and immutably white. For that matter, so were those who played for the Agricultural and Mechanical College.

Mary waited until Robert and Sammie were discharged before making her pitch for James to join them in St. Louis and enroll in evening school. With or without educational considerations, the subject of leaving Mississippi was, in fact, a standard one in the local black community. The years between 1900 and 1920—roughly the span of James's life at that point—still represent the only period on record in which Oktibbeha County's population has decreased, coinciding as it did with the start of the Great Migration of African Americans leaving the rural South for jobs in the industrial Northern cities. Before 1910, 90 percent of the United States' black citizens lived in the South. At mid-century, the figure was down to 68 percent and still dropping rapidly, bottoming out in 1970 with just over half of the country's African Americans remaining in Southern states.

But while, overall, employment was the principal reason for pulling up stakes and schooling figured in as well, racial violence was a fact of regional life that further informed Mary Nichols. Earlier in the decade, an Oktibbeha black man accused of assaulting a white woman (whose surname happened to be Bell) was lynched by a white mob before the sheriff could take him into custody. It was not an anomaly, nor, for the Nichols household, the most unsettling local atrocity. As an adult, Cool Papa confided to his St. Louis nephew, journalist Ken Webb, that his flight from Mississippi stemmed at least in part from the unprosecuted murder of an uncle whose farmland was coveted by white farmers who left his body straddling a fence.

All of that notwithstanding, James was now reluctant to leave Oktoc. He was having a fine time beating Starkville and generally enjoying his provincial status as the left-handed wunderkind of shape-shifting curves and knuckleballs. Even his batting, while still not especially lusty—and, unlike his throwing, right-handed—was invariably satisfying, for he'd found that the balls he put in play rarely made it to first base before he did. As it happened, his unwillingness to strike out was a splendid match for the conspicuous speed with which he was still coming to terms.

There was an aspect of the local terrain, however, for which his tolerance was wearing thin. Jim Crow policies prohibited black teams and players from using the well-kept fields available to whites and included the prospect of being arrested for such impertinence. James's penchant for common sense—not to mention his affinity for baseball—made it difficult to process such a state of affairs, which, in turn, softened his resistance when his St. Louis brothers urged him in their direction. Word from home had reached them about the pitching prodigy that their very own Jamie had become, and they happened to know a nearby team that would welcome such a fellow.

They even sent money for the train ticket and assured Mary that they'd get him into night classes. Once James had safely arrived in St. Louis, the brothers moved him in with their sister, ushered him to a job where most of them worked—the St. Louis Independent Packing Company, a sprawling, stinking, sixteen-acre facility at Choteau and Vandeventer that processed pork, beef, and mutton—and presented him as twenty years old, which was the cutoff for adult wages, fifty-three cents an hour. The meat man asked him why his last name was Nichols when his brothers were Bells, and James explained that he'd been raised by his mama down the road.

What's your father's name?

Jonas Bell.

Then your last name is Bell.

And so it became.

It's apparent that James was already butchering cows and hogs when he joined his brothers on the Compton Hill Cubs, an African American semipro team that played on Sunday afternoons before lively crowds of up to a couple thousand people and donated the proceeds to local churches after the players received their $20 apiece. On October 15, 1920, his name—his *new* name—appeared in a newspaper for what is believed to be the first time. It was a black publication, the *St. Louis Argus,* under the headline of CUBS WIN AGAIN:

The Compton Hill Cubs defeated the East St. Louis Cubs Sunday, October 10, 15 to 4. The feature of the game was J. Bell, pitching, and R. Bell, catching, for the Compton Hill Cubs, who have won 18 out of 22 games. The same teams will play on the East side this Sunday. The last Sunday's game was for the benefit of Calvary Baptist Church.

CHAPTER TWO

THE SLAUGHTERHOUSE

T HIS IS THE STAGE OF JAMES BELL'S JOURNEY at which we might imagine his baseball ambitions burning fiercely inside him. Ambition, however, is not so easily discerned across the generations; it traffics in context. Bell delighted in the game, and it retained a significant place in his plans, but the fact was those plans were being quite nicely realized on Sunday afternoons with the Compton Hill Cubs. He was playing alongside older brothers whom he looked up to, in front of spirited, appreciative crowds, for take-home pay that nearly matched his weekly wages at the slaughterhouse. What else *was* there?

That's not to say there wasn't better baseball being played around St. Louis. Like Chicago, Boston, and Philadelphia, there were two major-league teams in town—New York had *three*—and in 1920 the Cardinals, even with Rogers Hornsby claiming his first of six straight National League batting titles, were the lesser of them. The St. Louis Browns of the American League, whose distinguished first baseman, George Sisler, that year set a record for hits (257) that stood until

Ichiro Suzuki broke it in 2004, were more viable both competitively and economically.

The Browns played at Sportsman's Park and were joined there in July 1920 by the Cardinals, whose old wooden stadium had already caught afire twice. A northside landmark in which black fans were restricted to the right-field pavilion, Sportsman's Park was situated at Grand and Dodier, in close proximity to the city's prevailing African American neighborhood, locally known as the Ville. In the decade to come, the Ville would swell from 8 percent black to 86 percent and throb with electric streetcars (some left over from the 1904 World's Fair), gambling halls, and ladies of the evening singing blues on the sidewalks.

At the turn of the century, St. Louis's black population was second only to Baltimore's among American cities. When its growth accelerated with the Great Migration, the snarls of white citizens precipitated in 1916 the passing of a local referendum that prevented the purchase of a home by any buyer of a race different from 75 percent of the neighborhood in question. It was the first legislation in the country to sanction segregated housing, and although it was invalidated the following year by a Supreme Court decision in a related Kentucky case, its spirit was preserved by racial covenants in which homeowners of a particular St. Louis block or subdivision would agree in writing never to sell the house to an African American.

As intended, this served to artificially isolate the black citizens and severely restrict the areas available to those who continued to stream in lugging the baggage of Southern culture. Some settled on the other side of the river in East St. Louis, where in July 1917 nine whites and somewhere between thirty-nine and a hundred-something blacks were killed in a race riot that sprang from labor tensions and lasted for most of a week. A black baby was tossed into a fire, locals were hung from streetlamps, and police shut down the bridge that provided an escape route into St. Louis. When frightened African Americans attempted to swim across the Mississippi, they were shot at by white folks with rifles.

To be near the packing plant, the Bells lived south of the Ville, across the Market Street divide between north and south St. Louis.

Sportsman's Park was not out of their reach, but this predated the advent of stadium lights, and if the Bell men worked day shifts there would have been little opportunity to watch Hornsby or Sisler from the right-field pavilion, especially with games of their own on Sundays. Nor did they go out of their way to catch a great player whom many consider the equal of Hornsby, Sisler, and, while we're at it, Ty Cobb, with whom he was often compared.

At the very time when James was enlisting in the Great Migration, a burly pitcher/manager/executive named Rube Foster, in an administrative effort to stop black professional players from their serial hopscotching between teams, was organizing and introducing the Negro National League. Its members included the St. Louis Giants, whose roster, for part of the 1920 season and all of the next, featured the magnificent and infamously combative center fielder Oscar Charleston—"the black Ty Cobb," as some called him. But the brand-new NNL and most of its franchises, including St. Louis, were widely underpublicized. Moreover, Giants Park was located north of the Ville and farther north of the Bells, to whom, consequently, the team's presence, along with Charleston's, was only faintly noted.

And so, with no higher station compelling him, James Bell represented the Compton Hill Cubs in relative contentment, but for one small item. Robert was considered the family's best player at the time—he'd been to spring training with the esteemed Detroit Stars of the NNL—and it had been generous of him to take up the catcher duties in spite of being left-handed (like most of the Bells), but he was not sufficiently self-assured at that position, or sufficiently indifferent about getting his fingers smashed, to allow Jamie to administer his knuckleball willy-nilly. Little brother was instructed, rather, to keep the blame thing under wraps until it was required for certain strike threes.

Bells typically occupied the top third of the Cubs' crackerjack lineup—although young James, as a rule, was not so prominently slotted—and it wasn't uncommon for all five brothers to be penciled in at once. Louis, however, sometimes appeared in the box score as L. Nichols, which leads one to speculate—since his original surname hadn't been overridden by the boss—that he, unlike the others, didn't work at the meat plant. Unencumbered by full weeks of repackaging livestock, Louis becomes the top suspect in the stumper about which brother ran a restaurant.

In any event, Louis manned second base for Compton Hill; Sammie, whom the brothers called Turkey, held down right field; Robert played the outfield when he wasn't catching; and James/Jamie/Jay did the same when he wasn't on the mound. On those occasions the pitching was carried out—in an entirely different fashion—by brother Fred, who answered to "Lefty." Fred Bell was tall and loose and threw as hard as Satchel Paige, according to the keen observer who was the brother of one and later the roommate of the other.

But at some point in the summer of 1921, the family found itself unable to muster a majority when the Cubs took the field. The missing Bell was Robert, who had been afforded a tryout with the St. Louis Giants. He plunged into the drills with characteristic gusto and little regard for the stitches in his arm, which during the course of the day were somehow torn open so malignantly that it put his ballplaying in peril for the short term at least.

Although a war veteran, Robert was only twenty-four years old at the time, and owing in large part to his comparative worldliness—he knew the urban landscape in ways that his half brother, fresh off the farm, couldn't possibly—his baseball aspirations ran deeper than James's. Years later Cool Papa would reflect whimsically upon how much his talented role model would have loved Negro League life. But unlike the newly minted James Bell at nineteen, Robert was not unburdened in his decision-making. He was married, and he had established a moderate amount of upward mobility at the packing plant. What's more, in light of his life experience, he considered himself a central figure in the resettlement of family members. And so, with his arm out of commission for the time being, Robert Bell made the solemn choice to leave baseball behind.

Such was James's admiration for Robert that, when 1922 came around, he was thinking hard about following big brother's example. Ditching baseball would allow him to take on weekend overtime shifts at the slaughterhouse and maybe get serious about night school, where he'd only dabbled, mostly in the winter months. (He blamed that on the large park across the street from where he lived, in which, spring through fall, people played ball through the twilight hours.) He'd all but made his mind up when he was approached in late April by the East St. Louis Cubs, the familiar team that had flailed so fruitlessly at his sundial curveball. The Cubs had a game arranged with the St. Louis Stars and wanted James to pitch it for them.

The Stars had just popped up as a brand-new iteration of the St. Louis Giants, still in the Negro National League but under different ownership and in the process of building a ballpark at Compton and Market, convenient to the Ville and even closer to the Bells. James figured there'd be no harm in pitching one little game against the Stars, whose pending relocation made them suddenly a team of interest. Besides, his brother would be joining him. *Which* brother—Fred or Sammie or even Robert, healed up and seeking one final fling—is unclear; the box score notes a Bell in the outfield but supplies no first initial.

The result was humbling for the Ebenezer junkballer, an 8–1 defeat, but he did strike out a fair number of professionals and smack a long fly off the right-field fence, enabling him to take a spin on the bases and display the stunning swiftness for which he was acquiring a local reputation. The year before, a report in the *Argus* about one of his Compton Hill games had described Bell as "the Cubs' speedy young southpaw," and it was assuredly not referring to his fastball.

For their part, the Stars may or may not have arrived in East St. Louis with knowledge of the young southpaw's speediness, but they positively left with it. Before James and his brother could start back across the river, the Negro Leaguers had offered to take the kid along on their upcoming road trip, reasoning that if his pitching wasn't too flashy, his feet certainly were, and perhaps they could be put to use in the outfield if a need arose.

This unforeseen development set off a whole new phase of mulling over. The Stars would pay James $90 a month, which was satisfactory but slightly less than he could earn at Independent Packing, where by this time he was working in the hog gang, which looked after the guests of honor as they were trucked in, penned up, shot, chained at the legs, hung upside down, stabbed, bled, shaved, gashed, gutted, hosed, frozen, and butchered into hams, loins, ribs, chops, and whatnot. The part-time pitcher was tasked with shaving the swine's extremities after they'd been run through hot water to get most of the hair off. The tool of the trade was a knife, and there was an unfortunate occasion when his cousin, working next to him, accidentally slashed Bell's non-pitching hand, leaving one of his fingers numb for a couple of years. He moved on to heads and was due soon for a transfer to the sheep gang, which pleased him, but just as imminent was warmer, steamier weather, when the stench in the stockyards and killing buildings was especially rank. In light of that prospect, the appeal of a long road trip—which it was sure to be, with two or three months of construction still remaining on the stadium—was not inconsiderable.

There was also the matter of James's schooling, which might have been easily dismissed had not Mary Nichols been visiting at the time. True to form, she argued on education's behalf, adding a word about his steady paycheck and throwing in maternal concerns about her sensitive son separating from his family to ride off with a crowd of older, footloose, disreputable strangers. Her reservations were shared by the sister he lived with, who in fact had brought the situation to her attention. To mollify those worries, Louis, whom Mary trusted and whose restaurant seemed to be a going concern—and who was not oblivious to the uncommon aptitude his younger brother showed for the family game—had vowed to make sure that James always had a dollar in his pocket and a place to come back to.

For James, the seminal moment demanded something of a choice between his mother and brothers, not to mention baseball and hog guts. In addition to Louis's encouragement, there was Robert, who had sacrificed his dream when he gave up baseball for responsibility; maybe this was a way to give him back just a little bit of it. As for his mother, well, she had never walked by a St. Louis slaughterhouse in late June.

Besides, he would still send her money once a month, which he did for the rest of her days.

CHAPTER THREE

TRICKY BALL

A MONG THE SEVERAL SEASONED PITCHERS AT his disposal, Big Bill Gatewood, the forty-year-old manager of the new St. Louis Stars, counted himself, if it should come to that. He still had spit left for his spitball, emery boards for his emery ball, and plenty of moxie piled up from his formative years with the far-flung teams he'd played for, a number that would reach fifteen before he was finished. Ten of those were named the Giants in one form or another, most of them predating the official Negro Leagues fathered by Rube Foster, alongside whom Gatewood had pitched with the famous Leland Giants and more famous Chicago American Giants.

By 1922, however, the authority commanded by Gatewood's stature alone—the imposing Texan stood 6 feet 7 inches and weighed 240 pounds in his prime—was best put toward shepherding the obstreperous players under his watch. There was George Scales, a quarrelsome infielder who once lost two teeth in a dispute with his roommate, occasioning the pair to sleep facing each other, gripping weapons. There was wispy outfielder Charlie Blackwell, a batting artist to whom neither size nor sobriety had yet demonstrated its merits.

There was ornery pitcher Bill Drake, nicknamed "Plunk" for obvious reasons, who avoided winter ball in certain Caribbean countries for fear of unchecked reprisals by defenders of players he'd plunked over the summer. Steel Arm Dickey, a talented pitcher from Tennessee, was a purveyor of Prohibition moonshine who, while back home following the season, was stabbed to death in an incident described three different ways in three different newspapers (and a fourth by Bell, who heard that the stabber was a bootlegger to whom Steel Arm had neglected to turn over some agreed-upon proceeds). Also under Gatewood's supervision, of course, was the demure young left-hander from Mississippi.

Bell's diffidence should not be mistaken for anxiety or lack of self-assurance. For one thing, he'd never encountered a baseball scenario that he couldn't reasonably manage, and for another, Negro ball, as far as he knew, was a proposition far removed from Cobb, Wagner, Mathewson, Johnson, Hornsby, Sisler, and the awe they invoked. Success in his new endeavor was hardly the stuff of his dreams. When he joined the Stars on the eastbound train, he'd already inhaled the reward, having outstripped the stinking business of the slaughterhouse.

James might have kept to himself on the ride to Indianapolis—his first destination—if duty had not directed his saltier teammates to make the new kid mildly miserable. But the verbal abuse seemed practically polite to a fellow who'd spent long days in the company of split-open hogs, and he no doubt suffered it patiently. Gatewood, meanwhile, turning to the more pertinent aspects of rookie life, recommended to his unaffected charge that, when they went about their business with the Indianapolis ABCs, he sit tight and take it all in for a while, because he'd surely be intimidated by the crowds on hand. Bell tacitly doubted that.

Sure enough, it wasn't the venue or the scene or the magnitude of it all that gave him pause at Washington Park. He found the atmosphere no more distracting than the clamor of a Compton Hill game, or even Artesia versus Starkville. And yet, there was, indeed, an element in play that stirred his humble regard: *the other side*.

The Stars were a fair-enough ball club, but to the former fetcher of loose nuts in the threshing machine, the Indianapolis team was a revelation. Among the ABCs—so named in reference to their founder, the American Brewing Company—were three fellows in particular who unwittingly conducted the first classes in James Bell's Negro League education: the young but cagey catcher Biz Mackey, a future Hall of Famer who took obvious pleasure in discomfiting batters with his banter and throwing out base stealers straight from his squat; first baseman Ben Taylor, one of four brothers from South Carolina who would make significant marks in blackball; and Oscar Charleston.

Presuming he knew that Charleston had spent the previous season with the St. Louis Giants, we can imagine Bell marveling at what he'd so regrettably missed by not going to see the broad-chested, swashbuckling slugger in action. More than half a century later, he would identify Charleston as the best all-around player he'd ever seen—John McGraw, the great New York Giants manager, made a similar observation—and a better center fielder than even Willie Mays. He could still see Oscar turning a flip before catching a high fly, snagging balls behind his back, powering home runs with his left-handed slash, collecting a toll from whoever might dare to tag him out, getting hauled off for slugging an umpire, and tossing Cuban soldiers around the infield when they came charging out of the stands after he'd knocked down the home team's shortstop and second baseman. Cool Papa didn't see Charleston pull the hood off a Ku Klux Klansman in Indiana, but he'd heard the story often enough to easily believe and certainly enjoy it. The so-called black Ty Cobb was not an especially big man in stature, but he was extraordinarily strong, fearless to a fault, and the toughest customer Bell ever knew, with the possible exception of Josh Gibson.

For three days, James watched earnestly as the ABCs pounded on St. Louis, which his teammates answered by pounding on *him*; also spitting on him, stepping on him, and pushing him out of the way in the shower, since, after all, he hadn't *done* anything. Between innings of the fourth game, in which Indianapolis was roughing up the Stars' best pitcher, Deacon Meyers, and the score was nine to nothing, Gatewood,

Oscar Charleston was the first great player whom Bell opposed, and Cool Papa never
laid eyes on a better one. Or a tougher one.

thinking to preserve his ace for a better day, finally told the kid on the
end of the bench to get in there.

If Bell was visited by apprehension, knowing that the fearsome
Charleston would be coming to bat just ahead, he opted to supplant
it with gamesmanship. The slugger's advantages—in addition to his
reputation—were roaring confidence and consummate talent. Bell's
was unfamiliarity, involving wrinkly, lollygagging pitches that met
none of the standard expectations.

So he pulled out the knuckleball, which Charleston wasn't
prepared for (strike one), and then the screwball that he'd been
working on—which he called an in-drop because it broke in the
opposite direction of the outgoing curveball—and Charleston
wasn't prepared for *that* (strike two), and then the big, tantalizing
curve that took its sweet time reaching the plate, by which point
Charleston had already completed his sweeping left-handed swing

(strike three). But he hadn't yet chucked his bat in anger, which immediately followed.

The next batter was Ben Taylor, who was just as left-handed as Charleston, which presents an especially difficult challenge when the pitcher uses the same hand in the perpetration of funk. The South Carolinian's luck was much like the black Ty Cobb's, except that instead of throwing his bat Taylor rubbed his eyes and muttered that there must be something wrong with them. In the Stars' dugout, Big Bill chuckled and said rather loudly, "Well, Ben, you ain't never seen a curve like that before."

NEGRO LEAGUE TEAMS tended to play other Negro League teams on the weekends, so as to ensure travel time between series and enable working people to attend. To capitalize on the days between, they regularly stopped along the way for informal or exhibition games against local outfits of varying grade.

The Stars, for example, were headed from Indianapolis to Chicago to take on Rube Foster's redoubtable American Giants, which would carry them in the general direction of Fort Wayne, Indiana, home of a semipro team known as the Colored Giants. The Fort Wayne game was the type for which, later on, an appearance by Satchel Paige would be touted on posters and in newspaper notices, and if he hadn't taken off fishing, Satch would toy with the townies for three innings or so and *then* take off fishing. But there was no Satchel on the St. Louis Stars, and, to rest his mainstays, Gatewood assigned the start to the pitcher he'd need least in Chicago. That, of course—notwithstanding the Indy business with Charleston and Ben Taylor—was Bell.

James had pitched to only a few batters when his catcher, Dan Kennard, realized that the Colored Giants were not about to connect with his dawdling curveball. It was as if they were swinging at the song of a nightingale. Seeing no reason to trade punches with the knuckleball, Kennard simply called for curve after curve, which resulted in strikeout after strikeout.

By the bottom of the sixth inning, the Stars led eleven to nothing, the sky was about to open up, and the home team hadn't managed a hit yet. Suddenly, with two outs and no umbrellas, Blackwell and his outfield buddies took it upon themselves to make a dash for shelter. The next batter was the Fort Wayne pitcher, Dicta Johnson, who'd played for both the ABCs and American Giants, and he poked a fly ball to center field that fell unchallenged and had the run of the place. It kept rolling, Johnson circled the bases, the no-hitter was gone, so was the shutout, the rain took over, the game was ended, and the winning pitcher—whose work, according to the *Fort Wayne Journal-Gazette*, "was of high caliber, he displaying fine control and a good curve"—slept cozily on the way to Chicago.

RUBE FOSTER'S FATHERHOOD of the Negro Leagues pertained not merely to their structure but to their style as well. The teams under his direction schemed and scratched for every base, emphasizing speed, resourcefulness, and manifold bunting. In one game, it was said, Foster, orchestrating from the dugout in his suit and roadster cap, watch chain across his vest, pistol in his coat pocket, waving or tapping or puffing on his corncob pipe to cue the plays, ordered eighteen bunts in a row.

The American Giants availed themselves, naturally, of all the traditional bunts—sacrifices, squeezes, drags, etc.—and if, with a runner on first base, the other team's third baseman was charging in to field a sacrifice bunt and not paying proper attention to his station, Rube would call for a *steal* and bunt, in which event, often as not, the runner swiping second would just turn left and keep on trucking to third. As hard as he worked that pipe—sometimes he did it as a decoy, the real sign coming from somebody else on the bench—Foster had to change the signs virtually every day.

He was a hefty man, having "let myself go" while still a brilliant pitcher—the smartest there was, according to Honus Wagner. Perhaps the extra weight made him extra-sensitive to pesky players who couldn't hit him but forced him, instead, to scramble off the mound and field his position. As a manager, Foster solicited speed and knew just what to do with it. The machinations deriving from the Chicago bench were, in fact, so sacred and serious that he would tolerate no laxity on it—no cursing, untucked shirts, eating peanuts, spitting tobacco, or smoking or even *holding* cigarettes. (Cigars were okay.)

Rube's objective, it seemed, was to drive the other team crazy. In St. Louis generations later, Cool Papa chuckled at the irony as Whitey Herzog successfully managed the Cardinals with a similar approach and the media called it Whiteyball.

Bell's name for it was "tricky baseball," which he enthusiastically studied in Chicago in his second week of Negro League classes. At Schorling Park on the South Side (named for part-owner John Schorling, who ran a saloon nearby), Foster had customized the infield by wetting it down to deaden the ball and raising ridges into the foul lines so that bunts would stay fair. His fastest player, Jimmie Lyons, was proficient at drag-bunting the ball along the first-base line, often crossing the bag without a throw. Other American Giants, including second baseman Bingo DeMoss and even Cristóbal Torriente, a power-hitting outfielder from Cuba, thrived in Foster's audacious game.

The weaponization of fast feet got James's attention, especially in concert with Chicago's baseball intelligence. The whole fusion—the electricity of speed and brains, in synergy, in action, on a ballfield—brought the game to light. Suddenly he could see himself in that circuit. He could see himself on that *team*.

For two days the American Giants ran wild. Bell was awed when Foster's dazzling squad won the first game 15–4 without hitting a ball beyond the infield. The second, at least, extended into extra innings, and when it was over, Gatewood dropped his big hand on the rookie's shoulder and told him he'd be pitching the next day.

James couldn't wait. It would be the kind of baseball he was wired for.

His comfort level kicked up another notch when the Stars scored five runs in the top of the first inning against Richard "Big" Whitworth, a former ace whose well-known whiskey habit, occasionally accommodated between innings, was perhaps catching up with him. Tall and powerful, Whitworth was, however, slow afoot, which did not go unnoticed by Bell, who extended the rally by successfully bunting with two strikes. It was a piece of trickery—requiring, of course, the skill to keep the ball in fair territory, lest it become strike three—straight out of Foster's playbook.

In part to test the unfamiliar pitcher, presumably, the American Giants came out bunting as well. James threw out DeMoss in the bottom of the first, and when Jimmie Lyons dropped one down between the mound and first base, Bell flashed to the ball, scooped it up, took after Lyons, and tagged him on the back. The unsuspecting Chicago star looked around and said, "Who touched me out?" From the dugout somebody yelled, "The pitcher did!" From his reaction, it appeared that Lyons had never considered that possibility.

Bell's curveball and fielding—in all, he foiled half a dozen bunts and slaps—kept the American Giants in check, and the Stars still led 5–2 when Torriente came to the plate in the bottom of the seventh with two outs and a runner on third base. On a two-two count, Kennard, the prudent catcher, summoned up the courage to call for a knuckleball. As the pitch floated in, spinless and fickle, Torriente let loose a wild left-handed swing that missed emphatically. The ball landed in the dirt, where Kennard, grinning broadly, snatched it up and tagged the future Hall of Famer where he stood, humbled and twisted.

An inning later Chicago's hopes were rekindled by a leadoff single from Lyons, but James promptly picked him off first base. That seemed to validate the newcomer's arrival. When he returned to the dugout, Sam Bennett, one of the Stars' more traveled players—along the way he'd given the incomparable Tris Speaker some pointers about playing the outfield—approached collegially and said to Bell, "Hey, kid, you're mighty cool out there."

Soon after the Stars had secured their 6–2 victory, Foster walked over to the visitors' side, sought out the fuzzy-cheeked lefty who'd beaten the American Giants at their own game and asked him if he'd ever care to play in the outfield. "Yes, sir," James replied. "I like to play every day, as much as I can." That part of the conversation went no

The paternal Rube Foster was the architect of not only the Negro Leagues but "tricky ball" as well, which to Cool Papa was equally monumental.

further, but Foster, ever the impresario, proceeded to set up a race, right then and there, between Bell and Lyons, about seventy-five yards down the right-field line.

That was fine with James, although it occurred to him that Lyons, stockily built and famously indomitable—the year before, he had fallen three floors down an elevator shaft and returned to the field in four days—was wearing the most notorious pair of spikes in the league, while here *he* was in his dollar-fifty sneakers. Then again, those sneakers were undefeated. And they remained that way, rather easily, at the expense of the American Giant who, just seconds before, had been considered the fastest man in the Negro Leagues.

Foster enjoyed that immensely, in spite of his own player going down. He threw his arm around Mary Nichols's astonishing son—engulfing him, nearly twice the size—and told him to stop in at the Spalding sporting goods store before he left Chicago, pick out the best set of spikes in the house, have the clerk put them on Rube Foster's account, and pay him back whenever he could; and if he couldn't, that would be all right. The next day Bell strode out of Spalding with a pair of featherweight shoes made from kangaroo hide, one white, the other yellow. They cost $21, about as much as he made in a week with the Stars.

As graciously as he treated Bell, Foster sang a different tune in his own players' ears that evening, holding them at the park for a brisk extra workout. He was especially upset about the two-strike bunt. "Here's this young man, him just a teenager," he railed, "and he pulled that play on us!" The upshot was that the American Giants thrashed St. Louis twice more before the Stars headed off to Kansas City.

The westbound train found Bell's teammates with less compara-tive rank to lord over their junior associate. *He* was the one with the snazzy new shoes. James would just as soon have dozed off until his stomach spoke up—after the transformative trip out of Missis-sippi on the Illinois Central, he never again rode a train he couldn't immediately fall asleep on—but some of the fellows were fussing over him, reading aloud from a newspaper article about a certain new left-handed pitcher for the Stars.

To their amusement, the sudden celebrity didn't lessen Bell's interest in a good snooze. They were reminded of what Sam Bennett had said to him in the dugout after the greenhorn had picked Jimmie Lyons off first base. Seizing on Bennett's remark, one of the pitchers, Jimmy Oldham, proposed that they start calling him "Cool." The veterans nodded and chuckled, and then Gatewood said, "Nah, that's not enough. . . . Cool *Papa.* That sounds better."

It seemed to James that he'd been acquiring new names right and left since he got to St. Louis. This one was particularly unlikely, him being, in his own mind, a far cry from either of those things. But there was a pleasant ring of camaraderie to it, three beats of brotherhood. Maybe, if she were to see it that way, his mother would be pleased to know that her Jamie was not entirely without family in his unfore-seen new life.

The bond, it turned out, was already stronger than he could have imagined. Later that very week, word got out that Rube Foster had contacted Dick Kent, the Stars' freewheeling new owner, and offered him *seven players* for James Bell. When he heard about it, the former Compton Hill Cub couldn't fathom why Foster would offer seven American Giants for a soft-tossing, tenderfoot left-hander.

Or, even more perplexing, why Kent would turn him down.

CHAPTER FOUR

THE TURKEY STEARNES EFFECT

W HEN IT FINALLY OPENED IN JULY 1922, on property later occupied by Harris-Stowe State University, Stars Park was easily accessed by trolley lines that served Market Street and midtown. Less convenient was the location of the barn, as they called it, that housed the streetcars, which sat on ground that otherwise would have been used for left field. The building and the field shared a common wall, 35 feet high and 269 feet from home plate, which figured prominently in the architecture of not only the stadium but the games therein: from year to year the ground rules at Stars Park vacillated on whether a batted ball landing on the roof of the barn should count as a double or a home run.

At the behest of the highly diversified owner, whose legal enterprises already included a newspaper, a barbershop, two taxicab companies, considerable St. Louis real estate, and perhaps a few less transparent operations, the park was unofficially known as Dick Kent's Ballyard. That was certainly a self-aggrandizing option but not begrudged by the Stars' constituency, which appreciated the fact that few Negro League teams, and fewer of their ballparks, were actually

The defining feature of Stars Park, built in 1922 at Market and Compton, was the streetcar barn that considerably shortened left field.

owned by Negroes. It seated sixteen thousand fans and, through the courtesy of peepholes in the fences, indulged a good many others.

The inevitable construction delays prompted the Stars to begin their home schedule with a series against the Kansas City Monarchs at the St. Louis Giants' old park on North Broadway. Bell had not faced the Monarchs in Kansas City, but, for the occasion of the belated home opener, Gatewood presented his accidental sensation to the paying customers on May 31. Pitching in front of very interested family members, no doubt, the newly christened Cool Papa stumped the visitors with his assorted slop and the various angles—sidearm, three-quarters, submarine, or over the top—with which he was learn-ing to stage it. The effect was a startling two-hit shutout that surely left his brothers beaming.

Days later Bell took another turn against Kansas City, matched up this time with Bullet Joe Rogan, one of the luminaries of the Negro

Leagues. Nine years in the Army—he served with the 24th Infantry Division in the Philippines and the 25th in Hawaii, both all-black units—had delayed Rogan's baseball career (although he was recruited and played for the highly regarded 25th Infantry squad), but he made up for lost time by doubling his production as he went along. As a pitcher, he was a no-windup, sidearming ace whose roaring fastball belied his modest size; one of his catchers, Frank Duncan, purchased a pair of thick steaks before every game that Rogan pitched and slid them into his mitt for padding. The rest of the time, the native Oklahoman was a distinguished outfielder, carrying the Kansas City offense from the cleanup spot. In 1922, Rogan may have (depends on the source) led the Negro National League in home runs as well as wins. Cool Papa was never lacking in humility, but he received a gratuitous offering of it from Bullet Joe that afternoon, in the form of a 4–0 defeat.

The Monarchs were followed to town by the American Giants, and Bell was selected to start the series opener against the team that had just offered a pile of players for his services. However, neither his gratitude for Rube Foster nor his admiration of Jimmie Lyons—he later cited Lyons and Oscar Charleston as the idols of his Negro League youth—deterred Cool Papa from beating Chicago not only that day, 10–5, but also the next, when he pitched the last three innings of a wild 19–16 affair.

His three victories over Chicago would nearly equal his total against the rest of the league that season. In the absence of more discerning modern metrics, Cool's 7-7 record made him the second-best starter, behind Deacon Meyers, on a team that finished 29-37 for posterity (and no-telling-what altogether).

But the highlight of 1922, and the main event at Dick Kent's Ballyard—a series of such significance that the Stars imported Oscar Charleston from Indianapolis to play center field—was a postseason visit from a reasonable semblance of the Detroit Tigers. It was not unusual for Negro League teams to play exhibitions against the mainstream big-league clubs and hold their own, but that's not to say the custom was fully endorsed. The Stars' forerunners, the St.

The St. Louis Stars' team photo for 1922, Bell's rookie season, was presumably taken very early in the schedule. He's the only player without a star on his sleeve or "St. Louis" across his jersey.

Louis Giants, had in recent years beaten the Cardinals and the Philadelphia Phillies and in doing so provoked sporadic outrage in the press. Over a period of decades, baseball commissioner Kenesaw Mountain Landis, a dramatic, aristocratic Ohioan with an angular face and crowning mane of white hair, would set forth various sanctions and edicts to forestall the troublesome possibility that a black team would take the measure of an established white one. That very year, in fact, Landis—who, after being named commissioner in 1920, had made his mark by banning eight players for their parts in the Black Sox gambling scandal, thereby restoring the game's integrity—declared that barnstorming major leaguers could not compete as a team in the uniforms of a National or American League franchise.

Undermined from multiple directions, the interracial matchups became increasingly watered-down, and that was the case when the Tigers—most of them, anyway—squared off against the Stars in early October. "All except Ty Cobb and Harry Heilmann," noted Cool

Papa, when interviewed for an oral history project conducted by the University of Missouri–St. Louis in 1970. "They had played down in Cuba and said they wouldn't play against black ballplayers anymore. But we played Detroit at Compton and Market over there, beat 'em two out of three."

Had Cobb and Heilmann made themselves available, other Tigers would have been lopped from the roster and its makeup rearranged a bit. "See," Cool Papa said, "Judge Landis wouldn't let 'em play with their whole team intact, because they was keeping blacks out of the major leagues and if we could beat 'em, why not let us play? And so, they would let us play an *all-star* team, and if we beat 'em, we hadn't beat no *big-league* team."

It's not surprising, as sensitive and self-respecting as he was— and as inexplicable as he found oppression by color—that Bell would remember particulars of a racially significant event from nearly half a century prior. But his lucid recollections were not confined to matters of exclusion and discrimination.

Gary Ashwill, a diligent baseball historian and publisher of the Negro League website Seamheads.com, came to appreciate the integrity of Bell's recounting when he set out to resolve discrepancies between the myths and many versions of Cool Papa's coming of age in the Negro Leagues. Zeroing in hard on 1922, Ashwill found himself comparing the accounts of one source with another, legend with transcript, book with article, and invariably concluded that the most likely scenario had derived from the fast man himself. "Cool Papa Bell's memories of his rookie season—fifty years after the events he describes and all off the top of his head, apparently, without the elaborately constructed spreadsheets and timelines collating dozens of sources that I've been relying on—are remarkably accurate and detailed," he wrote.

Bell only pinch-hit in the series with the Tigers—one time, without success, in the ninth inning of the final game—but we can well imagine that it was a memorable three days for him nevertheless. In his ragtag team getting the better of those big leaguers, he would acquire fundamental, eye-opening perspectives on both the world of professional baseball and his place in it.

THE FIELD LEADERSHIP of the Stars was taken over in 1923 by the best manager Bell ever had. Candy Jim Taylor, of the prolific Taylor baseball family from northwest South Carolina, would become the winningest manager in Negro League history by more than two-fold over the next guy, but that was a long way off. What Cool Papa liked about him was his way with young players: patient, attentive, intelligent.

The son of a Methodist preacher and brother to a dozen siblings—including Ben Taylor and two other Negro Leaguers, C.I. (also a distinguished manager) and Steel Arm Johnny—Taylor was a smallish man who still played some third base at the time, put up nice numbers with the bat, and made a salutary connection with the mannerly pitcher from Mississippi. Bell was also his *ace* pitcher that year. Without a fastball to speak of, and too scrupulous for the advantages of saliva, scuffing, or petroleum jelly, he somehow posted an impressive 11-7 official record on a mediocre team that went 20-42 in the rest of its games.

Four of *those* victories, and four of the losses, were attributed to Cool Papa's much harder-throwing brother Fred, a year older but a Negro League rookie. It was a happy reunion—a family triumph for the former sharecroppers—and at season's end Fred joined James on an all-star outfit sponsored by the Stars and ticketed to Los Angeles to play in the California Winter League.

The CWL was a progressive concern wherein one black and generally three white teams competed in a unique, pacific atmosphere that seemed to offend nobody but the austere Judge Landis. For his part, the commissioner, who took nothing lightly, was compelled to visit and see for himself the degradation going on in Southern California. Thereafter, active major leaguers could occupy only so many roster spots on a particular club and do so for only a portion of the season, although some stayed for the duration under assumed names.

The Bells shared a hotel room near the train station with Norman "Turkey" Stearnes (one bed for Fred and Jay, as James was known in California, the other for Turkey), a spectacular slugger and center fielder who that year had stormed onto the scene with the Detroit Stars. "Ooh," Bell declared, "that Turkey Stearnes was *some*thing!" A left-hander from Nashville, Stearnes was a player without discernible fault. He lived cleanly, fielded smartly, hit for both power and average—out of an unusual stance that had his right foot pointing upward—and ran nearly as well as Bell.

Cool Papa mostly pitched until Stearnes left for Cuba, which necessitated that he lend a hand in left or right field when available. As it happened, though, Turkey's replacement in center was not up to the task, and one day, in Pasadena, Bell found himself ranging out of position to flag down a number of fly balls that were too much to handle for the poor fellow beside him. Thankfully, Fred was around to take over some of the pitching duties for the remainder of the season—he carried a shutout into the ninth inning against the Universal Studios club—because his little brother's services were now required in center field.

IT'S NOT APPARENT how or when Cool Papa hurt his arm. Candy Jim had Bell back on the mound at the start of the 1924 Negro League season, although his pitching burden was lessened by, among others, Fred and a teenaged rookie from Oklahoma named Roosevelt Davis who had no compunction about throwing beanballs, spitballs, emery balls, shine balls—loaded with so much Vaseline that they practically blinded the batter on a sunny day—or whatever would keep him gainfully employed. Tapping into his gift for guiding young players, Taylor was piecing together a team to compete more vigorously in the Negro National League.

His leading left-hander was still pacing the staff into July, commended by the *St. Louis Post-Dispatch* for his work in an 8–2 victory at Stars Park against the Memphis Red Sox: "Bell did some brilliant hurling and was especially effective in pinches . . ."

Candy Jim Taylor, Bell's favorite manager and the winningest in Negro League history, would ultimately skipper five teams that Cool Papa played for.

But he also took some turns in the outfield while Candy Jim, mindful of putting Cool Papa's singular speed to best advantage, mentored him in the art of switch-hitting. Bell batted strictly right-handed when he first joined the Stars, and Big Bill Gatewood had urged him to try the other side, a step closer to first base. The tinkering continued under Taylor in 1923, with Bell instructed to frequently bunt, of course, and more frequently to chop downward and pound the ball into the ground, no matter how deviously the trolley barn taunted him in left field. He had orders to never swing hard and dutifully pledged to follow them. In the heightened interest of making contact, he used a thick bat for maximum surface, and to abet his control of it he choked up a bit and placed his hands an inch or two apart.

To Bell, it was all in appropriate deference to the kind of "tricky baseball" he'd come to admire in Rube Foster's teams. But if *throwing* left-handed felt perfectly natural to him—it was, after all, the family tradition, and his ride to the Negro Leagues—*batting* that way was a couple of steps out of his comfort zone. Frequently, that first season or so of switch-hitting, Cool Papa would start his turn in the left-handed batter's box and stride back across the plate when the count reached two strikes.

All the while, his ability to catch a fly ball was never in question, and he covered more ground than a liberal arts degree. Curiously, the only shortcoming in Bell's center-fielding was the weakness of his throwing arm, which testifies that there must have been an injury involved. After that "brilliant hurling" in early July 1924, the records show him pitching only two more innings over the remaining twenty-two years of his professional career. For all practical purposes, the curveball and knuckleball were shelved with the mothballs.

In truth, though, Cool Papa's departure from the mound was not much lamented. Not when the upshot for the Stars—the big boost for Candy Jim's development program—was a future Hall of Famer in the everyday lineup.

Make that two. . . .

CHAPTER FIVE

THE STARS COME OUT

V ERY EARLY IN THE 1924 SEASON, THE STARS' capable shortstop, a twenty-four-year-old Indiana native named Eddie Holtz, took ill with pneumonia. He never recovered and died in July.

By that time his replacement had arrived, a small, leathery, bow-legged Texan with a magical glove and a mean streak. Willie Wells, son of a Pullman porter, was only eighteen, father of a two-year-old boy and a two-year-old girl born five months apart, when he came under Candy Jim Taylor's care. His mother, who took in laundry, had wanted him to be a pianist and a college man. Willie was devoted to her, but he'd been smitten by baseball even before he was getting into semipro games for free by carrying Biz Mackey's catching equipment. To soften Cisco Wells's disappointment about her son's career choice, Willie did her the small favor of opting for the Stars over the Chicago American Giants because St. Louis was an overnight train ride from their home in Austin.

He and Cool Papa were best friends almost from the start. Both were reserved, unworldly, mindful of their moms, and serious about their craft. Their idea of a big night was talking baseball on the train—drag bunts, hook slides, opposing pitchers, and stealing the catcher's signs, the last of which Willie had a particular genius for—until they fell asleep. Wells didn't live quite as cleanly as Cool, who he said "wouldn't dissipate at all," but his degeneracy was confined mostly to betting on horses, playing the numbers, eating way too much—his equals were few in that area, nonexistent in his weight class—and maybe that time he tried to mix tobacco and Coca-Cola, which didn't turn out well.

Opponents, however, might have questioned Wells's innocence in the martial art of baserunning. His aggression, at least, was well informed. In the dugout, Cool Papa's buddy kept a keen eye on members of the other team who stretched the boundaries of sportsmanship, in his estimation. It was for them—most of whom, he duly noted, were much bigger than he was, and eager, he was certain, to take advantage of it—that Cisco's pride and joy kept a spare, extra-sharpened set of spikes. The great third baseman and gentleman Judy Johnson was accompanied in his old age by knee scars that reminded him daily of the occasion when Wells, sliding into a tag, tried to kick the ball out of his grip and somehow missed the grip altogether. The gashes were administered in spite of the shin guards Johnson wore under his pants for just such an eventuality—for Willie Wells, basically.

The magnificent shortstop was no less menacing afield. Dink Mothell, a fine player with his own prickly edge, may or may not have been noted on Wells's mental hit list, and that may or may not explain what happened when Mothell one day approached second base standing up in his attempt to disrupt a double play. Undeterred, Wells fired the ball in the direction of first base, a course that ran through the baserunner's face. Mothell lost a couple of teeth in the transaction. "Oh, he had the prettiest teeth you ever saw," Cool Papa lamented.

To more emphatically combat the larger likes of himself, Wells would collect little rocks and brick fragments from the Mississippi River bed and stuff them into the fingers of his glove to slap across the jaws of opponents attempting to slice him up or bowl him over while arriving at second. If he sometimes seemed less than discriminating in his purveyance of punishment, it was understood that the endangered runner might have represented a convenient surrogate for a pitcher who had targeted Willie's knees or noggin. He was hit by so many pitches that, long before the advent of batting helmets, Wells came to the plate in a customized coal miner's hard hat.

The compleat Willie Wells, however, entailed much more than ill temper. "Baseball is a beautiful game," Wells would often say, and more often he illustrated it on the field. Decades later Bell would think of his old friend as he watched Ozzie Smith perform his ballet at the shortstop position, the difference being that Wells's sleight of foot was carried out on much cruder surfaces. Acrobatic and improvisational, he was adept at making adjustments, one of which was necessary to compensate for his mediocre arm: He used a flat fielder's glove with most of the padding removed, making it easier to transfer the ball to his throwing hand and release it in a jiffy. It was a skill that Cool Papa, dealing with his own arm troubles, was able to observe and incorporate.

In 1924, with Wells a rookie and Bell an outfielder for the first time, both reliant mostly upon their raw talent, the future Hall of Famers performed better with the glove than the bat. Wells had difficulty with curveballs, and Cool Papa was often overmatched in his switch-hitting experiment. When they got on base, though, the party started.

In Bell and Wells, Candy Jim's transformation of the Stars had found its legs. One flaunting speed, the other intimidation, the two were bound by a creative cunning and relentless resolve to reach the next station. It was a micro game that they played to the utmost, a manifestation, in part, of the ideological reverence they both held for Rube Foster. Wells, the more talkative of the two, would visit the office of the Negro League icon whenever the Stars played in Chicago, discussing baseball theory clear up to game time.

Through the stylings of Bell and Wells, Taylor's ball club began to reflect not only Foster's prototype but the burgeoning jazz movement that was sweeping north from New Orleans. In the early twenties, Louis Armstrong, a New Orleans native who would become Cool

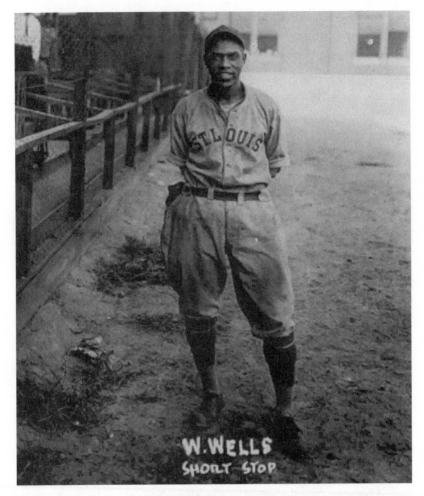

The great shortstop Willie Wells, Bell's best friend in baseball, backed up by the
Stars Park trolley barn

Papa's closest friend in the music industry, had taken his horns and
froggy vocal cords first to Chicago—a baseball fan, he likely caught
an American Giants game or two—and then to New York, seat of the
Harlem Renaissance. Improvisation was stirring black America, and
the St. Louis Stars were right in step with it.

Flourishing in the fresh culture, the Stars prospered like never
before, finishing the season with their first winning percentage over
.500. With that, they ascended to the top half of the NNL behind

Kansas City, Chicago, and Detroit, paced respectively by Bullet Joe Rogan, Cristóbal Torriente, and Turkey Stearnes. And when the last summer scab had hardened, the best St. Louis players headed west to get better over the winter.

Under the banner of the St. Louis Giants, they enlisted with the Southern California Winter League, whose numerous major leaguers that year included Goose Goslin, a Hall of Famer in the making who had just batted .344 for the Washington Senators and led the American League in RBIs. In such company—bear in mind, St. Louis would play far more games than the other teams—the Giants' young first baseman, Willie Bobo, would win the winter league home run title; their broad-shouldered third baseman, Dewey Creacy, would smack the most doubles and triples; William Ross would pace all pitchers in complete games and strikeouts; Fred Bell would share the lead in victories; and Fred's blazing half brother would claim the batting crown at an even .400. Among those statistical champs—all of them Stars in the regular season—only Cool Papa could say (but surely didn't) that his achievement, being a matter of percentage, was not advantaged by the superabundance of opportunities.

And yet, the stream of games was invaluable to Bell, who sorely needed repetitions and confidence from the left side of the plate. As the hits kept coming—he led the league in those as well, and among the bunts and chops there was even a home run, which matched his regular-season total—they provided him with vital confirmation that switch-hitting was, indeed, the way to go.

Willie Wells was in California, too, and joined up every now and again with his St. Louis mates. He was generally busy playing for another paying club, however, and conducting his principal business of the winter: learning to hit a curveball. To that end, his accommodating mentors were kind enough to tie his left leg to home plate and terrorize him with practice curves that he couldn't escape. Using his bat for defense, Wells eventually began to fend them off with increasing proficiency.

Come spring, the difference in his hitting was so conspicuous that when the Stars took the field in 1925, Candy Jim had moved his scrappy shortstop from the eighth spot in the batting order to the third, two places behind the suddenly self-assured center fielder.

IT WAS, IN fact, quite a batting order. St. Louis had added a slugging nineteen-year-old outfielder named Wilson Redus, who was variously called Frog or Babe Ruth; the talented catcher Mitchell Murray batted cleanup; and there were Willie Bobo, the formidable young first baseman; Dewey Creacy, supplier of power and speed; and Bell and Wells and the well-rounded right fielder, Branch Russell, who would serve many years as a supervisor with the city's parks and recreation department. The larruping Stars led the NNL in batting average (.316 as a team, 28 points higher than the next club), on-base percentage, and slugging percentage, although, surprisingly, not stolen bases, even though Cool Papa took league honors in that area.

He also led the parade in doubles and even managed ten home runs, suggesting that it must have been one of those years when balls hit onto the trolley barn roof were ruled as four-baggers. Nevertheless, Bell remained committed to not swinging hard, although he had no objection to the power supplied by the heft of his thirty-five-inch, thirty-eight-ounce Spalding club.

The Stars' dynamic offense attracted both black and white fans—separated by a rope, of course—some of whom might have been enticed by game accounts in the *Post-Dispatch* that, making no attempts at first names for the Negro Leaguers, at least twice pointed out Bell's "brilliant catches" in center field and another time his "excellent base running." The better the Stars played, the more attention they drew, and the more attention, the better they dressed. Cool and Wells, in particular, were rather famously wont to "dude up" (as a later teammate of Wells described it) after a successful game: suits, ties, dapper hats, and pocket handkerchiefs.

It amounted to considerable duding, because, with the offensive juggernauts complemented by adequate pitchers, Candy Jim's fast-rising outfit went 59-30 that year. Fred Bell faded from the scene early in the season, but the slack was picked up Percy Miller, William

Ross, hometowner Slap Hensley, and especially Roosevelt Davis, now the staff ace. The NNL standings were divided into half seasons, and after the Kansas City Monarchs won the first half, the Stars, now the toast of the Ville and a giddy distraction for the bloodied labor force of the St. Louis Independent Packing Company, stormed to the second-half title and a spot against the Monarchs in the 1925 league championship series.

THE SERIES BEGAN in St. Louis, but not without a fuss. All season, the Stars, who prided themselves on their independence from anything white—money, authority, facilities, personnel, etc.—had utilized the umpiring services of an African American barber named Henry Cooper, who naturally expected more of the same for the championship matches. But when all had assembled at Stars Park, it was discovered that Rube Foster, as NNL president, had brought with him a pair of Caucasian gentlemen to conduct the officiating. Cooper, whose contract ran a couple more weeks, sued the league for $239.57.

"It's not the money," the barber told the *Post-Dispatch*; "it's the principle of the thing, a matter of race pride. The St. Louis Stars is the only one of the eight clubs in the league that is owned and operated entirely by negroes, and St. Louis negroes always have been proud of that."

They were proud as well of the stylish, energetic team that had piled up runs all summer. Among the impressive routs was a 7–0 shutout of the Monarchs in Kansas City, featuring a grand slam by Cool Papa. Nevertheless, the Stars' postseason opponent—the victor would face the champ of the Eastern Colored League in the Negro World Series—was a seasoned squad with a tradition of winning big, its standard of excellence set by Bullet Joe Rogan and shortstop Dobie Moore, a World War I veteran known as the Black Cat. Kansas City, in a nutshell, was the kind of established, widely respected ball club that the youthful St. Louisans were itching to become.

That mission was well served over the three games at Stars Park. After an 8–6 opening defeat (in spite of a home run by Willie Wells),

Candy Jim's upstarts evened the series with a 6–3 victory that Bell instigated with an infield hit and a couple of steals. He also doubled home a run in the rain-delayed third game and later scored the winner when Dobie Moore—whose distinguished career was prematurely ended the following year when, under murky circumstances, his girlfriend shot him in the leg—was unable to properly grip a wet baseball and let loose a wild throw.

But there was still the matter of Joe Rogan to be resolved. The teams repaired to Chicago, and the fourth game was tied in the ninth inning when Stars pitcher Percy Miller was instructed to intentionally walk Rogan with the potential winning run on second base. Miller was unable to execute that order, and his failure was Bullet Joe's fourth hit of the afternoon, which squared the series at two games apiece.

Bullet Joe Rogan could dominate a game with his arm or his bat,
and he consistently did both.

Rogan, playing center field, was all set for follow-up heroics in game five. With the score again tied in the ninth, he caught a fly ball with his back to the infield, whirled, and shot a bullet to second base in an attempt to double up the runner, only to see the Monarchs' fine second baseman, Newt Allen, drop the ball as the winning run scored for the Stars. With that, and a doubleheader to follow, St. Louis was a game away from advancing to the Negro World Series. William Bell—no relation to Cool Papa—beat the Stars in the first game of the twin-bill and then handed the ball to Bullet Joe, who settled the whole business with a 4–0 shutout, improving his season record to an inconceivable 26-2. The magnificent Rogan also led the series in hitting with a .455 average, an epic performance that had the effect of reducing young Willie Wells to tears on the train back to St. Louis.

There would be no such heartbreak for the Philadelphia Hilldales, the serendipitous representatives of the Eastern Colored League. Before the World Series began, Rogan was playing with his toddler son when somehow a rusty needle found its way into the great player's knee, sending him to the hospital and clearing the way for the Hilldales' rout, five games to one.

But Rogan wasn't the only one to take a break from the game at that point. In Cool Papa's case, it's hard to say why he didn't return to California for the winter. He might have been worn-out from the extended season or nursing an injury or aching to spend some time with his family or determined to beat Willie Wells in at least one game of pickup basketball at the YMCA or simply attracted to a regular paycheck.

He knew, at any rate, that the slaughterhouse would not smell its worst from October to March, and it was good enough for his brothers.

CHAPTER SIX

WILLIE'S GIRL

I N THE ABSENCE OF ORGANIZED SCOUTING, A systemic minor league, statistical intelligence, and significant newspaper coverage in many black communities—especially those in rural areas—the arrival of talent to the Negro Leagues was seldom signaled by advance notice. There was no script, no process, no buildup. Year upon year, extraordinary players would simply appear in the spring like a scarlet tanager at the bird feeder. In 1922 it was Cool Papa Bell. In 1923, Turkey Stearnes. In 1924, Willie Wells.

And in 1926 the St. Louis Stars were gratuitously and abundantly beefed up by a Southern strongman who developed his crushing stroke in the Birmingham coal-mining leagues. When Mule Suttles lumbered to the plate at Stars Park, hauling his fearsome fifty-ounce mace of ash, the expectant crowd, and teammates as well, would cry out, "Kick, Mule, kick!"

And what a kick it was to see the kindly big man grip his colossal club at the very bottom, two fingers on the knob, and answer the call. Improbably—even given the built-in advantage of the trolley barn in left field—the wrecking-ball rookie that year led the Negro National

League in the unimaginable grand slam of home runs, doubles, triples, and batting average. He likely would have set the pace, also, in RBIs, runs, slugging percentage, and OPS (on-base percentage plus slugging percentage) had those stats been kept, or yet devised. In step with the times, the *St. Louis Globe-Democrat* summed up the strapping Alabaman as "a listless colored boy in his street clothes" but "a human dynamo" in his Stars uniform.

"Kick, Mule, kick!"

Of course, in burly contradistinction to the prevailing spirit of the Stars, Suttles did not matriculate in the Rube Foster school of tricky ball. The burden of that movement, in fact, would henceforth rest upon Bell and Wells, because the father figure of the Negro Leagues had involuntarily withdrawn from the arena. In September, more than a year after exposure to a gas leak in an Indianapolis boardinghouse and following subsequent episodes of memory failure, evident stress, and erratic behavior, Foster was admitted to a mental institution in

Kankakee, Illinois. He was never again to carry his iconic pipe or girth or wisdom onto a ballfield.

While cranking seventeen home runs that year—fourth in the league and third on the Stars behind Suttles and Dewey Creacy—Bell, as if in tribute to the founder, led the NNL in stolen bases for the second time. The credited total of twenty-three, however, seems rather spare for a sprinter so dashing, daring, and determined.

To that end, the accounting must be considered. *It* was spare, to say the least. In the Negro Leagues, there were no statisticians, only keepers of the scorebook, and those could be the second-string catcher, a pitcher between starts, the manager's nephew, or sometimes, in an exhibition road game between league stops, nobody. One team took the initiative to engage a reporter from an African American newspaper to maintain its book, but the scribe had a habit of showing up late and asking the players to catch him up on what had taken place. They called the fellow "Single to Center" because that's what he invariably wrote down to account for a runner who'd reached first base by means the indifferent journalist hadn't quite witnessed. For outs, the default was fly to center.

On the occasions when a contest was rigorously scored, the results may or may not have been sent along to an interested paper, which, depending on the timeliness of the dispatch or the newsiness of its contents or the whim of whoever might have been putting together the sports page that day, may or may not have entered them into the public record. Some teams might have bothered to report non-league games, others might not have. Some teams might have bothered to include such items as RBIs and stolen bases in their totals, others might not have. Those statistics, however, were typically not noted in published box scores, making them difficult for historians to tally. The scorebooks themselves, often as not, were thrown away once they were filled up or the season ended.

And so, while the coal miner's prodigious clouts were comparatively tracked and some of the longest ones even measured, most of Cool Papa's stolen bases simply piled up in a critical mass of myth.

THE SEMIPRO, HIGHLY competitive Birmingham coal leagues—some of the mines and factories sponsored separate white and black teams—gave rise eventually to the Birmingham Black Barons of the Negro Southern League, a confederation from which the Black Barons, in 1927, graduated to the Negro National League.

Their first visit to St. Louis as a league opponent occurred in June of that year, accompanied by subplots. One involved the Barons' manager, Big Bill Gatewood, the former Stars skipper—the sage who had embellished Cool with Papa—whose departure from the river city, for whatever reason, had been somewhat light on hugs and kisses. The other storyline centered around Gatewood's latest protégé, a long, lean, uninhibited pitcher just a few years removed from the Mount Meigs reformatory in Alabama.

The Black Barons had been stung by Suttles's move to St. Louis the season before, and their switch to the NNL was perhaps calculated to discourage more of the same. The Stars, in fact, had been one of the suitors for Satchel Paige when the long, lean right-hander—some newspaper stories would describe him as "elongated"—made it clear, as he always would, that he was available to the highest bidder, even though his previous team, the Chattanooga Black Lookouts, had already given him a Ford Model A to come back.

Birmingham won that derby, and by the time Paige arrived at Stars Park with the Black Barons—at which point the spelling of neither Paige (Page) nor Satchel (Satchell) was settled upon, although his actual first name, Leroy, had apparently been dispensed with—he had already gotten a calculated start on superstardom. This development was equal parts fastball and showmanship. Ultimately, Paige would exercise legendary control with his various speeds and angles and windups, but that part of his game was still down the road, a shortcoming that didn't diminish the colorful right-hander's conspicuous sense of eminence. Accordingly, his first strut to the mound in St. Louis was a deliberate, attention-centering performance unto itself, a grand entrance of astonishing presumption.

What happened next was classic Satchel Paige folklore, a cartoon of events sketched by conflicting accounts, the latitudes of oral tradition, and of course the puckishness of Paige himself. He would later claim that he broke the thumbs of the first three St. Louis batters, an almost certain fable insofar as the first would have been Bell, who over the years reflected upon the memorable afternoon without reference to any busted extremity.

More likely, the incident occurred in the second inning, involving one or more hit batsmen prior to the arrival at home plate of the Stars' fine catcher, Mitchell Murray, who the previous season had finished second in the league in batting. Paige proceeded to hit Murray in either the hand or the back, and Murray, still clutching his bat, lit out after the gangling Alabaman, with the crowd howling and Satchel fleeing toward either second base or the visitors' dugout. When Murray was in range, he flung the bat at Paige, who may or may not have picked it up and begun to chase Murray. In any event, both teams and assorted fans had joined the fracas by this time, with the police in close pursuit. Paige and Murray were ejected, and when Gatewood refused to

By 1926, the St. Louis Stars' lineup included three eventual Hall of Famers:
Bell (front row, fourth from right), Suttles (second row, far left),
and Wells (next to Suttles).

send the Black Barons back onto the field, the game was forfeited to
St. Louis.

THEY SAY THAT one of the vital characteristics of a special ballplayer is the capacity of carry on at peak performance in spite of
personal circumstances that would distract or dispirit a less focused
athlete. So it was that Willie Wells, at the age of twenty-one, took his
game to the top of the league in 1927.

His efforts were shaded somewhat by baseball's fixation that year
on Babe Ruth and his historic sixty home runs and, closer to home,
by the injury to Mule Suttles, who was bashed not on the thumb by
Paige but in the head by Chet Brewer, a tall, promising right-hander
with the Kansas City Monarchs. Suttles missed most of the season,
and while his career continued at a productive pace thereafter, he was
never quite able to replicate the outrageous slugging of his rookie year.

Wells, however, covered for him in the short term. The little
shortstop batted .380 and led the NNL in homers, all of it in the face
of a turbulent period with the girl he intended to marry.

Clara Belle Thompson was eighteen at the time, small, fair, and
spunky. As a child, she had moved to St. Louis from Nashville with
more than a few members of her large extended family. Wells was
serious enough about Clara Belle to make his marital wish known to
his mother, presumably still in Texas, and Cisco Wells was serious
enough in her resistance to forbid it. Conceivable reasons would
include Clara's youth, her mixed race, her Catholic faith, her uncon-
ventional family, her lack of education, her ties to St. Louis, her sharp
tongue, the two children whom Willie was already responsible for,
potential complications with the moms of those children, and the
unlikely possibility that Cisco simply didn't care for the young lady.

Disinclined to cross his dear mother again, Wells accepted his fate
and punished the pitchers and basemen of the Negro National League.
One night, though, in his melancholy after a road game, he pulled out
his photograph of Clara Belle and shared the sad story with Cool Papa
while the two of them played cards in their hotel room.

As the tale has been told, Bell took a good look at the picture, paused a moment, and said, "So you're not going to marry her?"

"No," Willie replied softly.

"Well, if you ain't gonna marry her, I think I might like her. Is that all right?"

"I suppose so."

FOR ALL THE voltage in their lineup and the sizzling records it produced, the Stars, throughout 1926 and 1927, played third fiddle to Kansas City and Chicago. When the 1928 season commenced, however, they were having no more of that, galloping off to nine wins in their first ten games.

All summer, the hitting never slackened. Bell even solved Bullet Joe Rogan of the Monarchs for four hits in one game, as St. Louis staked its claim as the best team in Missouri at last—or at least the best *black* team in Missouri, as the Cardinals were in the process of winning their second National League pennant in three years, with hopes for their second world championship.

Cool Papa stroked *five* hits one afternoon against Memphis, including a pair of triples. Another day, reprimanding Chet Brewer for beaning Suttles the year before, he roughed up the Kansas City pitcher for a homer and triple. Suttles himself ripped three triples in one game and three homers in another. Five-foot-seven Frog Redus of Muskogee, Oklahoma, who would share the same outfield with Bell and Branch Russell for seven years, placed second in the league in home runs that season, trailing only Turkey Stearnes.

In spite of batting .332, Bell was nowhere to be seen among the stolen-base leaders. This undoubtedly reflected not upon Cool Papa's speed or piracy—that very year, the *St. Louis Star* alluded to "Jim Bell, center fielder, and the fastest man in the league"—but on the willy-nilly record keeping. To wit, the top four base stealers in the NNL, according to the available statistics, were Kansas City Monarchs. No player on any other team was credited with as many as ten steals, strongly suggesting that few or none of those clubs kept track; certainly the

Stars didn't. It's not unlikely that Bell stole at least fifty, perhaps a hundred or more bases that went undocumented in that season alone.

The statistical neglect of Cool Papa's most salient skill, coupled with Suttles's injury, abetted the rise of Wells as the Stars' most celebrated player. In the absence of an official league MVP, historian John Holway, who generations later assembled the first comprehensive, season-by-season tabulation of organized blackball, conferred that distinction upon Wells for 1927. By 1928 the great infielder was reportedly bringing in the largest share of the team's league-maximum, $2,750-a-month payroll, enabling him to indulge his passion for big Buicks. (Negro League teams carried as few as a dozen players on their rosters and almost never as many as twenty. It wasn't unusual for the sum of them to earn considerably less in salary than a single major-leaguer. Research by Gary Ashwill in the blog *Agate Type* revealed that the twelve Indianapolis ABCs of 1923, led by Oscar Charleston and his $1,950 in wages (assuming a six-month season), combined for a total payroll of $12,870. On a corresponding major-league team that year, the Cleveland Indians, player-manager Tris Speaker (the ABCs also had a player-manager, Dizzy Dismukes) was paid $30,000—more than fifteen times Charleston's earnings. The top dozen Indians made $90,900, seven times as much as the Indianapolis players.

It should be noted, meanwhile, that the friendship between Wells and Bell was unshaken by either the acclaim of the shortstop or the attentions of the outfielder toward the lovely, wavy-haired girl who lived on Lawton Avenue and was becoming quite a baseball fan. Cool Papa had made several walking passes by the house where all those Tennesseans lived—Lawton continued on past Stars Park, where its pavement was periodically visited by another of Mule Suttles's home runs—before one day he finally caught Clara Belle sitting outside on a green bench and made her acquaintance. They were mutually smitten.

She attended games and couldn't help but observe, as the exciting summer unfolded, that while her new boyfriend and her old boyfriend, as well as Suttles, Frog Redus, Dewey Creacy, and the others, were more than capable of pummeling their overmatched opponents, it was the much-improved pitching that elevated the Stars to the summit of the NNL. Over the 1928 regular season St. Louis, finely and finally balanced, easily surpassed the Monarchs, Detroit Stars, Chicago American Giants, and less threatening rivals.

The Stars' staff was spearheaded by Ted Trent, a tall, side-arming, curveballing college man who had nearly as many nicknames—"Highpockets," "Big Florida," "Stringbean"—as breaking pitches. Trent's legend tells us that he struck out Rogers Hornsby three times in one interracial game, fanned the great Bill Terry *four* times in another, and seldom lost to Satchel Paige. That year Big Florida posted a stunning 21-4 record, two of the victories coming in a doubleheader against the Monarchs. What's more, despite his chronic thirst, it's estimated that most of his work was accomplished sober.

But it was the depth of the St. Louis pitching that kept the train rolling all the way into the league championship series against Chicago: chiefly, Roosevelt Davis (11-1), Luther McDonald (11-6), and Slap Hensley (13-5), whom Clara Belle Thompson preferred to call Eggie. Half a century later, she would speak of him with whimsical fondness.

"Eggie Hensley," Clara said to *St. Louis Magazine*, "is the reason Cool Papa made the Hall of Fame. He let the other team hit lots of long drives so my man could make great catches."

CHAPTER SEVEN

WE'LL ALWAYS HAVE CUBA

ATTENDED BY THEIR SOUTHERN FAMILIES, Cool and Clara were married on a sunny day in early September, two weeks before the opening of the nine-game Negro National League championship series in Chicago. Four games would be there, followed by five in St. Louis, where bright-eyed Clara Belle Bell would be keenly interested but not so economically involved as the many patrons who placed wagers on the games and stuck dollar bills in the wire screen for home team players to snatch after slamming a ball over the trolley barn. Those were customs shared at most of the Negro League venues, except for the trolley barn.

The American Giants were of course no longer orchestrated by Rube Foster, but his considerably younger half brother, lengthy left-hander Willie Foster, was their ace pitcher, and he was the leading figure of game one, claimed by Chicago. In the following match, Ted Trent, aiming to embellish his spectacular season for St. Louis, was unable to cope with the unseasonable chill or a clever little right-hander known variously as Willie or Wee Willie or Ernest or Wee Ernest or Piggy or Pigmeat or Pee Wee Powell. By any name, Powell was the American Giants' second-best pitcher, and he stopped the Stars cold with a three-hit shutout, leaving them in significant arrears to the defenders of the league's last two championships.

But Eggie Hensley, for whom Cool Papa's bride was so grateful, salvaged game three for St. Louis. The *Post-Dispatch*, in fact, corroborated the favorable symbiosis between Eggie and Clara's man, noting in its game report that "air-tight support saved Hensley. The fielding and hitting of Bell featured."

Bell's unsettling speed was featured at the outset of the last game at Chicago's Schorling Park, when it provoked a two-base throwing error. That led to an early score, which was soon trumped by a three-run homer off the bat of Chicago's Steel Arm Davis, representing the Negro League's most common nickname. (No team was truly complete without a Steel Arm.) The Stars regrouped with a fourth-inning rally that culminated in a go-ahead single from Wells, and Trent was summoned from the bullpen to protect the sudden lead. Flashing his demon curveball, Big Florida did so in style.

And thus the clubs were even, two games apiece, when they reconvened amidst the rowdiness of Dick Kent's Ballyard.

IN THEORY, THE three days set aside for travel and rest should have benefited the American Giants, whose top two pitchers, Foster and Powell, had proven themselves quite equal to the task of subduing the loaded St. Louis lineup. And that's how it played out in the first game at Stars Park, in which Foster, a Hall of Famer down the road, bested Eggie Hensley, owing in large part to a tiebreaking, eighth-inning home run by the Giants' outstanding shortstop, Pythias Russ of Cynthiana, Kentucky.

But if the break refreshed Foster, it was not so salutary for Pee Wee Powell. In place of relaxing family time in the Powell household, there was a domestic spat and a shotgun and an accident, they called it, when Pee Wee's father-in-law shot him in the face. The man of many monikers survived the incident and would pitch again, but not, as scheduled, in game six or the rest of the NNL championship series.

Trent, however, was off his stride that particular Sunday, and Chicago charged in front, 6–1, before the Stars cranked it up in the bottom of the fourth and chased off Powell's unfortunate replacement, Harold Treadwell. To a St. Louis crowd dressed for an occasion and wondering when the party would start, the sudden rally was like the band showing up.

A typical Negro League grandstand, the spectators well turned out and segregated.

The scene was duly and poignantly recorded. In deference to the ruckus being raised at Stars Park and a convenient quirk in the schedule—the Cardinals had wrapped up the National League pennant and it would be more than a week before Babe Ruth and the World Series arrived from New York—the *Post-Dispatch* favored the Negro Leaguers with a rare splash of attention.

> The grand stand at the Negro ball park at Compton avenue and Market street rocked like a shanty in a wind yesterday with the shouts of a capacity crowd of 5,000. . . . The per capita lung power

of the crowd cannot be challenged by the most exuberant of Sportsman's Park crowds. Every practice play was greeted with howls of glee and every howl spurred the fielders to greater effort till they scampered about and speared balls miraculously and tossed back and forth like supermen of the diamond.

. . . Many of the fixed stars of Negro baseball are performing in the present series. There is Willie Wells, St. Louis shortstop, whose hands "are worth a million dollars" but whose salary is about $250 a month, a ball player whom Negroes like to compare with the stars of the big leagues.

If one prefers sluggers, there are "Mule" Suttles of St. Louis and Davis, from whom the Chicago team must take its name, for he is a giant who grips the earth with his spikes and swings more Homerically than Babe Ruth and to quite as much avail.

There is Bell, fastest base runner in the league, who scored from second base in Saturday's game upon an infield out. . . . There is Russell in right field for St. Louis who roams an expanse quite as wide as that of the fleet Douthit [the Cardinals' center fielder], and who prances gleefully, his white teeth gleaming, as he spears the ball. . . .

Every play is made with a flourish and the stands howl their appreciation of the consummate grace of the athletes, a grace that anyone who has seen the Negro playground children dance in the annual fall festival in the Municipal Theater will understand.

In the author's depiction, however, consummate grace was pretty much confined to the playing field. Among those within earshot of his press box seat was a rhyming fan with a megaphone and another equipped with a roaring impatience for Big Florida's control troubles. The latter patron was financially vested and liberally quoted, primarily addressing Trent:

"Boy, you must been sick. If you sick, why don't you say to them: 'I'm sick; I ain't had my breakfast,' and go out? . . . Look where you threw that ball. You been pitching baseball all your life and you ain't

> never threw no ball like that before. You don't know you is pitching
> for a pennant. You don't know I got $75 on this game."

And yet, in the gallery of attention-getters, the agitated gambler was scarcely conspicuous. There was also, for example—coincident with the St. Louis comeback—a certain "fevered rooter" who was visibly moved by the Stars' six-run fourth.

> He jumps upon the rail separating two boxes. He runs along it
> like a cat. He clutches the wire netting. Up the netting he goes . . .
> till he reaches the very roof of the grand stand. There he clings,
> yelling raucously. The crowd rolls in glee. Hot dog. Who says this
> ain't an inning?

The ringing blow in that monumental frame was a home run by Dewey Creacy, which gave the home side a 7–6 lead and qualified the Stars' slugging third baseman for spontaneous remuneration. Apparently, though, some of the benefactors opted for a currency not easily redeemable.

> "Why throw straw hats? Dollar bills is better," says one [fan], and
> tosses his money toward the hero. Another and another. Creacy
> calmly gathers up the spoils. "Huh," he says, "sometimes I get as
> much as $10 for a home run." A championship game should be
> more profitable.

The American Giants would rebound to tie the score, but the Stars now had their lumber and mojo working. There was a shtick involved wherein the St. Louis hitters carried a whitewashed horseshoe out of the dugout for their turns at the plate. Stopping short of the box, they handed the horseshoe to the batboy, who spat on it, then spat on the player's bat. Once more—horseshoe, bat—and the battle was joined.

The ritual came through again in the seventh when Suttles stepped up and mightily cleared the bases. At day's end, the series had been evened once more, and in the next *Post-Dispatch* the entertained reporter pointed out that all of the above was a mere sixty-cent proposition for the satisfied folks on hand; ninety-five for those who enjoyed box seats.

EVEN WITHOUT RUBE Foster's stewardship of the American Giants, his aura was felt at Stars Park—and painfully so for the home team in the final inning of game seven. The Stars were trying to protect a one-run lead and gain the series edge for the first time when Rube's managerial successor, Dave Malarcher, called successfully for a squeeze play as if the patriarch had signaled with his corncob pipe from the hospital. Extra innings ensued, and Chicago took advantage two innings later when Pythias Russ—who would die of tuberculosis two years later—scored the game winner on a single by Mitchell Murray, the former Stars catcher who, the previous year, had chased Satchel Paige around the ballpark.

If there was a consolation for St. Louis, it was the strain put upon Willie Foster in the continued absence of Pee Wee Powell. Rube's brother had been given the ball in game seven, and when decisive game nine came around three days later—after the Stars had tied the series for the third time—Malarcher called on his ace lefty yet again, matched against Ted Trent.

Evidently, Trent ate his breakfast on the morning of the climactic Sunday. He kept Chicago off the scoreboard until the eighth inning, by which time wonderful Willie Wells had homered twice against Foster, tripled to boot, and pulled off a barehanded catch. The dollar bills he snatched out of the screen that day set him up nicely for the off-season, if not another Buick.

Regarding worn-out Willie Foster, the *Post-Dispatch* remarked that "the St. Louis hitters smashed him to smithereens." Over the course of the nine games, the most persistent smashing was produced by Cool Papa, whose eleven hits and .407 average tied Pythias Russ for the series lead. And while Wells was the center of attention in the celebration that rocked Stars Park—there was no ensuing showdown that year with the Eastern Colored League—John Holway, in his historical summary of the 1928 series, awarded the MVP title not to Clara Belle's would-be groom but to her actual one.

THE NEWLYWEDS HAD arranged a working honeymoon in Cuba, leaving behind the slaughterhouse, two families (they were living with hers), and a city whose enchantment with the Stars had been quickly routed by disappointment in the Cardinals. With Lou Gehrig and Babe Ruth ganging up for seven home runs and a .593 batting average, the Redbirds were unable to wrest a single World Series game from the indomitable Yankees.

James Thomas and Clara Belle Bell, Cuba, 1928

It was Bell's maiden voyage to the Caribbean, a journey he would often undertake in subsequent off-seasons and even some *regular* seasons. It was, in effect, the beginning of a companion career to his primary work in the Negro Leagues.

What Cool Papa found in Cuba was serious baseball in terms of both talent and stakes. For years, black and white American players had brought their games to the Caribbean nation for the winter, the blacks teaming with Cuban nationals to compete against the major leaguers. That lasted until Ban Johnson, the appropriately named American League president, took note that the big-timers were losing as often as they won and prohibited them from returning.

But the African Americans kept coming, mixing with the locals on two Havana teams and two outside the city. Immensely proud of the baseball it played—some Americans thought it was of better overall quality than the domestic variety, or at least the black leagues—Cuba had spawned the young Negro League marvel Martín Dihigo and, before him, powerhouse outfielder Cristóbal Torriente. The lively island had even sent some light-skinned players—Armando Marsans, Rafael Almeida, and the colorful, occasionally brilliant pitcher Dolf Luque—to the major leagues.

Bell, in fact, sailed with the presumption that the islanders were generally of Spanish descent. "I thought all the Cubans, in a way, was white," he told an interviewer. "When I went down there, naturally, I couldn't speak Spanish. We had loads of mail [to send], and we didn't know a mailbox from nothing else, and we were looking at one [fellow] we thought was an American—a Negro, dark—and we'd say something to him and he'd start speaking Spanish . . ."

For their part, the Cuban fans made no distinction between Caucasian and black, judging the athletes mostly on their likelihood to win them a wager. Betting was so prevalent that players were forbidden to drink lest they muddle the outcomes.

That, of course, was no restriction for Bell, whose exploits on the field were a winning proposition to the appreciative locals. On New Year's Day he set a Cuban record with three home runs, which would have been vastly out of character had not all of them stayed

Cool brought a box camera to the island and turned it on his bride.

in the park. Adding a couple more along the way, he actually led the league in long balls, if you could call them that—outslugging Dihigo, Oscar Charleston, and Judy Johnson, among others—and also, less surprisingly, stolen bases, which were more meticulously tracked than they were in the NNL.

While Clara Belle took pleasure in the fawning accorded her new husband in restaurants and drugstores, she would have preferred that fewer of his open admirers were so lovely and enthusiastic. She knew that she had married a trustworthy man but at the same time a handsome, popular, disarming one who circulated in a profession that winked at infidelity.

Taking stock of the situation, Mrs. Bell vowed right then to accompany Mr. Bell on as many subsequent trips as she could, especially if they took him south of the border.

CHAPTER EIGHT

LIGHTING UP BIG LEAGUERS

I N THEIR ASCENDANCY NOW, STARS AMONG THE Stars and Negro League champions of 1928, Willie Wells and Cool Papa Bell began the new year with a little extra cachet. Wells acquired a new and lasting nickname—the Devil—and Cool Papa's celebrity ushered him into the world of product endorsement.

To that end, there was this item, unimpeded by particulars and printed in the *Pittsburgh Courier*, the nation's leading black newspaper:

> BRIGHT HAIR WINS SAYS POPULAR STAR
>
> James Bell, the snappy shortstop [*sic*] of the St. Louis Giants [*sic*] of 1928, says he likes the new La-Em-Strait hair dressing better than any he has ever used—"because it is so easy to use and really does keep my hair smooth and bright without all that greasy condition I used to think was necessary." . . . All drug stores have the 25c and 50c sizes.

In 1929, with Wells, Suttles, and a new power-hitting catcher, Spoony Palm, thundering behind him in the St. Louis lineup, Bell ran amuck on the basepaths. The fellow who perhaps came closest to slowing him down was a local car salesman who in mid-May figured that the diamond at Stars Park was just the place to test out his new models. His handiwork, however, did not escape the attention of the aggrieved groundskeeper, who summoned a constable.

The upshot was a court date at which the little caretaker told the judge, "I spent two and a half hours last Wednesday morning combing the infield for the game with the Detroit Stars that afternoon. I was resting up in the grandstand when this man drives into the park and speeds around the infield, making a lot of ruts, and then drives out again. Judge, I got real mad. I called a cap [police captain] and we sat up in the grandstand some more. Then this man drives in again and does the same thing, and we arrest him." The fine was ten bucks, and the basepaths were groomed again for the churning cleats of Candy Jim's high-scoring fleet.

The Stars that year were a wrecking crew once again. The St. Louis batsmen had a way of demoralizing pitchers of less mettle than, say, Joe Rogan or Satchel Paige—and didn't make a point of sparing *them*, either. They pounded Satchel in a 10–8 victory— Cool leading the charge with four hits, including a triple—and then again 8–3, with every player in the St. Louis lineup getting a lick in. But Paige got off easy compared to a Memphis hurler named Robert Poindexter, who was on the bootheel side of a 14–3 trampling in late May in front of a crowd of five thousand.

Poindexter was so distraught by the beating that one of his teammates, first baseman J. C. "Sunny Jim" McHaskell, dropped by his room at the Grand Central Hotel around one A.M. As Sunny Jim later explained to the Associated Press from City Hospital No. 2, "Robert was down in the mouth over his punk pitching and I tried to kinda sympathize with him. I told him today was Ladies Day and he should do better with the girls all there. Somehow, he took offense at that. He thought I was razzing him, so he pulled out his pistol and shot me in the foot." McHaskell's wounds were grave, and he never played again. Poindexter's career ended there as well, undone by incarceration, depression, and a suicide attempt.

Less tragically, the whole 1929 season seemed shot in the foot. Rube Foster was still confined to his mental hospital in Illinois, and the league floundered badly without his leadership. While the Stars and Kansas City Monarchs had their ways with the rest of the NNL, the standings that year tended to vary from newspaper to newspaper, depending on which team had reported to which paper. Players made cameo appearances with rival clubs. Swaps and signings went unprocessed. Home teams chose their own umpires.

And yet, in September, a thousand Stars fans traveled clear across Missouri to watch their brilliant shortstop and their fearsome first baseman and their speed-of-light center fielder, among others, take on their only equal in the Negro Leagues. Perhaps the St. Louis faithful were seizing the last opportunity to see some championship-caliber baseball that year, knowing in advance that, in the dysfunction of 1929, neither the Stars nor the Monarchs would participate in a systematic postseason.

In the end Wells would lead the league in homers, Bell would finish second in doubles and stolen bases—the latter, of course, being a patently questionable tabulation—Kansas City would secure first place, and, instead of a proper championship, a series would be contrived between the Chicago American Giants, who finished third in the Negro National League, and the Homestead Grays from just outside of Pittsburgh, the third-place club in the Negro American League.

Those were *roughly* the sides, anyway. There were heavy-duty ringers involved both ways. For Chicago, those included Wells, Suttles, and Cool Papa from the St. Louis club. Homestead's ranks were fattened by Oscar Charleston and Judy Johnson of the Philadelphia Hilldales.

The moonlighting of the three Stars went swimmingly. Bell singled home the first run of the first game, and it was a run more than the Grays would manage, combined, in the first *three* games. Cool, Wells, and Suttles were finally aligned with Willie Foster, and between Foster and his fine fellow pitchers, Webster McDonald and Double Duty Radcliffe, the first peep out of Homestead was a four-run report in the top of the first inning of game four. That only cued Chicago to respond with *eight* in the bottom of the inning. It was an easy five-game sweep.

In effect, the set with Homestead was merely a tune-up for another unsanctioned but much more purposeful series. Bell, Wells, Suttles, and Foster remained in Chicago with the American Giants, who would now be visited by an impressive collection of major leaguers—including Harry Heilmann, Charlie Gehringer, and Heinie Manush, all future Hall of Famers—for five captivating games. This was not like the interracial competition in the Cuban or California winter leagues, where Ban Johnson and Judge Landis had radically restricted the participation of major leaguers. The Chicago series was an ad hoc event arranged expressly for the intrigue of prominent big leaguers squaring up against prominent blackballers, best team wins.

Bell spent ten seasons in a St. Louis uniform.

It was good baseball, but more important to Cool Papa, when he looked back upon the series, it was *respectful* baseball, each side admiring the other. Major leaguers like Gehringer, whom Bell would befriend long term, appreciated the alertness and dazzle that characterized the Negro Leaguers, who in turn were impressed by the pitching and especially the depth of the organized ballers.

When Suttles walloped two triples and a single in the opening match, it was the first time he'd faced a white professional pitcher: Willis Hudlin, a seventeen-game winner that year for Cleveland. When Wells won the game by stealing home and knocking the ball out of the hands of catcher Wally Schang of the Browns, whom he'd often watched at Sportsman's Park, it was likely the first time Schang or any of his teammates had lost in such a way. And when the Devil stole home in the *next* game as well, after one of his two triples, and the Giants won again—a 10–1 rout behind Willie Foster—eyes were opened all around. No doubt, the Negro Leaguers impressed *themselves* with their vivid success against the mainstreamers, and found it validating—perhaps even ironic, in a deeply satisfying way.

The All-Stars salvaged game three when Earl Whitehill of Detroit, a left-hander whom Bell later named as the toughest big-league pitcher he ever encountered, stopped the Negro Leaguers in a tight 1–0 shutout. But the American Giants bounced back with a 7–6 win in game four, which featured Suttles and Wells again and rendered moot the 2–0 decision for the All-Stars in game five, when George Uhle of the Tigers outdueled Foster. By that time the series had already mocked the color line.

"I sure am glad you colored players aren't in our league," Manush admitted to the American Giants after Cool Papa's extraordinary fly chasing had deprived him of a presumptive triple. "I wouldn't *ever* hit three hundred." The well-intended praise may, in fact, have ached as much as it flattered.

Bell, as usual, was circumspect about the relative prowess of the two parties. "Now, our league, on the whole, wasn't as strong as the major leagues, because a lot of the ballplayers wouldn't play because they wasn't making enough money; a lot of them had jobs," he said, reflecting upon his interracial experiences in interviews with the University of Missouri–St. Louis and John Holway. "But you pick an all-star team and you have the same chance at beating any major-league team. In later years, you could pick three teams out of each Negro League and put 'em in the major leagues and they could hold their own there, if they had enough men. But you see, we didn't carry but about fourteen to eighteen men. In the major leagues, they carry, you see, about twenty-five.

"Now, in a short series, we could beat 'em. For five years we played a postseason series against the Cardinals-Browns all-stars, and they didn't win one series. We didn't play baseball like they play in the major leagues. Our pitchers would curve the ball on the three-two [pitch]. They'd say, 'What, are you trying to make us look bad?' We'd bunt and run and they'd say, 'Why are you trying to do that in the first inning?' When we were supposed to bunt, they'd come in and we'd hit away. We'd go into third base standing up so the third baseman couldn't see the throw coming and it might go through him. Oh, we played tricky baseball.

"But you play more [games] than that, our pitchers, you know, wouldn't have enough rest. We kept about five pitchers. Sometimes, we'd have three outstanding pitchers. It's not that we couldn't get the pitchers if they was making enough money . . . but it wasn't paying anything. When I started, I didn't start playing ball just for money."

Of course, Cool Papa wasn't married when he started playing ball. Now that he was, and needed to keep the paychecks coming, another winter voyage to Cuba was in order for him and Clara Belle. His company also included Paige, Dihigo, Wells, and Suttles, whose league-leading barrage of home runs included one colossal blast that was measured at 598 feet. It was so historic a shot that the Cuban authorities memorialized it with a plaque.

In spite of so many friends in so compelling a locale, Bell rarely strayed far from Clara, which was well-advised. It meant that he was not party to the craps game that involved two members of the Baltimore Black Sox: their diminutive player-manager, Frank Warfield, and star third baseman, Oliver Marcelle, a Creole from Louisiana known as Ghost. No doubt, money, so hard to come by, was also material to that diversion, quite possibly at the center of a spirited quarrel that ended when Warfield bit off part of his third baseman's nose.

Such was 1929, not counting the Black Tuesday in late October that crashed the New York Stock Exchange and set off the Great Depression.

OUT OF THE darkness of the Depression came artificial ballpark light, carted around the Midwest by the Kansas City Monarchs. The portable lighting, brainchild of Monarchs owner J. L. Wilkinson, was an ungainly, gasoline-powered arrangement requiring two Ford trucks for transport and various players to help raise the expandable steel poles fifty feet above the field from the beds of the trucks. The generator made a racket, the gas produced an odor, blue smoke shrouded the premises, and pitchers could scarcely see their catchers' signs; the illumination, in fact, was insufficient for Kansas City's own spacious stadium. But there was money to be made playing games at night, and by mid-May 1930, when the Monarchs arrived at Stars Park for a league series after well-attended trial runs in Enid, Oklahoma; Independence, Kansas; and Des Moines, Iowa, the system had already paid for itself.

It was the first night baseball ever staged in St. Louis. Among the four thousand curious witnesses that landmark Monday—about three thousand, five hundred more than the Stars typically attracted—were Hack Wilson of the Chicago Cubs, whose team was in town playing the Cardinals (and who was in the process of setting a major-league record of 191 RBIs in a season, which still stands); most of the Cardinals; and their team president, Sam Breadon, who was considering the installation of lights for his organization's minor-league affiliates.

The Stars won that freighted matchup 4–0 and prevailed again two nights later 6–5 in front of six thousand folks. The events of the week would be instrumental in St. Louis edging Kansas City for the league's first-half title and even more significant in the decision of Stars owner Dick Kent to spend $19,000 for permanent lights at Stars

Park (the equivalent of nearly $300,000 today). A number of minor-league facilities were already equipped for night baseball, but the Stars would be first among Negro League teams and five years ahead of the major leagues.

The lights were up and running for an early September game with the Homestead Grays, and five thousand fans made a Wednesday evening of it. They were treated to an eleven-inning 6–5 St. Louis victory and an historic bonus: their first glimpse of Homestead's powerful eighteen-year-old catcher, Josh Gibson, just getting started on a career that would distinguish him as the Negro Leagues' most illustrious hitter.

Night baseball, in fact, was responsible for Gibson's early opportunity. A resident of Pittsburgh, he'd been present when the Monarchs brought their traveling lights to that city for a game against the Grays, whose catcher, Buck Ewing, was having a tough time receiving the ball in the relative darkness. When Ewing left the field with a gash in his hand, Judy Johnson, the Grays' esteemed third baseman, approached Gibson in the stands—the burly youngster had already developed a reputation in the amateur ranks—and asked if he'd like to strap on the catching gear.

"Yes sir, Mr. Johnson," he replied.

Gibson took a beating, but he made the team and the trip to St. Louis. There, batting against Double Duty Radcliffe and Ted Trent under cutting-edge candlepower, he also made an impression on the Stars, who wished to check him out away from the shadows, without the mask. "We said, bring him up close so we can look at him," Bell recalled. "He was just a boy!"

In his long career, there were few games that lodged in Cool Papa's memory like that one. Naturally, the reasons included Gibson and the novelty of playing baseball in a stadium unbowed by the setting of the sun. But, to Bell, the most indelible aspect of the consequential occasion was the far-reaching, durable indifference that attended it.

When the first major-league night game took place in Cincinnati in 1935, the lights at Crosley Field were theatrically switched on by President Roosevelt in the White House. Over the ensuing decades, history's lamps have shined back on that celebrated event. And every time he heard or read about Cincinnati and 1935, Bell bristled at the wrongness of it all.

As far as he was concerned, the first night game under permanent artificial lighting was played at Stars Park in 1930. And what's more, "no white man was connected with it," he told the *New York Amsterdam News*. "We did a lot of things for ourselves and the United States that we have never gotten credit for. We helped build this country."

As a practical matter, the lights at Dick Kent's Ballyard enabled the Stars to host four nights of bonus baseball late that summer over a five-game, handily won "little World Series" with the Houston Black Buffaloes, "colored champions of the South." There were also popular exhibition games against visiting white semipro teams, and a year later a pair of provocative encounters against a loaded club of major leaguers, the Max Carey All-Stars.

The first of the Max Carey games, a 10–8 victory for the Stars, was the occasion on which Ted Trent struck out Bill Terry four times. Big Florida split four more strikeouts between Paul Waner and Babe Herman, the latter being the only one of the three victims not later elected to the Hall of Fame.

In the second match, Cool Papa stole three bases—including home, of course—*on three straight pitches*, and the Stars cakewalked by an 18–1 count. That lopsided spectacle left the big leaguers and the *Post-Dispatch* in a scramble to rationalize the result and perpetuate the prevailing narrative in support of white superiority.

> Since then the boys have been trying to find an explanation for the All-Stars' downfall. Most of them refuse to believe that even the admittedly strong Negro Stars team is the equal of major league talent, even though they did belt the redoubtable pitcher, Heine Meine [a St. Louis native who that year, pitching for the Pittsburgh Pirates, led the National League in wins], for 12 hits.
>
> Most of the boys blame the lighting system, which is not of sufficient power, but to which the Negro players have become accustomed. At that flood lights have not bothered the many minor

league teams which play most of their games by electric light. Some measure of credit must go to the St. Louis Stars.

A unique explanation was offered by a veteran baseball player who requested that his name not be used. "I saw that game and I walked all around the park before the contest to get an idea of the effects of the lights. I found that there was a glare in the eyes of every player on the field and that even the batter suffered from this handicap, especially the white-skinned ones. The light, glancing on the white skin beneath the eyes was reflected back, affecting the batsman's vision.

"If the white players in those night games would darken their faces beneath the eyes, I feel sure that both their batting and their fielding would improve."

And that's that. Undoubtedly players performing under flood lights for the first time, are not able to do their stuff.

In his firm and quiet manner, however, Bell would never concede that that, indeed, was that. Nor would he ever, for that matter, accept the supposition that the achievements of black athletes or black scholars or black scientists or black clergy or black patriots or black farmers or black mothers or black butchers back at the St. Louis slaughterhouse were somehow insignificant.

"They kept the black hidden," he said, "not only in baseball—in any form of life that we had outstanding black people. Just like our baseball; they just said it was sandlot baseball.

"I want the young black kids to know what blacks did for this country. The black man has made the white man rich in this country. And all the time we were helping to build this country, they were treating us like dogs. We couldn't eat in the restaurants, sleep in the hotels, and they wouldn't let us play with them. We took great delight in whipping those major-league all-star teams after their season was over."

CHAPTER NINE

"THE GREATEST NEGRO BASEBALL TEAM EVER SEEN"

V ERY EARLY IN THE 1930 SEASON, BEFORE THE traveling lights arrived at Stars Park and long before the permanent lights were installed, the St. Louis team romped in the shadows. A rout of the American Giants, for instance, in which Cool Papa homered, was noted in the *Post-Dispatch* just below the dog-racing results. "It would seem," observed the competing *St. Louis Globe-Democrat* in a feature story on the Stars, "that here in St. Louis is an athletic institution that has been flourishing for a decade or more without the majority population of the city being aware of its existence."

The Negro Leagues were struggling to stay afloat in a troubled economy that exacted a heavy toll on discretionary money for the likes of going to baseball games. Bell was described as their highest-paid player, but there's no telling how many of the agreed-upon dollars he actually saw. Teams passed the hat to make payroll and still couldn't. A few NNL players, including Mule Suttles, Satchel Paige, and Turkey Stearnes, headed east in the hope that clubs on the more concentrated coast would be less burdened by travel and thereby less susceptible to the ravages of the Depression. Most of those fellows—Suttles, Paige, and Stearnes included—came back after a month or two.

Bell stayed put in St. Louis but missed several weeks in late spring, presumably due to an injury, which may or may not have been the painful corns between his toes, for which he conjured up a brew of soap, turpentine, and secret ingredients. Otherwise, he had seven hits in a doubleheader sweep of the Monarchs; four (and six runs scored) against Chicago, on which occasion the *Post-Dispatch* referred to him as Cool Papa for the first time (the *Pittsburgh Courier* had done so a few months earlier); four more hits (with a pair of triples) in a shutout of Kansas City; and a bunch, it seemed, every time the Stars played the Memphis Red Sox.

Candy Jim Taylor had relocated to Memphis, replaced as the St. Louis manager by Johnny "Sparkplug" (also "Speed Boy") Reese, a protégé of Rube Foster's. But Reese's deference to Foster—and Bell's and Wells's, for that matter—didn't stop the Stars from pounding his old team, the American Giants, fifteen times in a row. They were more hospitable to Kansas City, loaning their intimate rivals a couple of players, Frog Redus and Roosevelt Davis, when two of the Monarchs were hurt in an auto accident. And they were thoroughly submissive to Birmingham one day in July when Paige, gaining retribution for prior abuse, shut down St. Louis without breaking any thumbs or allowing a runner to reach second base.

While Satchel managed to make himself the centerpiece of most games he pitched, that one happened also to be the professional debut for Jimmie Crutchfield, a swift outfielder from Moberly, Missouri, next to whom Bell would later play for several special seasons. Crutchfield delivered three hits in support of Satch, winning the game on an inside-the-park home run deep to right center. "I hit it between Cool Papa and the right fielder," he reported, "and they said it had to be hit pretty hard and I had to be pretty fast to get a ball past Cool Papa and then beat his throw in."

Back in Moberly, Crutchfield worked as a barbershop porter at the Merchants Hotel, in competition with a left-handed fellow named Leroy Matlock who shined shoes nearby at the White Palace Barber

Shop. But Moberly's loafers and wingtips would be scraping through an extended period of inattention, for Matlock, too, was becoming a long-term Negro Leaguer, spinning a medley of breaking pitches for a stout St. Louis staff. Ted Trent, armed with perhaps the best curveball in blackball, was in his prime; Double Duty Radcliffe, when he wasn't catching, might have led the NNL in earned run average had it been an item; and Slap or Eggie Hensley, take your pick, paced the league's pitchers with eighteen victories.

As in the major leagues, however, 1930 was a notoriously hitting-heavy season on the Negro side of the aisle. The most robust of the batsmen were Stars, with Suttles and Wells, respectively, running first and second in the league in batting average—both exceeding .400—and the other way around in homers. The slugging style suited Reese, who boiled down his managerial philosophy as "Sock 'em and keep 'em socked." The net effect, according to the proud *Moberly Monitor-Index*, was a comprehensive club "that sports writers over the country acclaim as the 'greatest negro baseball team ever seen.'"

But another squad of Stars, the Detroit edition, would not permit that superlative to go unchallenged. There would be a legitimate league championship series this time—in the Negro Leagues, you could never be certain if, how, and at whose convenience that would happen—with St. Louis aspiring to a second title in three years and Detroit, paced by the return of the remarkable Turkey Stearnes, riding the best record in the season's second half.

Stearnes had acquired his nickname by virtue of a conspicuous chest bulging above his slender waist. "Turkey's gonna strut his stuff today," his fans would say, and he did so at the outset of game one, banging a two-run homer in the top of the first to put Detroit ahead. Bell answered summarily, leading off for St. Louis with a long ball of his own. The back-and-forth continued until Trent was summoned from the bullpen and Big Florida threw down five scoreless innings.

Homering again and going five for five in game two, Stearnes staked the visitors to a sizable lead that was seriously threatened in the eighth. John Henry Russell stood on third base for St. Louis and Bell was on second with no outs and five runs already in. Offering a best guess at what happened next, it appears that George Giles, a skilled first baseman whom the Stars had signed when Suttles sought a greener pasture, ripped a line drive to the right of Detroit's third baseman, Bobby Robinson, who snagged it barehanded, stepped on third to double Russell, and threw to second to triple Cool Papa, effectively and theatrically squaring the series.

In 1930, the path to the NNL championship had to go through Turkey Stearnes.

The third game, played under the new lights at Stars Park, was won by St. Louis on the strength of a home run from Suttles and more stalwart pitching from Trent. But when the action removed to Detroit—more specifically, to the commodious new stadium in Hamtramck—the Michiganders took command with a pair of tight decisions. The go-ahead victory was secured by clutch relief pitching from Pee Wee Powell, the little right-hander who, playing for Chicago, had stymied St. Louis in the 1928 championships before his wife's father accidentally discharged a shotgun into Pee Wee's stunned expression.

The series was scheduled for nine games, but the weather forecast was skeptical in that regard. The drama was consequently heightened in game six, which included a leadoff single, steal, and run scored by Bell in the first; a stunning 450-foot home run by the wiry Stearnes in the fourth, the first ever to clear the distant right-field fence at Hamtramck Stadium; an inside-the-park response from Wells the very next inning, in the very same direction; and a two-out, eighth-inning, run-scoring single by Cool Papa that left the teams level at three wins apiece.

The Stars' advantage was depth of both batting and pitching, and when Stearnes went hitless in game seven, the issue was all but settled. Cool and Wells led a St. Louis assault that ended at 13–7 and beat the rain that pelted Detroit immediately thereafter.

In place of games eight and nine, there was a parade in St. Louis for the greatest Negro baseball team ever seen, for the time being.

IT IS PERIODS such as this one that frustrate the seekers of Cool Papa Bell. We can say with certainty that, because of baseball, he was not among the 25 percent of Americans unemployed in 1930, and because of baseball he was not surviving hand-to-mouth in one of the Hoovervilles—shantytowns of cardboard, tar paper, and scrap metal hovels that rose up on the margins of cities, often along riverbanks—that altered the national landscape that year. But we don't know, entirely, about the *baseball*. Certainly not all of it.

There's a tantalizing hint of the Stars chasing their championship with a team trip to Cuba, but no chronicle of it. There's a mention or two but no particulars regarding an exhibition series played in Chicago and Milwaukee in which Cool and his St. Louis cohorts won six of eight games against a major-league collection that included some of the friendly foes they'd successfully engaged the year before, notably Charlie Gehringer, Harry Heilmann, George Uhle, and Wally Schang. ("It is interesting to note," pointed out the mainstream *Globe-Democrat,* "that in several post-season contests in which Negro all-stars have been pitted against white all-stars from the big leagues, the former have won the greater percentage of games. Competent judges have frequently remarked that numerous of these agile performers would be holding down positions in the white man's leagues today were there not the barriers of race.") And there's a more generally acknowledged allusion to Cool Papa playing that year in the California Winter League, where he reportedly opposed and influenced the St. Louis Cardinals' late-blooming outfielder Pepper Martin.

Martin, subsequently dubbed the Wild Horse of the Osage, had spent seven years in the minor leagues and appeared sparingly for the Cardinals in 1930. But he was possessed of speed and chutzpah, and in California he took note of the way Cool Papa utilized those assets for mischief making and extra bases. Or so both of them testified. However, the California Winter League literature shows evidence of neither that year, even though, in Bell's case, the rosters included Wells, Suttles, and Dewey Creacy, his regular-season running mates. Perhaps Cool and Martin competed in a less organized barnstorm setting, which would not have been abnormal.

At any rate, and wherever they met, Martin marveled at the manner in which Bell and his blackball accomplices "drove us nuts" stealing bases, advancing from first to third on sacrifice bunts, scoring from second on fly balls, and generally seizing opportunity where none appeared obvious to the conventionally trained eye. To the unprivileged black players, improvisation was a way of life. Cool Papa's first-to-third gambit was so frequently perpetrated that sometimes "the pitcher would field the ball," attested Bell, "and instead of throwing it to first base he'd throw it to third and maybe get me in a hot box."

Finally, the Wild Horse approached Cool about his bold baserunning, and the kind Mississippian shared his thoughts on maximizing leadoffs, studying outfielders as they fielded base hits, and maintaining vigilance at all times. "I made up my mind I would play that type of ball in the majors," said Martin, privately wishing he could do so in the same lineup as Papa.

The following year, the colorful Cardinal broke through with a .300 batting average, backed up by a sensational World Series in which he hit .500 over the seven games and stole more bases—five—than everyone else combined. St. Louis unseated the muscular Athletics of Philadelphia, reversing the outcome of the previous season, and when journalists questioned Martin about his conspicuous daring on the basepaths, he credited Cool Papa Bell.

Meanwhile, the inspiration for *Bell's* running game succumbed to his miseries in the final month of 1930. Wherever Cool had spent the aftermath of the Stars' triumph in Hamtramck, we know that he was back in St. Louis in early December, because it was from there that he and Willie Wells caught a bus to Chicago for Rube Foster's funeral at St. Mark's Methodist Episcopal Church on the South Side.

Their arrival was not early enough to gain them entrance alongside the three thousand admirers who packed the church, which was decorated with a two-hundred-pound baseball made of white chrysanthemums, with red roses for seams. So they stood outside, in the freezing rain, with another three thousand. Despite the cold, the windows of the sanctuary were left open so those in the elements could at least hear the moving service.

Cool and the Devil had themselves a good cry when Rube's casket was carried out and the choir sang "Rock of Ages."

AFTER THE PASSING of Foster at the close of 1930, it seemed as though the Negro National League, reeling from the Depression—many of the owners, their fortunes built on vice rackets, suffered severely in the absence of customers who had the cash to sin with—lost its will to live. The American Giants floundered under their new owner, who was, appropriately, an undertaker. The Kansas City Monarchs, making the most of their portable lights, eschewed their regular league schedule in favor of an extended, more profitable tour with the popular House of David barnstorming team, which represented an Israelite colony in Benton Harbor, Michigan, but was better known for its players' beards and unbarbered hair.

The Stars' 1931 season began auspiciously enough. On opening day, their 1930 pennant flag was raised amidst speeches and ceremony, and they whipped Detroit, 8–2. Cool Papa, in his prime now at twenty-nine, showed the way with three hits and as many stolen bases.

A notable entry in the box score for that game, as a substitute catcher, was eighteen-year-old Quincy Trouppe, a strapping athlete who just the year before had finished playing scholastic ball for Vashon High, situated across the street from Stars Park. The ballpark, in fact, was the center of the youngster's universe. "I was thrilled just to see the famous players pass on the street," Trouppe would write in his autobiography, *20 Years Too Soon.* "Whenever Bell walked around, sometimes with his pretty wife, Clara, he was always tagged after by two or three kids, and one of those kids was bound to be me. Cool Papa Bell was a good-looking man, one of the best dressed in baseball, and it was no wonder he attracted so many young fans eager to walk in his shadow down the streets of Compton Hill."

Vashon played its home games at Stars Park, and Bell had observed Trouppe there from time to time. For Vashon's 1930 championship match with Sumner, the other black high school in the city, Cool Papa was joined by Suttles and Trent, watching with critical eyes.

A native St. Louisan and fan of Cool Papa, Quincy Trouppe (batting) had hopes for a long career with the Stars. He settled for a long career in baseball.

Trouppe's talent was evident, as was his enthusiasm for baseball, and the Stars gladly brought him on as a batboy, even sneaking him into a game or two as a player that summer. He had the throwing power to pitch and the batting power to play anywhere else—Bell, along with Frog Redus, worked with him in the outfield, urging Trouppe to ratchet down his arm and hit the cutoff man—but the big fellow's heart was set on catching. On that score, however, there was a hitch: The Stars' manager, Johnnie Reese, was reluctant to entrust those vital duties to an untested player, no matter how impressive. So, as the roster for 1931 was being set, Bell intervened on the teenager's behalf. "And then," Trouppe wrote, "there it was. I was looking at my first professional baseball contract, thanks to Cool Papa Bell." It was for $80 a month, a tad less than Bell's starting wages at Independent Packing.

In a May game at Detroit—part of a doubleheader in which Bell, who would bat .330 that year, was six for eight at the plate—Trouppe was called in to pitch in relief of Leroy Matlock, struck out Turkey Stearnes, then came to bat and tripled in a run. By all appearances, he was destined for a fine career with his hometown team. But that was about to become impossible.

Two months later, after dominating the NNL over the first half of the season, the Stars sold their stadium to the city of St. Louis for $100,000. It would be converted into "a playground for Negroes."

The sale of the ballpark assured the imminent demise of both the franchise and the NNL. In a sense, it was the Stars' own fault, having demoralized the competition. An article two years later in the *St. Louis Star* explained that the collaborations of Bell, Wells, Suttles, Trent, and influential owner Dick Kent, among others, "became so strong that they broke up the Negro National Baseball League. . . . Interest in other cities began to wane because of the Stars' steam-roller victory march. After winning two pennants and piling up a commanding lead in 1931, the Stars found themselves without opposition."

After the transfer of Dick Kent's Ballyard and before it was dismantled for the children, the club did play some games there, but not many and not for a while. It's curious, consequently, that the Stars were generally described, and still are, as league champions that year,

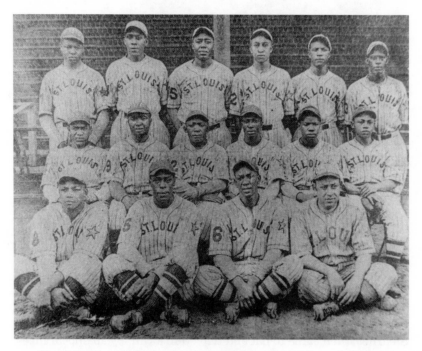

The 1931 Stars were in the process of perpetuating the team's NNL supremacy when their ballpark was suddenly cashed in.

in spite of a so-called World Series contested between Kansas City of the NNL and the Homestead Grays of the East league. It's curious, too, that during a twelve-day break in said World Series, which Homestead would win, St. Louis hosted three games against the Grays, featuring Cool Papa's five-for-five hitting performance in the first of them.

The NNL had come to be characterized by a capricious, haphazard state of affairs that contributed, certainly, to its charm and mystique but ultimately to its mortality as well. The league would be out of business at the anticlimactic conclusion to the 1931 season.

The Stars, unable to get games with vanishing and resentful league members, played out the string with an eye toward paydays that the regular agenda could no longer provide. They took a trip to Moberly, Missouri, and let Matlock pitch before a sizable audience of his home folks. They took on a team of Cardinal minor leaguers, winning with an eleventh-inning homer by Bell and an emphatic shutout by Slap Hensley, who struck out twenty-one of Branch Rickey's famous farmhands. They took the measure of the Max Carey All-Stars, thumbing their noses at the color line. And they brought in the flowing-haired wonders from the House of David, whose ranks included forty-four-year-old pitching great Grover Cleveland Alexander, retired from organized ball for more than a year.

Lovingly known as Old Pete, Alexander was a St. Louis icon, his salient moment having come as a Cardinal in a legendary, possibly hungover game-seven relief outing against the Yankees in the 1926 World Series, following two complete-game victories of his own. Judging by the coverage in the *Post-Dispatch*, Alexander's appearance in '31 was of far more importance than the farewell of the Negro League team that had just claimed its purported third championship in four seasons.

> The crowd gave him a good hand as he peeled off his old Cardinal sweater and stalked out to the pitcher's box with the old familiar gait. He snapped three balls to the catcher and was ready for the game. His first offering was a high hard one which "Cool Papa" Bell, the Stars' center fielder, let go for a strike, and the crowd roared its appreciation.
>
> The two games attracted many who followed Alexander's career in the big leagues. Saturday it seemed less than half of the crowd of 1500 were Negroes, and yesterday there were many white men and women.

The Stars knocked Old Pete around a bit and won both games, but that was scarcely a footnote. Their time had passed.

In the late thirties, the Stars name would be revived for a while. The magic, however, would not. The second iteration of the St. Louis Stars would come without Bell, Wells, Suttles, Big Florida, stadium lights, a significant following, or distinction of any meaningful kind.

By that point Cool Papa was covering center field for the franchise that would make people forget the *previous* greatest Negro baseball team ever seen. If they hadn't already.

CHAPTER TEN

MUTINY

T HERE WAS MUCH TO COMMEND THE
California Winter League. In spite of the steadfast efforts
of the commissioner's office to minimize interracial
competition—or white players being outclassed, as the case seemed
often to be—the CWL continued to provide the struggling, scrambling
black players with platforms and paychecks.

Their livelihoods were particularly unsteady in the off-season
that followed the undoing of the Negro National League. For those
with enough cachet to be recruited for a Winter League gig—among
the former St. Louis Stars, that included usual suspects Bell, Wells,
Suttles, Creacy, and Trent—Los Angeles was a place to regroup and
thrash some white teams. Throughout the 1920s, the league's annual
black team had been confined to cavernous White Sox Park in South
Los Angeles, but in the thirties, when racial restrictions were lifted
from nearby Wrigley Field, a Pacific Coast League venue, Negro Leaguers dominated in that historic stadium also.

The Philadelphia Royal Giants, as the black entry was called in
the winter of 1931–32, were put together by a Tennessee entrepreneur

named Tom Wilson, whose ownership of a bus line, a ballpark, a nightclub, a gas station, and considerable real estate, among other commodities, had made him one of the wealthiest African Americans in the land. As the founder of the Negro Southern League and a vital figure in the California Winter League, he was also one of the country's leading advocates for black baseball—Tom Wilson Park in Nashville housed spring training for various Negro League teams—and a fellow who certainly knew how to stack a ball club.

On his Royal Giants, the starry St. Louisans were joined, most notably, by Satchel Paige and Willie Foster, who would post respective records of 6-0 and 9-1. In addition, Big Florida was 3-0 with a pair of shutouts when he up and quit, having determined that he could no longer deal with the booing he received for striking out Caucasians.

Bell, Wells, and Suttles all banged the ball for batting averages that exceeded .400—Mule led the league with a preposterous .586—and Wilson's overwhelming club burned through the schedule with an eye-popping record of 22-2. Satchel, meanwhile, was in his element for the first of his many celebrated showdowns with big leaguers, milking his mismatches with an almost vaudevillian flourish. He, like Trent, put up two shutouts, one of them resulting in a tight 1–0 victory over San Diego, a game presumably played under the lights just installed by the Pirrone brothers (Joe and John), the owners of White Sox Park and architects of the CWL.

Paige permitted but one hit in that defensive struggle, struck out thirteen, and got all the help he needed from the speediest of his new best friends. According to the *Pittsburgh Courier*, "The Giants scored the only run of the game when catcher Warren missed the third strike on J. Bell, who reached first base by some fast running. He stole second and scored on Vic Harris's single [apparently the Giants' only hit]. This was the greatest game ever played at White Sox Park."

As the poundings proceeded, the regrouping efforts were also coming along, every man endeavoring to find his own way in the year ahead. In the absence of the Negro National or any other established league, and with delineations between the Midwest and East rubbed out, blackball that winter was a carnival of teams and players in desperate, opportunistic, unregulated pursuit of each other. There was no acknowledged commissioner to lay down the guidelines, and every roster spot stirred a vigorous spirit of open marketing on the midway.

When spring was nigh, Bell, Wells, Suttles, Creacy, Trent, and Vic Harris all decided to cast their lot with the Detroit Wolves (no longer the Stars, and no longer headlined by Turkey Stearnes), assembled by manager Dizzy Dismukes and owned by highly respected Cumberland Posey of Pittsburgh, the longtime honcho of the Homestead Grays. A former college athlete whose father was a shipbuilder, industrialist, publisher, and the wealthiest black man in Pittsburgh, and whose mother was the first black teacher at Ohio State University, Posey—who still ran the Grays as well—was in the process of instituting the new East-West League.

For his part, Dismukes, a well-traveled former pitcher, moonlighted as a columnist ("Dizzy's Dope on Baseball") for the *Pittsburgh Courier*, over which Posey's father had presided for fourteen years. In mid-March, the Wolves' skipper used his convenient forum for an important announcement:

> After weeks of dickering, James Bell, baseball's fastest human, finally affixed his signature to a Detroit contract. Bell was born at Starksville [*sic*], Miss., May 17, 1903. He began his baseball career as a member of the Compton Hill Cubs, St. Louis, Mo., playing the seasons of 1920 and 1921. He broke in as a pitcher.
>
> James [Candy Jim] Taylor . . . placed Bell in the outfield where he has established himself as one of the game's greatest outer gardeners. Bell is a turn around [switch] hitter, throws left handed, is five feet nine inches tall, weighs 157 pounds, and is happily married. Bell is affectionately called "Cool Pappa" by his team-mates.

What it lacked in pedigree, the East-West League attempted to make up for with good intentions and publicity. It resolved, specifically, to engage Negro League fans with a steadier presence in the black newspapers—the "race papers," they called them—emphasizing game reports and statistics. The objective was not only to apprise readers more thoroughly about their local teams but, with the geographical barriers giving way, to familiarize the fans of the East with the stars of the West and vice versa.

Late in the 1932 preseason, that cause was taken up by Dick Lundy, an illustrious player—among Negro League shortstops, he is eclipsed only by Pop Lloyd and Willie Wells—who at the time managed the Baltimore Black Sox and corresponded for the *Baltimore Afro-American*: "We have developed, in the past few years, some great young ball players, but the fans, throughout the country, don't know anything about some of them because the owners neglected to advertise them properly," Lundy wrote in his baseball column, "Dick's Diamond Dope." "We have some of the game's greatest players, men with plenty of color. Take men like our own [Showboat] Thomas, first baseman, who proved a sensation wherever he played; and Wells, the boy who performs with just as much dash and brilliance as Thomas. 'Cool Papa' Bell has been labeled the fastest ball player that ever drew on a pair of spiked shoes. And there are numerous others."

WITH SO MANY recent St. Louis Stars on hand—also coming over were Quincy Trouppe, John Henry Russell (better known to some as Pistol Johnny), and a promising young pitcher named Bertrum Hunter—the Detroit club was an instant powerhouse. The Wolves sprinted out to a dazzling start of 25-5; or maybe it was 20-6, 29-13, or 38-12, depending on which source you consulted. The premium the league had placed on record keeping wasn't quite having the desired effect.

By June, it was apparent that Cum Posey's hastily formed federation was no match for the Depression, which, in some cities, assaulted African American communities with unemployment rates three times the national average of white citizens. Most of the league teams proved unsustainable, and most of the second-half schedule went unplayed. The East-West League wouldn't last the season.

A few of the franchises soldiered on, but prolific winning, by whichever account, was not enough to save the Wolves. The Homestead Grays, Posey's *other* team, were closer to his heart and hearth, and his resources would now be fully devoted to them. The deep-rooted Grays were in dire need of nothing less, having suddenly found themselves in contentious competition with a new crosstown rival, the Pittsburgh Crawfords.

Operated by impresario and racketeer Gus Greenlee, freewheeling proprietor of the popular Crawford Grill, the Crawfords had been founded the year before as an ambitious extension of a successful local amateur team. In a time of Depression economics, banking on the support of an impoverished black community, Gasoline Gus (a moniker Greenlee had acquired by selling whiskey from the trunk of his taxi) promptly built his new team a splendid stadium in the north side's Hill District. Owned entirely by African Americans, Greenlee Field was dedicated in the spring of 1932, with marching bands accompanying the flamboyant owner as he was carried onto the diamond in a red convertible to throw out the first pitch in a white silk suit.

Greenlee saw to it that his ballpark, like his grill, would stage only first-class entertainment. To that end, he signed Satchel Paige, who was now hitting his stride; and even more dramatically, from the Pittsburgh perspective, he spirited the great Oscar Charleston and the slugging local wunderkind, Josh Gibson, from the Homestead Grays.

And so the battle was joined, the bootlegger's team against the privileged college man's. The two sides were not *league* opponents—disinclined to share Pittsburgh, Posey had effectively prohibited the Crawfords from gaining membership in the East-West by demanding untenable terms for their admission—but they would play each other from time to time and tussle unceasingly for audience and talent.

In that respect, the premature demise of the Detroit Wolves was not altogether inconvenient for Posey. His original team, after all, having lost Josh Gibson and Oscar Charleston, was now in jeopardy of losing *Pittsburgh*. There were some erstwhile Wolves who could be useful to him in preventing that.

Gus Greenlee, kingpin of Pittsburgh's Hill District,
with two friends, a smoke, and his wife, Helen (right)

And that was how Cool Papa Bell became a Homestead Gray.
Along with his sidekick, Willie Wells.

IT WAS AROUND this time that Negro League teams stopped
taking trains, instead transporting their players in buses or multiple,
overcrowded automobiles. They sometimes drove all night, sleeping
on each other's shoulders and shifting in unison when somebody
called out, "Swing!" Other times they would pull up at a dim hotel for
"coloreds," grab their suit rolls—uniform (if they weren't still wearing
it), shirt, socks, trousers, ball glove, etc.—and claim their rooms by
tossing their hat or suit roll on a bed that didn't sag too much, if possible. The whole team might share a toilet and tub. On one occasion,
the Grays spent the night in a hotel that wasn't quite as affordable as

they'd hoped and, to settle the bill, the local sheriff auctioned off their car right there in the parking lot.

Flexibility was the rule of thumb. If public accommodations were simply not available and the collective grime no longer tolerable, a stop might be made at a sympathetic household with a backyard and oversized kettle, in which water was heated and the players would scrub off two or three ball games. Teams would sleep in a YMCA just for the common shower. Negro Leaguers, athletes who excelled at the most popular game in America—the best of them playing at the level of Lou Gehrig, Jimmie Foxx, Bill Dickey, Lefty Grove, and Dizzy Dean—would curl up next to farmworkers at a dusty migrant camp.

In the Depression, expenses were not just monitored but assailed. Even in the unsinkable major leagues, attendance dropped by 40 percent over the first four summers after Black Tuesday, prompting franchises to pare rosters from twenty-five players to twenty-three and slash salaries by 25 percent. Circumstances in the Negro Leagues were naturally more dire. When the East-West sputtered to a halt and Bell and Wells hooked up with Homestead, Posey did away with salaries and paid his roster with a percentage of the gate. It was never a large percentage and rarely a large gate.

Cool and his teammates understood that times were tough. By 1932, more than thirteen million Americans were unemployed. But the Grays had jobs. They played hard, often, and well. And still, they bathed in kettles.

The Homestead players—mostly Bell and Wells, in different ways—took out their frustrations on Cum Posey. Cool Papa, a gentleman objector but unflinchingly firm, couched his grievances in terms of fairness and obligation. The Devil was less diplomatic, particularly when he was sleeping in the Grays' locker room one morning and Posey woke him to get going for a game that night in Toronto, whereupon the worn-out shortstop advised the parsimonious owner that he valued his health more than the pittance he was making on percentage.

The situation came to a head on the last Saturday in June, during a doubleheader in Detroit—go figure—between the two Pittsburgh teams. At some point of the first game, Wells expressed his displeasure with a call at first base by tossing dirt in the umpire's face. In a flash, all the Grays and Crawfords were on the field in a fighting mood.

Cool Papa rapped out three hits in that contest, then informed Posey between games that they would be his last for Homestead unless the players were paid in advance of game two. When his terms were declined, Bell walked out with Wells and three others.

"William [*sic*] Bell (Cool Papa) led the mutiny which threatened to leave the Grays without a full team five minutes before game time," reported the *Pittsburgh Courier.*

The next game he played was with the Crawfords. As was the next, the following day. Greenlee made him an offer, and Cool was tempted by the audacious wheeler-dealer and the sweet new ballpark and the Crawford Grill and Satchel and Gibson and Charleston and Pistol Johnny and Double Duty.

But Wells was already headed to the Kansas City Monarchs and there had been conversations and Cool Papa had made a commitment—at least, *sort of* a commitment, or what loosely qualified as one in the Negro Leagues in 1932. Whatever it was, honoring it would bring a semblance of integrity into his professional life, which was what he really needed right about then, almost as much as a regular paycheck.

The Monarchs would be his fourth team that year, and it wasn't even July.

THERE'S A FADED black-and-white photograph of the 1932 Kansas City Monarchs, thirteen strong, standing in the grass, shoulder to shoulder, hands behind their belts, caps pushed back a bit, shadows on their foreheads, baggy trousers, striped socks riding high, "Monarchs" arced or slanted across the chests of their light-colored jerseys, block lettering on a few, script on the rest. Above some thin, distant trees, in the upper left corner, within the hand-sketched outline of a pennant, the solemn squad is labeled tidily as World Colored Champions—which is curious, because Kansas City didn't play in the East-West

League that year, showed up only periodically in the Southern League, and is not known to have won any crowning tournaments.

You wouldn't call it a snapshot, because it's a wide-angle arrangement, but then again, just about any Negro League team photo might be considered a snapshot of sorts, as famously fluid as the rosters tended to be, each alignment a moment in passing. To wit, more than half of the baker's-dozen Monarchs in the picture—Bell, Wells, George Giles, Quincy Trouppe, Newt Allen, Bertrum Hunter, Thomas Jefferson "T. J." Young—had been St. Louis Stars the previous season.

The other six were Chet Brewer, an accomplished pitcher and Monarch mainstay; veteran catcher Frank Duncan; utility man Dink Mothell; Hooks Beverly, a curveballing lefty; nickname specialist Popsicle Harris, also known as Moochie, depending on which part of the country his current club was situated in; and, holding down the far left in the eloquent photo, Newt Joseph, a fireplug third baseman who excelled at shooting rabbits or the occasional pheasant through the windows of the old Dodges in which the Monarchs crisscrossed the rural Midwest.

After bolting from the Homestead Grays in midseason, Bell and Wells found their way into the Kansas City Monarchs' team picture.

Joseph sported an additional talent that held an abiding place in Cool Papa's heart. It enabled Bell to prove—at least to himself— that, contrary to folklore, his baseball skills were not confined to his accelerator.

"I wouldn't want nobody to call me the greatest all-around

ballplayer, because I've seen too many great ballplayers," Papa said in an interview with Charlie Harville for the Society for American Baseball Research (SABR). However, in regard to the actual inventory of his toolbox, he was compelled to point out, "I had power. They say now that I couldn't hit a long ball. But they didn't want me to do that.

"The longest ball I think I ever hit [was] in 1932. [The other team] had Lester Williams—he was a white boy—pitching for them. We had a guy named Newt Joseph; he could steal signals. He said, 'Lookit, if I tell you what's coming, could you hit it?' I said yes. He said, 'Now, when I tell you, *take your time*, it's a curveball. When I say, *come on, get right on it*, it's a fastball.'

"They had a highway out there over the fence, and a cornfield, and [when the pitch came] he said, 'Get right on it!' You know how there's always a boy to go get the ball if it goes over the fence? They threw it and I hit that ball to center field, over the highway, so far into the cornfield that the boy wouldn't go out and get it; it was too dark. That was in Oxford, Nebraska. [Newt Joseph] said, 'Get right on it,' and I knew it was a fastball. I was going to write and ask them if they ever found that ball and measured how far it was."

Bell was identified that year as an all-star in both the East-West League and the Southern. Amidst all the upheaval of 1932, it was actually one of the better years for the Southern League, which appropriated more than its usual share of blackball standouts. The Chicago American Giants played in the Southern League that season, for lack of a friendlier option, bringing along Turkey Stearnes, Willie Foster, Pee Wee Powell, and Alec Radcliffe, Double Duty's less versatile brother. The Nashville Elite Giants, owned by California League activist Tom Wilson, boasted Wild Bill Wright and Black Bottom Buford.

But all the while, Gus Greenlee was scheming ahead, maneuvering to put the Negro National League together again. He strove, primarily, to assure that his Pittsburgh Crawfords would be associated with an entity over which he, and not Cumberland Posey, exercised a great deal of control.

By the time the Monarchs returned from a monthlong, economically challenged postseason tour of Mexico—midway between Franklin Roosevelt's landslide defeat of Herbert Hoover and the ushering in of his New Deal—the California Winter League had knocked off early, Gasoline Gus had pieced together a seven-team revival of the NNL, and the Crawfords' latest offer was waiting for Cool Papa. This time he accepted.

CHAPTER ELEVEN

BEHOLDING JOSH GIBSON

I N LATE MARCH 1933, AN OLD TEAMMATE OF COOL
Papa's, pitcher Leroy Matlock, and a new one, outfielder Jimmie
Crutchfield, meandered down from Moberly, Missouri, to meet
up with Clara Bell's soft-spoken husband in St. Louis, where the Bells
lived on crowded Lawton Avenue with Clara's aunt and uncle and a
few others. There, the three players would fill up on the last home
cooking they'd see for a while, pack some leftovers, and wait for the
Crawfords' twenty-two-seat, smartly painted, handsomely stenciled,
custom-built Mack bus, with genuine grain leather upholstery and
vacuum-boosted foot brakes.

A bold replacement for the two Lincoln Model L town cars
that had facilitated the club's unrelenting road-tripping, the new
bus departed from Pittsburgh with nine Crawfords aboard, including Josh Gibson, Judy Johnson, outfielder Ted Page, and manager
Oscar Charleston, headed, ultimately—after picking up the St. Louis
contingent—to Memphis, Tennessee, for spring training and a month
or so of Southern exhibition games. Of course, Satchel Paige was not
among the card gamers and highway nappers; as always, he had his

own automobile and his own agenda. Matlock and Bertrum Hunter were preparing to outpitch him, anyway.

It felt strange for Bell to embark on a season without Willie Wells at his side, or Mule Suttles, for that matter—they were now in Indianapolis, where the Chicago American Giants set up shop because their old park was being converted to a dog track—but he'd fallen in easily with Matlock and Crutchfield and Page, and he seemed cut from the same cloth as Judy Johnson, the thoughtful son of an East Coast seaman and coach. He considered Johnson the greatest all-around third baseman he ever saw, but that was just for starters.

A former boxer and stevedore, Johnson was, most of all— notwithstanding his considerable skill at stealing signs from opposing coaches and players—a gentleman of consummate integrity. Ted Page recalled when the Crawfords were in some forgotten small town and Johnson came up a penny short of paying the barber in full, whereupon he walked a mile back to the motel, fetched a penny, then turned around and walked back to the shop to square his bill. "Judy was the best," Cool Papa said. "You could trust him in every way. He would never let you down. When things were tough, Judy would say, 'Just keep goin', boys, the sun will be shining up there someplace.' Judy Johnson and Jimmie Crutchfield are the two finest people I met in baseball."

Bell was intrigued also by young Josh Gibson, whose preternatural power he'd already heard so much about. It didn't betray itself in the brawny catcher's demeanor on the bus. What showed, though, was the mentoring he'd received from Judy Johnson when both played for (and Johnson managed) the Homestead Grays. Gibson's only vice appeared to be eating too much ice cream—too much *everything*, really. His manner was innately sweet, disarmingly goofy, eminently likable, and so innocent that his older teammates minded their manners when discussing women in his presence.

In short order, Papa would see for himself the brute force that the sharecropper's son—whose father had moved the family from Georgia to Pittsburgh when he took a job in a steel plant—could bring to bear on a baseball with his blacksmith arms and forty-inch, forty-ounce

Judy Johnson: a third baseman Cool Papa could trust in every way

bat, which was simply too much lumber for anyone else but Suttles. He saw it when Gibson, feet spread wide in the batter's box, little finger wrapped around the knob of his imposing bludgeon, became the first man to clear the roof at Yankee Stadium; when Gibson clubbed a ball over a tree and a guard shack and onto the railroad tracks in Monessen, Pennsylvania, and the watchman ran out to grab it; when Gibson shot one over the high and distant center-field fence at Griffith Stadium in Washington, D.C.; when Gibson's home runs kept coming and coming and going and going. They were not lofty, aesthetically pleasing clouts, like Babe Ruth's, but screaming, supercharged missiles, launched with a short, efficient, wrist-driven swing that reminded Bell of Lou Gehrig's.

But the comparison that most interested him involved Mule Suttles. Cool Papa's longtime teammate had become his standard for power hitting, and Cool was curious to find out whether, as word had it, Josh had truly supplanted his old pal as first among fence busters.

When Bell joined the Crawfords, "they told me they had a guy who can hit the ball further than Mule," he recollected to Rod Roberts in his Hall of Fame oral history session. "I said, 'Further than Mule?'" Even if that were true—and it soon became apparent that it probably was—could he knock it out of the park as *frequently* as Mule? Skeptical, and unimpressed by Negro League record keeping, Cool Papa resolved, for 1933, to do some arithmetic himself in the matter of Gibson's home runs, tracking them in a little private ledger.

And while he was at it, he'd tabulate his own stolen bases, thank you very much.

WHEN WORKOUTS COMMENCED in Memphis—where the players could visit a local movie theater by entering through an alley and up the fire escape to the "buzzard roost" next to the projector— Bell found himself in competition for center field with a commanding thirty-six-year-old whom many, including Cool Papa, would come to regard as the greatest everyday Negro Leaguer. As it happened, Oscar Charleston was also the Crawfords' manager.

In that capacity, Charleston, who by dint of his very nature wouldn't abide the thought of putting less than his best team on the field, set up a little contest: Another player would hit fly balls to be caught by whichever center fielder got there first. Charleston was a faultless fly chaser, but after a few minutes of chasing *Bell*, fly after fly, he wisely repurposed himself as a first baseman.

With Bell in center and Page and Crutchfield on his flanks—both nearly as fast and spectacular as he—fly balls against the Crawfords were overmatched. Later, when Sam Bankhead replaced Page, the Pittsburgh outfielders acquired the sobriquet of the "Raindrop Rangers," able, it was said, to keep a field dry by catching the raindrops until the clouds blew over. But Page, too, was a player who put his speed to considerable advantage.

Much like Cool Papa, he was an excellent bunter and a baserunning dynamo. With the New York Black Yankees the year before, Page had spoiled the grand opening of Greenlee Field, scoring the game's only run in the ninth inning with a single, a steal, and so on. Not long after, Greenlee had encouraged him to jump to the Crawfords, and to ensure that Page didn't leave Pittsburgh the same way, the generous racketeer gave him a second job as a lookout at the side door of the numbers operation, with a bell to ring if trouble showed up. Page was worldlier than most of the Crawfords, his family having been the only black one in the Monkey's Nest enclave of Youngstown, Ohio, a neighborhood of steel-working immigrants from Eastern Europe. A necessarily rugged sort, the lefty swinger had turned down a football scholarship to Ohio State and redirected his aggressiveness toward basemen attempting to tag him out. Or combative roommates: He'd been the other party in the infamous George Scales fight, in which Scales lost a couple of teeth, Page was nicked by a knife, and they went to bed that night armed and watchful.

Crutchfield was a less menacing fellow, the smallest man in the league and the best team player, in the opinion of Cool Papa. Labeled "the Mite from Moberly," he was often compared to Lloyd Waner, the Hall of Fame outfielder who played next to his brother Paul on the Pittsburgh Pirates; Little Poison and Big Poison, respectively. "I used to think about that a lot," said the courteous Missourian, who was known to snag an occasional line drive with his throwing hand. "He was on the other side of town making twelve thousand dollars a year and I didn't have enough money to go home. I had to borrow bus fare. It seemed like there was something wrong there.... [But] when you're doing something you love to do, there's nothing lousy about it."

The Crawfords, in general, seemed to feel that way about playing ball, even in the face of Charleston's ferocity. As they pulled out of camp for their tour of the South, fully enjoying their teammates and collective clout, their enthusiasm was a rather remarkable thing after two years of shattered leagues and folded teams and disappearing wages. The synergy was soon apparent to John L. Clark of the *Pittsburgh Courier*:

> There is a different spirit, a hustling, hitting combination that has tucked under their belt 25 straight wins.

> Two men with the Charleston clan this year stand out. [Bertrum] Hunter, the 22-year-old shark, who lost 5 and won 49 last year. And Cool Papa, the base-running streak and fly ball hawk. Both are unassuming and appear to be anything but the stars they are. . . . [Bell is] a sensational fielder, a hard hitter and the fastest man in the game. He is a most dangerous man on bases.
>
> The team as a whole is a most interesting one. . . .

Times being what they were, though—U.S. Steel, headquartered in Pittsburgh, was operating at a capacity of only 14 percent—the Crawfords' tours were not entirely about winning. The ball club was entertainment for hire as well, a circumstance that, when it compromised the integrity of the product, Cool Papa simply couldn't countenance. On one occasion, the event was a donkey baseball game. Bell bristled at the indignity, refused to make a fool of himself, and told Charleston he was having none of it. The fearsome skipper threatened to fire him, but Cool called his bluff, knowing that Greenlee wouldn't allow that to happen.

It wasn't the only time that Papa's pride placed him at odds with the game's toughest man. When the Crawfords hired multisport star Babe Didrikson, the most famous female athlete of the day, to pitch against them in a series of exhibitions, the players were instructed to not hit the ball hard against her, inasmuch as that might spoil her value as a gate attraction. So Bell bunted his way to first base. Charleston was furious.

"I thought I told you not to hit her," he thundered when Cool returned to the dugout.

"I didn't hit her. I just bunted."

"Well, it's just the same. Don't do it again."

So next time he doubled off the wall. Charleston charged onto the field in a rage and Bell was certain that the ever-ready fighter came with intent to bodily punish. But before a blow could be landed, Josh Gibson had his bullnecked manager in a headlock. Oscar Charleston had finally met his match.

Actually, two matches. "One thing's for sure," Bell told James Bankes, author of *The Pittsburgh Crawfords*. "I wasn't going to let Charleston or anybody else tell me not to do my best on the baseball field."

Oscar Charleston didn't look so mean when posing with his wife, Jane.

Pride, in fact, was a conspicuous commodity in the Crawfords' makeup. Although Bell and Satchel Paige were exceptions, the composition of the Pittsburgh club happened to be more Northern in nature than many Negro League teams. Not that pride followed geographical lines, but throughout the leagues, Northern players tended to be better educated, more expensively dressed, and—with notable outliers among the Southerners (Cool Papa, Satchel, and Willie Wells among them)—perhaps more prideful in racial scenarios than their cotton belt counterparts.

In any event, the Crawfords found their spring road swing to be more challenging socially than athletically. When the team bus parked at a restaurant in Picayune, Mississippi, for example, folks inside came out to ask if there were any white people on board. Hearing there weren't, they advised that the ballplayers best be moving along before the law showed up and put them all to work on the county farm with the coloreds who had tried to pass through previously. In another small town a local stalwart pulled a shotgun on Page and Johnson for the indiscretion of dressing in too highfalutin a fashion. In Arkansas, with Cool Papa kneeling on deck, a fan threw a chair onto the field and sweet Josh Gibson climbed into the stands after him. At the evening's conclusion, Charleston, his reputation perhaps preceding him, confronted the chief agitator and negotiated an end to the open hostilities.

Bell was a little uneasy about Arkansas to begin with. On a previous trip with the St. Louis Stars, a white man had sat near their bench waving a .45-caliber pistol at various players and dispensing counsel on what they were and weren't to do. To Mule Suttles he said, "Hey, nigger, if you don't hit that ball over the fence you'd better find a hole to crawl in." Hearing that, Mule's teammates implored the opposing pitcher to deliver the sort of low fastball that the big slugger favored. The fellow thoughtfully obliged, and Suttles didn't hesitate to sock the ball over an outfield fence that wasn't far enough removed to trouble him much anyway.

A subtler incident, some years later in rural Kentucky, disturbed Cool Papa more profoundly. The players drove up to a gas station, spotted a well behind it, and asked the lady in charge if they might indulge in drinks of water. There was a gourd hanging from the side of the well for that purpose. She consented, they drank and thanked her, and as they drove off Bell was sickened by the sight of the woman smashing the gourd to smithereens against the side of the well.

"I know what prejudiced people can be like," he said to Bankes, alluding to his Southern upbringing. "Most of the bad things they do are because of the way they were brought up. They really don't know any better.

"Wherever the Crawfords played in the South, there were white people there at the game right along with the blacks. They always had to sit on opposite sides of a rope. A white man and a black man could be sitting right next to each other, but they had a rope between. Silly, isn't it? But that's the way it was." In Atlanta, black and white baseball teams were not permitted to play within two blocks of each other.

Fortuitously, the Crawfords traveled the South on the wheels of their own support system. The constant bus riding brought them together in a way not achievable through modern-day team travel, when players are shuttled to the airport, slip into seats on the chartered plane, clap on their headphones, arrive in a couple of hours, and meet their luggage in their hotel rooms.

On the Crawfords' bus, there was woman talk, money talk, fishing talk, poker talk, cracker talk, baseball talk (Bell's favorite), and always food talk, because getting something to eat was rarely an easy proposition. It helped to have a player aboard who could pass as white and walk into a restaurant or general store to pick up bread and cheese and lunch meat or maybe sardines. (On the occasions when light-complexioned Clara Belle traveled with the team, she sometimes filled this role.)

The designated off-white man in the Pittsburgh party was Harry "Tin Can" Kincannon, who now and then taunted his teammates by strolling into an ice cream shop that didn't welcome blacks, ordering a root beer float, and enjoying it at a seat by the window, grinning smugly as Bell, Gibson, Matlock, and the others paraded past in envy. Tin Can was also a fried-chicken fan. On one occasion he brought a fresh box of it onto the bus, ate some, and set the rest in the overhead rack. Before nodding off, though, he waved his gun and explicitly warned everyone not to touch his damn chicken. It almost goes without saying that, as Kincannon dozed, one of the Crawfords removed the bullets from the revolver, appropriated the chicken box, and passed it around. When he woke up a short while later, Tin Can was wearing a necklace of chicken bones.

The club rolled through the Gulf states, dispatching Southern League and town teams. It was a scraping, scrounging, tiresome existence, brightened here and there by bus amusement and Judy Johnson's sunshine. Then, for one memorable evening in Houston, the Crawfords escaped the grit and the grind and lived like men of means.

Their gracious hostess was a Creole woman they called Mother Mitchell, whose wealth and stately home derived from oil royalties. The players were seated in a spacious dining room appointed with lavish rugs and crystal chandeliers. There was fried chicken for Tin Can Kincannon and a sumptuous spread of roast beef, fresh-baked bread, salads, sweet or mashed potatoes, and plenty of fruit and pie for Josh Gibson.

When the Crawfords at last returned to Pittsburgh, ready for the long haul of their regular season, Cool and Judy set aside a few moments to coauthor a letter of thanks to Mother Mitchell. Her hospitality had nourished both their bodies and their souls.

CHAPTER TWELVE

SEE YOU IN CHICAGO

T HE INAUGURAL ALL-STAR GAMES OF BOTH THE
major and Negro leagues occurred in 1933 at Comiskey Park in
Chicago, two months apart. During that interlude, Babe Ruth,
who appropriately swatted the first home run in the former, had this
to say in advance of the latter, as reported in the *Pittsburgh Courier*:

> Interviewed in his suite in the Hotel Schenley, Babe Ruth, the
> Yanks' home-run king, declared "The colorfulness of Negroes in
> baseball and their sparkling brilliancy on the field would have a
> tendency to increase attendance at games. The game in Chicago
> should bring out a lot of white people who are anxious to see the
> kind of ball that colored performers play." Ruth said that he had
> seen many high-class colored players. Hans Wagner, Pirate coach,
> said that the good colored clubs play just as good baseball as seen
> anywhere.

Both extravaganzas were conceived by journalists. The big-league
model was the brainchild of Arch Ward, sports editor of the *Chicago*

Tribune, and the inspiration for the Negro League spinoff—known as the East-West game—came from Roy Sparrow, a sportswriter for the *Pittsburgh Sun-Telegraph* who doubled as the traveling secretary for the Crawfords. Sparrow and his enterprising baseball boss, Gus Greenlee, who was also the de facto commissioner of the NNL and a fellow who didn't hesitate to put the football under his arm once the hole was opened up, intuited quite correctly that a late-summer spectacle—a glittery cavalcade of stars—was just the ticket for a league that struggled with the unremitting logistics required to sustain an entire season. Sure enough, there was Babe Ruth himself talking it up (even if his remarks sounded suspiciously manufactured).

From its spectacular beginning, the East-West game would illustrate what the Negro Leagues could have been all along with sufficient capital and coverage, neither of which was reasonably available in their time and marketplace. Even at the height of the Depression, the maiden affair captivated what the *Chicago Defender* described as "a howling, thundering mob of 20,000 souls."

The howling mob had bought tickets in dime stores, department stores, and tailor shops around the country. The thundering souls had ridden special coaches along the Illinois Central rails from New Orleans, the New York Central from the East, and the Santa Fe from Kansas City. And all the while, the league itself careened through yet another season of dysfunction and disorder.

The Kansas City Monarchs elected again to barnstorm rather than affiliate. In May the American Giants were forced to move their home games to Indianapolis when the owners of their Chicago park decided to turn it into a dog track. In June the Homestead Grays were booted from the league for violating Greenlee's tampering rules by trying to sign two Detroit Stars.

In July the Crawfords and American Giants played each other in Cleveland, with Jesse Owens featured in a match race against another sprinter. The first half of the schedule ended in a disputed tangle between Pittsburgh, Nashville, and Chicago/Indianapolis, and neither the second half nor the interested newspapers provided much in the way of clarity.

The press was most attentive in Pittsburgh, where Greenlee and Cumberland Posey exerted influence and the *Pittsburgh Courier* took the lead among the nation's black papers. But they were weeklies, and no degree of diligence could keep them abreast of the daily particulars relating to undermanned, overextended franchises chronically preoccupied with getting to the next gate. It was a self-defeating state of affairs that was called out in midsummer by NNL secretary John L. Clark, who was tasked with circulating game results but frustrated by the lack of cooperation from the teams.

As quoted in the *Courier*, Clark charged that Negro League organizations "will not spend 60 cents or $1 for a score book. Owners seem to have adopted a public-be-damned policy on reporting the outcome of the games." On the rare occasions when a team representative took the trouble to file a result from the nearest telegraph office, "the local newspapers," Clark wrote, "must guess at hits, runs, errors, doubles, triples, strikeouts, stolen bases and the many other things which happen in a ball game—and which make records."

The embattled secretary didn't shrink from citing the source of the Negro League's perception problems. "Owners," Clark continued, "are deaf, dumb and blind to the fact that interest can be stimulated, maintained or killed outright by records alone. . . . Because this phase of the game has gone unrecognized is one of the genuine reasons why the status of Negro players cannot be proved."

While the Crawfords were better chronicled than other clubs, the numbers they occasionally presented to the public and posterity were more like narratives. On days or nights when a reporter from an African American or mainstream newspaper was charged with covering a game, it was not unusual for the correspondent to place a low priority on actually attending it, instead seeking out the players afterwards for a workable summary. Satchel Paige confided that some of the Negro Leaguers, mischievous by nature and resentful of the writers' indifference, were inclined now and then to respond with fabricated results and descriptions. Bell was sharply mindful of all that when he set out to quantify the deeds that were so vital to

Gibson's legend and his own, doing blackball a monumental service in the process.

The Crawfords had entrusted a chunky veteran pitcher, left-handed spitball specialist Sam Streeter, to keep their scorebook, and he often did, when he remembered to bring it along. But Cool Papa's dedicated tallies, which included nonleague games that otherwise went unreported—but, in Negro League reality, folded prominently into a season's body of work—would more usefully tell the tale.

It was obvious to Cool, from the outset, that young Gibson was clouting home runs at a livelier clip than Suttles—or anyone else—ever had, with the possible but uncertain exception of Ruth (whom Bell, incidentally, strongly suspected of some African heritage). Gibson's homers were slammed in every direction, but farthest, it seemed, to center field. No matter how high or distant, a fence could not contain him, although there were times, on country fields, when the *absence* of one would cause him to stop running at third base, either out of pity or fatigue. Mainstream sources set Gibson's total of round-trippers

In 1933, Cool Papa's personal tally of Josh Gibson's home runs verified, for him, that the burly catcher was indeed a slugger for the ages.

that year at as low as six and as high as twenty-three. But Bell kept a much closer watch. His final accounting was seventy-two. It would, of course, have been higher if the mighty catcher had completed every circuit within his reach.

"I've seen all the power hitters in my time," Cool Papa reflected to James Bankes. "Ruth, Foxx, Mantle, all of those guys. Most of them took long strides, waded into the ball, and took big swings. Many times, they could be fooled by pitchers who changed speeds because they were off-balance. Josh, on the other hand, had a short, compact swing and took a very short stride. He was almost never off-balance, never fooled. He also hit for a very high average. Hank Aaron and Ernie Banks had swings like Josh, short and compact with lots of wrist snap.

"[But] the first thing I remember about Josh was his courage. Everybody threw at him and tried to scare him. It didn't ever work. He just concentrated more. I'm surprised they didn't stop throwin' at him, but they never gave up."

Cool Papa was thirty-one years old that season, and while he was routinely described as the Negro Leagues' fastest player and leading base stealer, that consensus was not supported by statistics—or, more to the point, it was left undocumented by the lack of them. In 1930, for example, when he is credited by the leading authorities with either 5 or 15 stolen bases—one of those numbers is nonsense, the other baloney—Cool verifiably swiped 3 in the season's first game alone. In 1933, when he was keeping track himself, the published records show him with somewhere between 7 and 11 steals, even though he copped 5 in the final game. Using Streeter's scorebook, the Crawfords settled on 91. Bell, whose veracity has been borne out time and again, put the number at 175. But while the figure is staggering, even historic, comparisons with major-league standards are awkward at best, given the unspecified volume of non-league and exhibition games in the mix.

At any rate, reputation trumped statistics in the Negro Leagues, and Gibson and Bell were easily voted onto the East squad of the highly anticipated East-West game. If the fans had been alienated by the lack of Negro League data, they were now handed a precious feeling of franchise through the popular vote for all-stars. In advance of the alluring event, to be played on September 10, legions of them filled out ballots that were printed in the *Pittsburgh Courier*, *Chicago Defender*, and other leading black newspapers.

Not surprisingly, the polling sent seven Crawfords to the game—Bell, Gibson, Charleston, Johnson, Streeter, Hunter, and Pistol Johnny Russell. Satchel Paige declined the invitation—he later expressed regret about that—opting for a more lucrative, monthlong gig in North Dakota. Charleston led the voting, Cool Papa led off the top of the first, and so commenced what was soon acclaimed as the most significant annual event in America's black community.

Facing Willie Foster—which meant that he was batting right-handed—Cool belted a high hard one with such force that the ball carried over the head of the left fielder, Steel Arm Davis, but then, caught in the Windy City currents, it curled back into Davis's glove. Suttles, playing for the other side, was the game's big hitter in a high-scoring win for the West, smoking a double and a celebrated home run that, contrary to reports, evidently did not break the window of a taxi cab on Princeton Street, according to the *Pittsburgh Courier*:

> Streeter carried one through the letters for a strike. The next ball was to [Suttles's] liking. With hardly any effort he swung. Like a bullet from a rifle, the ball sped out into deep left center. There was power to the drive. "Cool Papa" Bell started to run. Suddenly he stopped. Pandemonium reigned. Straw hats filled the air. The noise reminded one of the machine-gun fire which, on occasion, rocked Chicago in its halcyon days. For "The Mule" had tagged one on the nose. Way up in the upper tier of the left center stands, the ball landed and bounced along as a hundred fans scrambled madly for the honor of getting the ball. It was the kind of swat which is worth the price of admission any day.

In subsequent years, attendance at East-West games would reach fifty thousand, the Grand Hotel would rock all week, and Cool Papa would lead off again and again.

DURING PAIGE'S ABSENCE, he was missed by the Crawford Grill almost as much as he was by the Crawford ball club. Maybe more, given his lackluster 7-9 record that year in league play (although other sources report his overall mark a trifle differently at 31-4, underscoring both the capriciousness of Negro League statistics and the extent of Satchel's moonlighting).

He and Greenlee had a mutually satisfactory arrangement for his frequent furloughs, entailing a kickback to the boss from Satch's extracurricular revenues. Nevertheless, the Caliph of Little Harlem—Gasoline Gus was awash in colorful titles—was always glad to have the great pitcher back in town, because Paige was a leading attraction at the Grill, even in a cast that included, at various times, Duke Ellington, Louis Armstrong, Count Basie, Bojangles Robinson, teenage songbird Lena Horne, the controversial boxer Jack Johnson, and the Mills Brothers, who occasionally traveled with the Crawfords in custom-made uniforms. The "elongated southern lad," as the *Courier* referred to Paige, was in his element at the bustling club with a piano atop

Satchel Paige holding court at the Crawford Grill

the bar and games of chance upstairs with Lena's father. (The Negro National League headquarters were up that way as well.) Satchel sat in with the bands, played whatever instrument he could get his bony hands on, sang boisterously, shot a sharp game of pool, spun stories that stretched the truth, and showed off for the waitresses, one of whom he would marry.

While Cool Papa got a kick out of Paige's company—they ended up as roommates whenever circumstances called for one—he was less at ease in Greenlee's eclectic club, the beating heart of broad and busy Wylie Avenue, where the streetcars ran. In addition to turning down Gus's offer to man the entrance around the corner, Cool gave Jack Johnson an unequivocal no when the former heavyweight champ, an American icon, approached him, of all people—"the epitome of respectability," as he was described in *The Pittsburgh Crawfords*—about fronting a hotel where drugs could be trafficked. But Bell was charmed by Lena Horne and gravitated toward Louis Armstrong not only at the Grill but in New York and Los Angeles as well, sitting with Satchmo in steam baths and talking baseball for hours at a time.

He also grudgingly admired Greenlee, notwithstanding the impresario's local monopoly on immorality. A veteran of World War I, Big Red, for all his vices, was a kindhearted, community-minded businessman to whom residents of the Hill District could turn for rent or grocery money, even tuition, in times of need, without obligation. Greenlee's soft spots stood in stark contrast to other gangster owners, including Bell's in St. Louis. "Some of those guys would do anything, including killing people," Willie Wells told James Bankes. "The first guy I played for was Dick Kent with the St. Louis Stars and he certainly had no conscience about anything. He was into protection, drugs, loan-sharking, all kinds of bad stuff."

Moreover, Cool appreciated that Greenlee was almost singlehandedly holding the Negro National League together in its uneasy reincarnation. The East-West game was certainly something on which to hang their sweat-ringed ball caps, but a more bona fide achievement would be to finally bring a season to its proper conclusion. And now Paige was on hand for the final push.

A strong case could be made that he and Gibson represented the most imposing battery in baseball history. In 1933, however, they were still works in progress. Satchel's fastballs were in full flower—although he hadn't named them all yet—and his gamesmanship came from the cradle, but his curve, his various deliveries, and especially his control were well short of their destinations. For his part, Gibson, whose youth had been diverted by such activities as swimming a lot and working at Gimbels department store, was just beginning to refine the nuances of catching.

Cool Papa was able to assist him with that. When Gibson had caught for the Homestead Grays, Willie Wells had easily pilfered his signs to the pitcher by watching the movement of Josh's elbow when he flashed them. After Bell alerted him to that troublesome habit, Gibson became hypersensitive about his signaling. At times he put his fingers down for a traditional call while the actual sign was conveyed with a turn of his catcher's mitt. He also used eye contact to communicate with Bell when he wanted the center fielder to rush in for a pickoff play at second base, a maneuver that the two of them took great delight in pulling off.

If Cool felt out of place at the Crawford Grill, it was a different story at the beautiful ballpark. He thoroughly enjoyed his first season in the blue-trimmed Pittsburgh uniform, batting .379 and running endlessly not only on the bases, piling up doubles and triples to go with his steals, but also in the vast, luscious outfield, with gazelles on either side and teammates he admired all around. The grass and handsome crowds looked even better under the snazzy lights of Greenlee Field.

The league schedule, meanwhile, played out in an apples-and-oranges kind of way, with teams, as usual, completing different numbers of games against different opponents. For what it was worth, the Crawfords recorded the most wins and Bertrum Hunter did the same among pitchers. More important, three clubs—Pittsburgh, Nashville, and Chicago/Indianapolis, which had competed so inconclusively in the season's first half—made it to the finish line, each staking a claim to the championship, or at least a shot at it.

A playoff was in order, and the first round was set for League Park in Cleveland, starting with a doubleheader in early October between the Craws and Nashville. Paige and Cannonball Willis staged a stirring pitchers' duel in the opener, with the Elite Giants tying the score in the ninth inning, at which point Satchel was relieved by Leroy Matlock. The outcome would not be resolved until the twelfth, when William Nunn of the *Pittsburgh Courier* picked up the action:

> The crowd . . . rose en masse as "Cool Papa" Bell, one of the greatest centerfielders in the game, caught a Willis pitch square on the butt end of his bat and drove a screaming liner into deep center field. And as the fleet [Bell] sped across home plate [with an inside-the-park home run], his flying spikes marked "finis" to as great a diamond struggle as we've ever seen.

The second game was rather less compelling. It was called for darkness after six innings, with Pittsburgh ahead 3–1 behind Bertrum Hunter. And there the series—scheduled as best of five—abruptly ended.

The title would be decided, then, between the Crawfords and the American Giants, starting with a game in Wheeling, West Virginia. The American Giants showed up in Wheeling with seven players. After a tie in Cleveland, they stopped showing up altogether.

It was January by the time the league—more specifically, Greenlee—got around to conferring the championship on Pittsburgh.

CHAPTER THIRTEEN

SNOOKERING SATCHEL

F OR THEIR OWN SURVIVAL, THE NEGRO
Leagues had become a system of stars. Of course, even the
brightest of them were of only casual interest to the metropolitan dailies, which still hadn't settled on "Satchel" or "Satchell"
or "Paige" or "Page." Needless to say, the headlines were reserved for
the leading lights of the designated major leagues, where, in 1934,
pillar-of-strength Lou Gehrig was claiming the Triple Crown in the
American League and piece-of-work pitcher Dizzy Dean—the white
Satchel Paige, if you will—was winning hearts and thirty games, the
latter of which no National Leaguer has done since.

Satchel himself won twenty that year on behalf of the Pittsburgh
Crawfords—he was the whole package now—but wasn't compelled to
answer their every call. In August, for example, he was off to Colorado
for the annual *Denver Post* national tournament, rocking a fake red
beard and blazing twenty-three straight scoreless innings for the
House of David, which won the title in a thrilling match against the
Kansas City Monarchs. Pitching to his familiar Negro League battery
mate, Bill Perkins ("Thou shalt not steal" was emblazoned on Perkins's

chest protector), Paige carried the House of David into the championship game with a 2–1 semifinal victory over Chet Brewer and the Monarchs, the first entirely black team in the tournament's history.

For the Crawfords, engaged in a pennant race, Paige's two-timing illustrated what can happen when a franchise permits itself to be held hostage by its marquee attraction. For the Negro National League, the scenario, like the season, was another function of an untidy alliance in which teams were merely vehicles, schedules were simply outlines, and championships figured in there somewhere, somehow, sometimes.

The star system was not Cool Papa's thing, necessarily, although he fit the bill manifestly. His baserunning was ballyhooed in virtually every town he visited; he had a continuing habit of playing for the winning side; as an outfielder he "nabbed everything hit in his direction, and kept base runners honest with his accurate throws," according to William McNeil, author of *The California Winter League: America's First Integrated Professional Baseball League*; and in the spring of 1934 he was coming off winter league titles in batting average and stolen bases. (In Los Angeles he'd played next to Stearnes and Wild Bill Wright, the three of them constituting what, in McNeil's estimation, "may have been the greatest outfield in the annals of baseball.")

Bell was the same player he'd been in St. Louis, but he was more secure in his station and dusted now with Crawford glitter. In Pittsburgh, Gus Greenlee's team was followed on both the sports and society pages, and there was plenty to write about. The entertainment for Paige's wedding at the Crawford Grill was provided by his best man, Mr. Bojangles Bill Robinson. At Greenlee Field, a nattily dressed patron might find himself sitting next to Joe Louis. When the ball game ended, Lena Horne was liable to croon on the grass. After dinner at the club, Duke Ellington just might strike up the band.

Meanwhile, at .364 (the best of his reported batting averages) or whatever it might have actually been, Cool Papa would significantly outhit Oscar Charleston, Josh Gibson, and Judy Johnson, the other

Louis Armstrong, Cool Papa's best pal in the music business (left, with jazz singer Ann Baker and *Pittsburgh Courier* reporter George Brown), would drop by the Crawford Grill from time to time.

three Hall of Famers in the Crawfords' lineup (when Paige wasn't pitching) for 1934. When William Nunn of the *Pittsburgh Courier* discussed the apparent inevitability that black players would soon integrate the major leagues—a movement championed by Heywood Broun and Jimmy Powers of the *New York Daily News*—he put the Pittsburgh center fielder on the short list of likely candidates.

"The phantom wall of race prejudice," wrote Nunn, "which for years has kept Negro players out of big-time diamond competition, is under a bombardment from which it cannot hope to stand. . . . And now, look at the cream of the crop . . . men of the type of Willie Wells, whom westerners referred to as the 'Colored Hans Wagner'; Dick Lundy, one of the admittedly great shortstops; 'Cool Papa' James Bell, who can trail a ball farther than any man in baseball."

Those were words that resonated with Bell. Integration, rather than adoration, was the shape that his ambition assumed. The gentleman from Mississippi had played too successfully, against too many white opponents, to settle for less. He was interested, also, in the comparative windfall that his talents would rightly command if he wore a major-league uniform, increasing his salary by a multiple of five to ten—there was, after all, Clara Belle to support, the monthly contribution to send his mother, a certain vesture to maintain, and, most of all, the pursuit of justness—but such considerations as celebrity and station were lower priorities. Cool Papa's stardom was not design but residue, a natural by-product of his speed and grace.

"When Cool and I played together in Pittsburgh, he was the most popular player on the team both among his teammates and the fans," Judy Johnson recalled to James Bankes in *The Pittsburgh Crawfords*. "All you had to do was walk down the street with him and you knew why. He was a beautiful dresser. Absolutely immaculate. He had perfect manners and you never heard him say even a hell or a damn. He had time for everybody. Signed autographs, talked to people, gave advice on baseball, anything they wanted. All the time showin' his big beautiful smile."

The front office, however, had a different perspective on Cool Papa's popularity. He was a bargain at $220 a month, and any heightening of his stature—any renown or publicity that might escalate his price—was a threat to that economy. For Bell, the harsh reality hit home on a road trip early in 1934 when his torrid batting began to overtake Josh Gibson's and he was instructed not to send back any out-of-town newspaper clippings in which his exploits were featured.

The Crawfords had decided that their rainmakers were Gibson, who was local as well as Olympian—his showstopping home runs could actually be *measured*—and of course Paige, the lanky force of nature to whom the game was equal parts sport and theater. The club's traveling secretary, wishing only to spread the word about good baseball being played, was fined for stating his intention to dispense unspun information about who on the club was doing what. "The self-effacing Bell," wrote Bankes, "as sweet a human being as was ever elected into the Hall of Fame, found himself in the shadows, both in fame and finances, of the two glamorous stars."

Cool Papa was kindly disposed toward the pair at the top of the bill and would begrudge neither his glory. He was not so forgiving, though, concerning the Crawfords' calculated denial of his own contributions. Wise to suppression from Southern custom and mainstream baseball, he hadn't counted on more from his own team.

"When I went to the Crawfords," Bell said to John Holway in *Voices from the Great Black Baseball Leagues,* "they had Charleston, Gibson, Paige. They weren't going to build anyone over them. They never did advertise you over those guys. The Crawfords advertised Satchel. They just kept dramatizing and dramatizing him, but we had guys who would win more games than him. Now, when we played in California, they would bill Satchel, and he would get fifteen percent. When they billed me, they had those wagons all going around saying, 'Bell's going to be here tonight.' But I didn't ask for anything. I only got a cut like the rest of the ballplayers got. I'm not the guy wants to be praised too much. I never wanted to be a big shot."

Even so, there he was again at the festive East-West affair in late August, leading off for the East and coming to the plate in the eighth inning of a scoreless duel. He'd played a part in the scorelessness, having hit his relay man, Dick Lundy, with a throw from deep center field, whereupon Lundy pegged out a runner at home plate. But the run prevention accrued mostly to the dazzling pitchers.

The starters were Cool's old teammate, Ted Trent, for the West, and a twenty-one-year-old rookie sensation named Slim Jones, a long left-hander who'd been turning heads all season for the Philadelphia Stars. For the East side, Jones was followed by Tin Can Kincannon and then Paige, who'd known better than to spurn the all-star invitation a second time. Big Florida's successors were Chet Brewer and now Willie Foster, who made the mistake of walking the fastest man in the sport to start the eighth.

Bell, as expected, stole second base, and he was still there with two outs when Boojum Wilson broke his bat on a flare to short center, which Willie Wells retrieved from his shortstop position but not in time to keep Cool Papa from scoring the only run of the game. Satchel did the rest, with no sign of his hesitation pitch but liberal use of the double windup.

NEGRO LEAGUE CALCULUS placed the Philadelphia Stars and Chicago American Giants in the championship playoffs that year. Never mind that the Crawfords, with what some consider their best team, won the most games by a long shot.

A cynic might suspect that Gus Greenlee was happy to forgo the title series for a more lucrative exhibition at Yankee Stadium. The special game was a showdown showcase for Satchel Paige and young Slim Jones of the Philly Stars. All season the precocious southpaw, winner of twenty-one games, had been stealing Paige's thunder, and Satchel was competitor enough—and showman enough and certainly mercenary enough—to have the score settled with baseballs from twenty paces, in front of thirty-five thousand people.

The crowd included fifteen-year-old Monte Irvin, a future Hall of Famer who would later describe the heavily promoted spectacle as the greatest game he'd ever seen. It was played on September 9, three days before the opening of the Stars' playoff against Chicago. (*They* weren't put off by the prospect of playing in both the exhibition and the championship series.) The night before, Satchel drove to New York from another extracurricular engagement and slept in his car outside the House that Ruth Built.

His entire season had been a road show, adventures in peripatetic pitching. Have arm, will travel. Often, when he wandered off from the Crawfords, Paige would tie a canoe to the top of his car just in case he came upon an irresistible fishing hole. In addition to bait and tackle, he also packed, at various times, a rifle, a handgun, a guitar, bongo drums, a Bible, a camera, clothes for all occasions, and bird books. He was a man of considerable knowledge and multifarious talents, the most acclaimed of which he was determined to put to full advantage.

In July, Satchel had thrown a celebrated no-hitter against Homestead and struck out seventeen Grays. Then it was Denver, the East-West game, a swing in North Dakota, and now, deep in the Bronx,

When Satchel Paige rolled into Harlem, he was ready for it.

heading into the seventh inning, he was embroiled in a 0–0 duel with the towering whippersnapper of the Philadelphia Stars. At that point the Stars broke the spell on a run-scoring double by Biz Mackey. The Crawfords, however, retied the game in the bottom of the inning with an unearned run against Jones, singled in by Jimmie Crutchfield. It was still 1–1 after nine, and the great match ended there, because, unlike Greenlee Field, Yankee Stadium didn't have lights yet.

So a rematch was scheduled, Satchel versus Slim, same place, a week hence, in the thick of the Stars' playoff series. This time, thirty thousand turned out for a less epic event, won 3–1 by the more epic pitcher, a two-hitter for Paige.

Shortly thereafter, Jones, back to the official business at hand, nailed down the Negro League championship for Philadelphia with a 2–0 shutout in the final playoff game. And for all practical purposes he was never heard from again.

Paige, meanwhile, was taking on all comers for the right price and turned his sights next to Dizzy Dean, the National League's Most Valuable Player. That challenge, for which the Crawfords would accompany their ace, was still a short ways off, however; the colorful Cardinal was preoccupied with beating the Detroit Tigers in games one and seven of the World Series while brother Paul took care of games three and six.

As the respective championships were being claimed, the Pittsburgh club simply carried on, far from the shouting. Bell was cool with that, and suited for it. In a nonleague, late-September match at Greenlee Field with the Homestead Grays, his subtle work in the field was insightfully admired by William Nunn of the *Courier*:

> The game was the fourth of a series between the two home-town teams, and saw the Grays even it up as they romped away with an 11-2 triumph. And we really saw things. . . . We saw "Cool Papa" Bell get rather heated up as he put on as fine a display of defensive fielding as we've ever looked it—and he didn't catch a fly. But the way he saved doubles from being triples and singles from being doubles reminded us of [African American football pioneer] Fritz Pollard the day when Dartmouth's big team ran Brown [Pollard's school] bowlegged. Making tackles all over the field, Fritz that day proved he was All-American—and the same goes for Bell.

Dean, meanwhile, wrapped up the World Series with a shutout and was $5,390 richer when he embarked on his autumn tour with Paige and the Crawfords. The series, covering Ohio and Pennsylvania, was characterized, as usual, by the competitive edge of the black-ballers. For starters, Satchel toyed with the awestruck white batters, striking them out at a flabbergasting rate—nine in three innings at Columbus, where he purposely walked the bases loaded and fanned the next three guys.

By contrast, the Crawfords so thoroughly cuffed around the MVP in one game that he repaired to the outfield. Dean had been known to appeal to his African American foes to please take it easy on him if he felt overworked, and the Negro Leaguers had been known to tacitly decline the invitation; the opportunity to defeat, even clobber, a premium major-league team or player was too precious to pass up. They held nothing back, as long as their safety was not at stake. Judy Johnson would keep his bag of dirty tricks on the shelf for most of a season, but bring on Dizzy Dean or Rogers Hornsby or Paul Waner and he'd hide a bottle cap in the thumb of his glove to scrape up the baseball for his pitcher, he'd fluff his shirtsleeves to engineer a painless hit by pitch, he'd read the other team's signs like the Sunday paper.

There was, also as usual, the obligatory fight, this one triggered when Vic Harris of the Crawfords pulled the umpire's mask and then let go, allowing it to recoil back into the poor fellow's face. Oscar Charleston rushed over to get the rumble properly going, and Josh Gibson was soon administering a headlock to the *other* catcher, George Susce. When Dean and Ted Page tried to pull him away, Gibson, still holding Susce, grabbed Dizzy with his free hand and shot-putted the strapping pitcher an impressive distance onto his back. Dean got a good belly laugh out of that, Josh broke into a smile, and all was well except for Vic Harris getting carted away in handcuffs by the local police. The Craws won that game on a late rally, capped by Gibson's home run.

Those outcomes—the disarming conclusion to the melee and the endgame victory for the Negro League side—were not the presumptive fare. Often as not, depending on the politics of the crowd and the mix of predispositions on the field, there was a pall of volatility to the all-star matches in black and white. "Sometimes," recounted Willie Foster, "we would be beating one of the all-star teams, there would be eighteen thousand people in the park, and the only sound you could hear was the ball hitting the mitt when I pitched and when the catcher threw it back to me. Our shortstop, Willie Wells, was real good at detecting when it was getting dangerous. We'd have to lose sometimes to keep from getting hurt. When he could tell it was getting tense, Willie would walk up to me and say, 'Forget it, Willie. Let's see if we can lose it. Try to make the ball hit their bats. Make these guys look good.'"

The Paige-Dean affairs, by contrast, were notable for the spirit in which they were negotiated. The vigor of the Negro Leaguers ultimately prompted from Dean a casual quip that, while not intended for Cool Papa, reached his ears and swelled his pride. It followed a game at York, Pennsylvania, in which Gibson had homered twice in a runaway victory for the Crawfords. As Diz crossed in front of the black players' dugout, he stepped toward the burly catcher and said, "Josh, I wish you and Satchel played with me 'n' Paul on the Cardinals. Hell, we'd win the pennant by the Fourth of July and go fishin' the rest of the season."

Dean obviously enjoyed the atmosphere of race-mixing baseball. He would catch Paige in warmups and make a show of his glove hand smarting from Satch's fastball. He and Paige would mimic each other's pitching motions. And when the tour was over—Dean said he made more money on it than he had by winning the World Series—the two characters apparently contrived to hook up again at Wrigley Field in Los Angeles for a legendary game that eluded the public record. Folklore, however, has Satchel prevailing in it 1–0 in thirteen innings.

Paige and Bell were headed out there anyway, to share a room and play for another absurdly talented team put together for Tom Wilson's entry in the California Winter League. Luminaries trailing Cool in the Elite Giants' lineup included Wells, Stearnes, Suttles, Wild Bill Wright, catcher Larry Brown, third baseman Felton "Drifty" Snow, and second baseman Sammy T. Hughes. Paige was joined on the pitching staff by able starters Pullman Porter and Cannonball Willis.

The CWL's inclusive posture was reflected by supportive Californians and the Los Angeles press, which took the maverick attitude that good baseball is good baseball. The winter season opened with a parade long enough that three bands could play simultaneously, and the *Los Angeles Times* described the Elite Giants as "a colored baseball club which is so good it ain't nothin' else but . . ."

The Giants were so good, in fact, that five of them—Paige, Bell, Wells, Stearnes, and Suttles, in chronological order—would end up in the Hall of Fame. At the time, of course, that was a preposterous notion.

For one thing, Cooperstown's maiden class wouldn't be announced for more than a year. And it would be thirty-seven before Paige became the Hall's first black member.

Immortality, however, visited two of those five well ahead of schedule. It happened after the mischievous Paige began telling folks about the mind-boggling speed of his outfielder friend. Satchel's words may have deviated from time to time, and decades of approximated accounts, oral and published, have assumed various forms, but the basics were always the same.

"Cool Papa Bell," he said, "is so fast that, when he goes to bed, he can turn out the light and be under the covers before it's dark."

The famous line almost certainly derives from the 1934–35 Winter League season. The likeliest version of its origin was offered by Bell at a 1981 Negro League reunion in Ashland, Kentucky, then printed the following year in *St. Louis Magazine*. It begins with him alone in their California sleeping quarters.

"One night," recalled Cool Papa, "before he got back, I turned out the light, but it didn't go off right away. There was a delay of about three seconds between the time I flipped the switch and the time the light went out. Musta been a short or somethin'. I thought to myself, here's a chance to turn the tables on ol' Satch. He was always playin' tricks on everybody else, you know. Anyway, when he came back to the room, I said, 'Hey, Satch, I'm pretty fast, right?'

" 'You're the fastest,' he said.

" 'Well, you ain't seen nothing yet,' I told him. 'Why, I'm so fast I can turn out the light and be in bed before the room gets dark.'

" 'Sure, Cool. Sure you can,' he said.

"I told him to just sit down and watch. I turned off the light, jumped in bed and pulled the covers up to my chin. Then the light went out.

"It was the only time I ever saw Satchel speechless. Anyway, he's been tellin' the truth all these years."

Perhaps not the *whole* truth, however. The episode may well have been predicated on the fluorescent lights that back then were found in some hotel rooms and boardinghouses, the kind that illuminate methodically, one end at a time. It may also have involved wagering.

One iteration of the story has Cool winning $10 from Paige on the initial gambit. And if that was the case, another twist seems highly plausible: that the enterprising roomies turned the trick a number of times for skeptical teammates willing to put a few dollars behind their doubts.

CHAPTER FOURTEEN

THE QUINTESSENTIAL CRAWFORDS

T HERE IS PERHAPS NO OTHER IMAGE THAT articulates the Negro Leagues like the iconic photograph of the 1935 Pittsburgh Crawfords neatly arrayed alongside their handsome team bus, caps shading their eyes, right knees dropped to the street, left arms resting on left legs, upper bodies angled and over-lapping so that the prominent *P* shows clearly on the left sides of their uniform shirts. The bus, now a tricked-out General Motors model, is parked in front of the Greenlee Field entrance, on the brick façade of which is posted a notice for an incoming boxing match featuring light heavyweight champion John Henry Lewis, whom Gus Greenlee was managing at the time. The kneeling line of Crawfords—it's as if each player waits in the on-deck circle without a bat—outdistances the motor coach, beginning at the left front tire with player-manager Oscar Charleston. Their championship that year is noted in cursive at the bottom of the frame.

The photo's power derives largely from the team's. With their five Hall of Famers and notable sidekicks, the Crawfords are almost unanimously hailed as the benchmark for Negro League quality. And yet, given the arbitrary nature of their 1933 championship, the 1935 title is their only objective, unambiguous one, the official validation of their obvious eminence. The historic picture stands for something fleeting and very special.

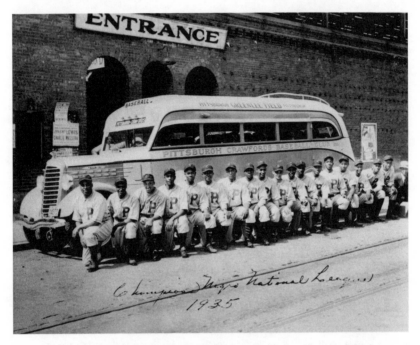

The 1935 Pittsburgh Crawfords, left to right: Oscar Charleston (player-manager), Jimmie Crutchfield, Dick Seay, Sam Bankhead, Bill Harvey, Sam Streeter, Bill Perkins, Chester Williams, Theolic Smith, Harry "Tin Can" Kincannon, Judy Johnson, Cool Papa Bell, Leroy Matlock, Ernest Carter, Josh Gibson, John Washington, Satchel Paige, unknown, team secretary Wendell Pearson

So did the bus, for that matter. It represented a barnstorming lifestyle even as the Crawfords and their confederates competed foremost in leagues. At that, the Negro League games, mostly weekend affairs, were effectively scheduled in chalk. It was altogether imperative that, in the critical interest of cash flow, the blackball clubs work the weekdays as well, cultivating the byways. Like musicians, they called it "hittin' the chitlin' circuit."

Their opponents blurred into an untidy travelogue of town teams, some of them semipro, most of them outclassed. Rather than run up lopsided, humiliating scores, the Negro Leaguers often tempered their performance with disarming humor, making plays and running bases with touches of slapstick and tinges of lightheartedness. They learned, however, to never take a reasonably close pitch in the presence of two strikes and a hometown umpire, who may or may not have concealed a firearm in his gear. And if racial venom made an appearance, the jocularity was off and the rout was on. In general, the games were more competitive on those occasions when two professional clubs converged at the same stopover, vying for the heavy side of a 60-40 split of the gate.

While to some, the bus life might seem romantic in the faint light of folklore, it was considerably less so for those to whom the rumbling transport sometimes sufficed also as hotel and dining hall. The hard-knocks aspect of the backroad existence had a palpably harsh effect on Cool Papa Bell, for one.

Late on one particular trip, he was sleeping soundly, which was what he did best on the bus, with the possible exception of shaving. (It was said that Bell was the only man in the league who could shave flawlessly at fifty miles an hour. All he needed was a cup of water, a slice of soap, and for whoever was in the back seat to switch places with him for a few minutes.) When, as he slumbered on the night in question, the wheels encountered a bump in the road, or perhaps dipped impolitely into a pothole, Bell's head bobbled fiercely and banged the side panel of the bus with such force that his eyesight was affected. Shortly thereafter, against Greenlee's preference—it was quite an unusual thing, after all—he was fitted for glasses that he wore for the rest of his days, on the field and off.

The time and place of his optical jolt was never reported, but a reasonable estimate would place it quite possibly on the spring tour of 1935, after the Crawfords left their training camp at Hot Springs, Arkansas, for warm-weather exhibition games in Mississippi and New Orleans. Presumably it was not before the club played in Greenwood, Mississippi, because Cool Papa pounded out six hits that day.

Meanwhile, his feet soaked up the salve and his knees, though suffering from mood swings, somehow always delivered him in short order to the next base or the ball in the air.

His eyes didn't prevent him from leading the team in hitting, nor his legs from leading the league in steals again, at age thirty-three. Bell's showstopping swiftness even got the attention of Jesse Owens—on hand this time as a spectator, rather than as a sideshow—one July afternoon in Cleveland, where the Crawfords and Chicago American Giants undertook a doubleheader. Particulars are provided by Chester Washington of the *Pittsburgh Courier*:

> We wondered what the bounding Buckeye was thinking as he sat sandwiched in between his mother, his bride, three sisters and a brother, marking up the runs, hits and errors as such flashing bolts of baseball flesh as "Cool Papa" Bell, [Jack] Marshall, [Jimmie] Crutchfield, Willie Wells, [Sam] Bankhead, "Josh" Gibson and Chet Williams thundered by his box for first base. Between games we asked him how Bell's speed compared with other runners he had seen. We recalled "Cool Papa's" bullet-like dash to first to beat out a perfectly-laid-down bunt to third. "He's just about the fastest ball player I've ever seen," Jess said. "And I believe he has more speed than Ben Chapman, the Yanks outfielder." This was a perfect tribute to the clean-cut Crawford centerfielder who had the amazing record of a triple, a double, four singles, two walks and one "flied out to left" in nine trips to the plate, scored six runs and had a couple of stolen bases thrown in for good measure in the two games.

The Crawfords were rolling from the outset that season. They won the league's first half, qualifying for the postseason championship series, if indeed there was to be one. And they did it without their rock star, Satchel Paige, who, following the money, joined Quincy Trouppe, Chet Brewer, and Double Duty Radcliffe on a racially mixed semipro team in Bismarck, North Dakota. There, perhaps for the first time—certainly not the last—Paige found occasion to have his fielders take a seat and carry on his business with the aid of only his trusty catcher, in this case Trouppe.

In Satchel's absence from the Crawfords, Leroy Matlock, the lefty from Moberly, Missouri, blossomed into an ace of historic proportion, carving out a record of 18-0. And Gibson—as if he could do otherwise—once more led the league in home runs.

The epic catcher, still only twenty-three, remained a playful soul and was only beginning to lose his innocence. In that endeavor, he was abetted by Sam Bankhead, a respected all-around player who in 1935 was new to the Crawfords. Bankhead was as fun-loving as Gibson, but in a more adult manner, and being best buddies entailed being drinking buddies. For the time being, though, it was not a discernible problem for Josh at the plate.

The Raindrop Rangers, so fast they could keep the field dry in a hard rain by catching the drops: left fielder Sam Bankhead, center fielder Cool Papa, right fielder Jimmie Crutchfield

Still, it was not Gibson who struck the most celebrated home run of the season. That occurred in the bottom of the eleventh inning of the third annual East-West game at Comiskey Park, with two outs and the score tied 8–8. The East side had stood in good stead early on, with Slim Jones, the prematurely faded star (at age twenty-two, his record that year fell from 21-6 to 4-5, and he would thereafter win only three games more, dying at twenty-five from pneumonia), pitching three scoreless innings and slamming a homer. But four hits from Gibson rallied the West, and Cool Papa led off the eleventh with a walk against the imposing Cuban star Martín Dihigo. Bell was sacrificed to second base by Sammy T. Hughes, and after a strikeout Dihigo intentionally and quite regrettably walked Gibson to pitch to Mule Suttles. With two strikes, the fearsome Alabaman drove a colossal home run to the upper deck in right-center field—a blow estimated at 475 feet—to end the game.

At the victory party that evening, Suttles was dressed for attention in a striking white suit. He happened to be socializing in the balcony when the band struck up "Hail the Conquering Hero," and on that cue the former coal miner swung himself over the railing, landing nimbly on the dance floor below.

PRIOR TO THE season, the Negro National League had made an investment in New York, admitting the Brooklyn Eagles, who would play at Ebbets Field, and the New York Cubans, who would occupy Dyckman Oval, a former skating rink and boxing venue, among other things, near the northern tip of Manhattan. The Cubans' park had been recently leased and renovated by their popular owner, Alex Pompez.

A native of Key West, Florida, where his father was a state representative and director of the local Cuban Revolutionary Party, Pompez ran a cigar store and numbers racket in Harlem, credentials that fit right in among Negro League owners. Generous and reputable, he was a princely figure among the citizens of his community—an understated, courtlier version of Gus Greenlee.

In the 1920s, Pompez had owned the Cuban Stars of the Eastern League, and by 1935 he was ready to invest more seriously in baseball, his numbers operation having been surrendered at gunpoint to Dutch Schultz. The Cubans roster included players from Cuba, Puerto Rico, and the Dominican Republic, headlined by Martín Dihigo—El Maestro—a rare player who excelled at every position and managed the team to boot. Dihigo was proficiently aided, however, by the likes of Dick Lundy, Rap Dixon, Showboat Thomas, and pitcher Luis Tiant, a Cuba native whose fabulous son and namesake would win twenty games for both the Cleveland Indians and the Boston Red Sox. Pompez, in fact, signed ten players that year who wound up in one country's Hall of Fame or another's. (Long after taking fugitive in 1936 and being arrested in Mexico as he ducked into a bulletproof car, Pompez, a National Hall of Famer himself, became a distinguished scout for the New York Giants, hooking them up with Juan Marichal, Orlando Cepeda, Willie McCovey, and Felipe Alou.)

Not too surprisingly, the Cubans claimed the season's second half and earned the spot opposite the Crawfords in the NNL title series. It began at Dyckman Oval and after two games—the second a shutout by the home team's Neck Stanley, a master scuffer of baseballs—mighty Pittsburgh was still winless.

Game three went the Crawfords' way when Charleston homered, Bell and Gibson tripled, and Matlock, who curiously hadn't started game one, came through with a shutout. At that point the series switched to Greenlee Field, where Matlock started for the second game in a row and was bested by Dihigo. Suddenly the Cubans were but a win away from the championship, with three chances to grab it.

The grind of the long season had evidently taken a toll on Cool Papa's legs, and he was not in the Crawfords' lineup for game five. He did, however, pinch-run at first base for pitcher Roosevelt Davis in the bottom of the ninth, with the score deadlocked 2–2. In the ensuing developments, there seems to be an acquired base that recorded history has not yet accounted for; but somehow, after a bunt, a wild throw, and an undetermined measure of presumably painful scampering, Bell made it home with the winning score to keep Pittsburgh in the picture.

The teams reconvened in Philadelphia—Negro League postseason matches were often held in neutral cities like Cleveland and Philadelphia, for purposes of convenience and/or attendance—for game six. It was even more dramatic than its predecessor. The Cubans carried a 6–3 lead into the bottom of the ninth, whereupon the great Dihigo—who would be elected to Halls of Fame in the United States, Mexico, and Cuba—elected to take over the vital pitching, title-clinching duties. Charleston, who no doubt sympathized with the perils of playing and managing at the same time, weighed in with a three-run homer to tie the game. The Crawfords continued to rally and won it when Judy Johnson, hitless for the series, pushed a bases-loaded single past the slick first baseman, Showboat Thomas.

Game seven, still at the neutral site, offered more of the same. The eighth inning began 5–5, but Gibson homered, Charleston followed in kind, and Cool Papa singled in Bankhead for the Crawfords' eighth run. It would ultimately be the decisive, all-the-marbles tally, after the Cubans scored twice in the ninth.

Thus, by pulling out three consecutive cliff-hangers, staring all the while into the grim face of elimination, the Crawfords had married extraordinary talent with indomitable heart, at last ensuring their lofty place in history. So immense was Pittsburgh's star power that the Crawfords have since conjured dreamy comparisons to the exalted 1927 Yankees, widely considered the greatest team of all time. It's a fetching comparison and a poignant reminder of what baseball was missing in those misguided times.

Imagine Cool Papa Bell atop a consolidated lineup that included Charleston, Ruth, Gibson, and Gehrig behind him, in whichever order.

FROM PHILADELPHIA, THE Crawfords rushed back to New York—to Yankee Stadium this time—for an extracurricular four-team doubleheader. With the freshly crowned champs opposing the Philadelphia Stars in front of twenty thousand fans—this, mind you, was the very next day after the conclusion of the playoff series—Cool Papa kicked off the game with a double, and Pittsburgh romped to a 12–2 victory.

The doubleheader events had become a Negro League fashion, and New York a favored location for them. "And it is a well known fact," noted the *New York Age* in an October editorial, "that the crowds who have turned out to see colored or mixed teams play in New York during the past two or three years have been larger than the average attendance at big league games." (In 1935, with lights installed at Crosley Field in Cincinnati and the national economy trending upward again with help from the New Deal programs of Franklin Roosevelt, major-league games averaged roughly six thousand fans.)

The cultivation of New York was advisable with respect not only to the nation's biggest market but also to its diversity of newspapers. Like most major cities, New York offered papers for the African American community—notably, the *Age* and *Amsterdam News*—but, unlike most major cities, some of the mainstream dailies showed a respectful interest in the bold, uninhibited, and often brilliant brand of baseball played by the likes of the Crawfords, Cubans, Stars, and American Giants. (It was Damon Runyon, writing for the Hearst newspapers, who gave Double Duty Radcliffe his nickname after watching him catch the first game of a Yankee Stadium doubleheader and pitch the next. Radcliffe, wrote Runyon, "was worth the price of two admissions.") What's more, the competing editorial voices of those publications, urged on by the ideological currents of a throbbing modern metropolis, called attention to the un-American backwardness that necessitated the Negro Leagues' existence.

The absurdity of segregated baseball was of course underscored when the blackballers took on major leaguers in publicized exhibition games, which was now happening in New York with increasing frequency. Babe Ruth, who had retired in May 1935, appeared at Dyckman Oval in late September for an exhibition doubleheader against the Cubans. (He smacked a first-inning double against Luis Tiant, but it was his only competitive trip to the plate. To please the crowd and earn his $3,000, the Babe belted a few batting-practice homers between games, both of which were won by the Cubans.) And in October, Dizzy Dean's so-called all-stars arrived at Yankee Stadium for a pair of Sunday games against the Crawfords and company.

Their series had already touched down at Dayton, Akron, and Shibe Park in Philadelphia, with the Negro Leaguers notching a couple of wins and routing Dean in one of them, but they were stymied in the Bronx. They were, in fact, shut out twice, although Cool Papa distinguished himself in the process with "several sensational catches," according to the *New York Age*. Lewis Dial of the *Age* credited players on both sides with exceptional work:

> The money goes to "Cool Papa" Bell. My, my, my, what a ball hawk that fellow was. Texas Leaguers, drives to the right, drives to the left, drives over his head, all were the same to "Cool Papa;" he had decided nothing should fall safe in his territory and take it from me, he was right after everything. Like the famous Mounted Police, he always got what he went after.

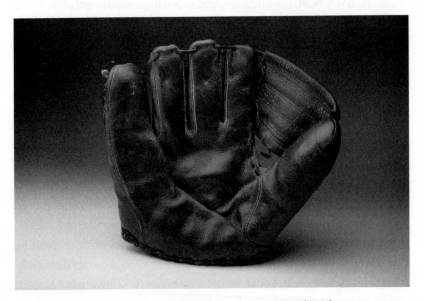

The glove with which Bell caught raindrops and everything else

And yet, as the years passed, neither his fly chasing nor its flattering description would stand out among Bell's memories from that New York afternoon. Rather, it was the day when a fundamental fact of his life and professional ambition—and his teammates' lives and professional ambitions, for that matter—was inadvertently but quite effectively clarified.

Dean was pitching in the first game of the doubleheader. He would work the whole nine innings, with some staunch defensive support from his young center fielder, Jimmy Ripple. Early in the game, Ripple had robbed Josh Gibson of a home run. The next time Gibson came to bat, with Bell on second base after his second double against the famous Cardinal, Diz turned and waved Ripple back toward the fence. Then farther back. And farther, until the freckle-faced prospect was approaching the headstone of former Yankees manager Miller Huggins in front of the flagpole.

Sure enough, the brawny catcher boomed a breathtaking fly in Ripple's direction, which he weaved under and tracked down four hundred–something feet from home plate. Naturally, Bell tagged up at second. Not so naturally, however, he disregarded the stop sign thrown up by Dick Lundy, who was coaching third, and kept churning. The relay from shortstop Billy Urbanski arrived at the plate around the same time as the speeding Crawford, who, in his enduring mental image, could see himself sliding in just ahead of the tag from catcher Mike Ryba.

"Out!" screamed the umpire.

When Cool Papa scrambled to his feet and pronounced his outrage, the man in blue was ready with an unflinching explanation.

"You don't do that against big leaguers," he said.

Bell understood perfectly, and never forgot, what the ump meant by "you."

CHAPTER FIFTEEN

LIMBO

T HE CRAWFORDS HAD BEEN BUILT TO DAZZLE, not to last. They were a starburst of a ball club, the showpiece of a fleshy, flashy man who was bound to lose a step at some point, and it would surely be the one that kept him just ahead of the law.

Gus Greenlee wasn't the first gangster who had employed Cool Papa Bell, but he was the most benevolent and least objectionable. Not to imply that Gasoline Gus lacked the sand for the rough stuff: back in the day, he had brazenly defied the likes of Dutch Schultz and Lucky Luciano when he picked off the Prohibition liquor they transported to New York and Chicago out of Canada. He'd also defended the hustlers of the Hill District against Luciano's encroachment. But, among men in his line of work, he was characteristically averse to knocking people off, a rumored exception being the hoodlums who'd demanded protection money from the moms and pops of neighborhood stores and small businesses. Greenlee took care of his community.

He'd come by baseball only at the behest of a strong local youth team—the one for which Josh Gibson played, representing a bathhouse—that was weary of scrounging for uniforms and packing into pickup trucks. Greenlee was happy to help the boys out, and mindful, besides, of the opportunity to letter the team shirts with the name of a county commissioner he was eager to elect.

It was the election cycle six years later, in 1936, that doomed him. With Luciano busted and Alex Pompez hiding out in Mexico—he'd been targeted by Thomas Dewey, the district attorney of New York County, for his Harlem numbers operation and especially his association with Dutch Schultz, who had been murdered the year before—the routing of racketeers was receiving excellent press around the country. Now that local governance was up for grabs in Pittsburgh, a crackdown on Greenlee had become politically expedient. The incident that effectively did the trick—the play by which the goods on Gasoline Gus were finally gotten—might well have been one described by Bell in *The Pittsburgh Crawfords:*

> There was a young boy who worked around the numbers rooms cleaning up. One time, he tipped off a couple of the cops who wanted to get Gus. He told them the time [when] most of the numbers money would be delivered. They pulled a raid and Greenlee lost plenty. I heard talk about killing the boy, so I went to Greenlee and begged him to let the boy go. I even offered to pay for a train ticket to send him to another town. I don't think Gus even knew about the kid. All he said was, "I'm not going to have any boy killed."
>
> All I know is that as soon as I told Greenlee, the boy was safe on his way out of town on a train. They didn't use my money.

Through the science of trickle-down, Hill District economics, Greenlee's misfortune was also the Crawfords'. The Grill stayed open and the ball club carried on, but not in the style to which either had become accustomed. Without vice money to sustain his operation, Wylie Avenue's impresario was hard-pressed to compensate his players and get them to their games. Paychecks were skipped. The bus was impounded. The schedule was compromised.

Independent of the money crunch, there was the additional complication of a local ordinance that year prohibiting games on Sundays, although the Pittsburgh Pirates, managed by the immortal Pie Traynor and starring the Waner brothers, continued hosting Sunday affairs at Forbes Field; Cool and his cohorts frequently attended. Perhaps to tweak his governmental tormentors, perhaps to salvage the substantial gate—most likely both—Greenlee got around that inconvenience by scheduling so-called milkman specials, in which the first pitch was delivered a minute after midnight on Monday mornings.

Any improvisation was on the table in 1936, if it paid the freight. The defending Negro League champions were again the class of blackball, and well on their way to the postseason playoffs, but that basic goal became expendable when Greenlee saw the chance to bring home the handsome purse offered to the winner of the annual *Denver Post* national tournament. He and Tom Wilson, the California League activist and owner now of the Washington Elite Giants, joined their best players with a few others for a crack at more than $5,000.

That placed Bell, Paige, Gibson, Jimmie Crutchfield, and Leroy Matlock alongside Wild Bill Wright of Washington and Buck Leonard of the Homestead Grays, with Candy Jim Taylor as the manager with little to do. "Without question," wrote Jay Sanford, author of *The Denver Post Tournament,* "the 1936 Negro League All-Stars were the best team ever to appear in the Denver Post Tournament. It could be argued that this club was the best ever to appear in Denver, including all major league teams."

There was but one challenging game among the seven it took for the dream squad to run roughshod over the field of eighteen teams: a pitchers' duel between Paige and a tall, left-handed cattle rancher from Colorado. The cowboy had given up but two hits—both tappers to the mound that Bell (who batted nearly .500 at Merchants Park) beat out—until Gibson took him deep in the ninth inning for the win. The final match was another shutout for Satchel, after which the tournament director vowed to not accept any more Negro League clubs.

Meanwhile, Cool Papa tied a purported world record with his timed circuit of the bases. From the gushing of the *Denver Post* sports editor, one might infer that Bell's feat was only slightly less impressive than the four gold medals Jesse Owens was winning in Berlin. Although the writer, C. L. Parsons, had himself been a decorated track star, he'd evidently never witnessed such velocity attained on two legs. Parsons was the scribe who openly rejoiced at finally finding a player who could steal first base.

The payout for the Denver tournament convinced Greenlee and Wilson to abandon their pennant pursuits in favor of jackpot games. The next of those was the East-West showcase in Chicago, when Bell's three hits inspired William Nunn of the *Pittsburgh Courier* to take the conversation to the next level, which is where so many conversations seemed to be going in 1936. Nunn implied that Cool and his cohorts shouldn't *need* the Negro Leagues:

> We know that many a major league would welcome the addition of Bell, either one of the Wright brothers or [Sam] Bankhead to their roster. . . . We don't believe the majors can produce three outfielders with the all-around ability of "Cool Papa," Bill Wright or Bankhead. They've got speed to burn. Two of the three are turn-around hitters. And in the outer-garden they really "go places" to get anything which is sent in their general direction.

In October, Bob Feller's sudden celebrity afforded another payday opportunity. After his success that season as a seventeen-year-old pitching sensation for the Cleveland Indians, the precocious Iowan was the toast of his home state. As it happened, Iowa was nearly as nuts about Negro League ball as it was about Feller. That was all Greenlee needed to know. He pulled together a team of mostly Crawfords, headlined by Paige—the matchup with the boy wonder was too good to pass up—and scheduled a series against a collection of major leaguers led by Rogers Hornsby. A rough edge was set in game one, when Oscar Charleston and the home plate umpire exchanged punches, but the hard feelings seemed not to spread to the competing teams or assembled Iowans, even when Satchel took the measure of Feller and, for the series, the Crawfords did the same to the big leaguers, time and again.

The legendary Hornsby also captained the starrier squad, managed by Earle Mack, that the blackballers took on shortly thereafter in Mexico City, the pregnant interlude so memorable to Cool Papa Bell. Equal opportunity was still but a concept when it came to race and baseball, but after Mexico—after his brief exchanges with Hornsby and Mack in 1936, and the flattering, haunting tease of $75,000 a year—Cool Papa never again wondered where he stood in regard to the "equal" part.

As the exhibitions played out, the Negro League season wasn't *totally* forgotten. Back in late September, at Philadelphia, the Crawfords—absent Paige, who naturally had his own show playing somewhere else—had engaged the Elite Giants in the crude beginning of a championship playoff. But after one game, which Washington won 2–0, the teams adjourned to greener pastures, with vague intentions to resume the series somewhere in the South the following spring.

As if *that* would happen.

IN SPITE OF the *Pittsburgh Courier*'s drumbeating for desegregation, the escalation of black-white competition, and the booming statement that the Negro Leaguers articulated in Colorado, the color line was going nowhere. Notwithstanding the theater of Jesse Owens, the rise of Joe Louis, the popularity of Satchel Paige, the New York press, the Dean games, the Feller games, the Hornsby games, common sense, ideological momentum, the moral imperative, the American spirit, the empathy of FDR, and the commissioner's pooh-poohing of the notion that baseball observed any sort of prohibition whatsoever based on race, neither Bell nor Paige nor Gibson nor Wells nor Suttles nor Leonard nor Johnson nor Charleston nor any other dark-skinned, tricky-ball barnstormer was about to become a Philly Athletic, a New York Giant, a New York Yankee, a St. Louis Cardinal, or a Pittsburgh Pirate.

And yet, increasingly, the two parties lined up against each other on the playing field. They competed, they fraternized, they periodically fought, and they got paid well enough to keep doing it.

During and shortly after the 1936 season alone—in addition to the interracial matches in which the Crawfords and company acquitted themselves so conspicuously—Paige and Double Duty Radcliffe played on a team that won a mixed tournament in Wichita, Kansas; the Newark Eagles and Homestead Grays collaborated to beat the Cincinnati Reds in Puerto Rico; a Cuban club split four games with the St. Louis Cardinals; and Cool Papa's team in the California Winter League (the Royal Giants) breezed to the title over five Caucasian squads (one of them named the White Kings) of mostly minor leaguers with a few legitimate major leaguers mixed in. When the tables were turned and the Crawfords were blanked by the white Brooklyn Bushwicks, it seemed so peculiar that Dan Parker of the *New York Daily Mirror* charged the Negro Leaguers with complicity in a gambling setup, which the players subsequently denied in an affidavit.

If they weren't reconfiguring the national pastime or taking down double standards on the spot, the Negro Leaguers were at least gaining admirers. Joe DiMaggio, a rookie standout for the Yankees that year, declared that he knew he was ready for the big time when he got an infield hit against Satchel Paige the previous winter in California.

As the racial games played on, the body of work would build and testify on the blackballers' behalf. Over a period of years in the mid- and late thirties, journalists and major leaguers alike served as witnesses to the obvious.

Arkansas native Arky Vaughan, an all-star shortstop for nine straight years with the Pittsburgh Pirates, recognized a peer when he saw one, and he saw plenty of them on the Crawfords plenty of times. "I have played against any number of great Negro players," Vaughan told the *Pittsburgh Courier*, "and I know that there were any number who could play in the major leagues. Some of the best ball players I have ever seen were colored."

Chester Washington of the *Courier* contended that Bell, Paige, and Suttles would not only strengthen the big-league product but "add more color." Hugh Bradley of the *New York Post* wrote that any of twenty or more black players could improve the Brooklyn Dodgers. Leon Hardwick of the *Baltimore Afro-American* went ahead and named them: Willie Wells, Turkey Stearnes, Mule Suttles, Sam Bankhead, Chet Brewer, Newt Allen, Biz Mackey. . . .

> There is no doubt about it that fellows like Paige and Gibson and Bell would bolster up not only the sagging Brooklyn Dodgers but many of the other wavering clubs such as the Boston Bees [the new owners of the beleaguered Boston Braves thought a different name might change the team's mojo, which, in a five-year experiment, it really didn't], Philadelphia's Phillies, St. Louis's Browns, Cincinnati's Reds, et cetera. In fact, this trio alone could weave miracles for any of the above mentioned clubs.
>
> . . . Where is Cool Papa Bell's superior as a fly chaser? This lad with the dazzling speed and intuitive knack of knowing just where to dash to bring down a fly.

Over his double-digit years of playing periodically against major leaguers, it's estimated that Bell batted .391 in those games. That doesn't include his .366 in a dozen seasons of California Winter League competition. Nor do those lofty numbers take into account Bell's most distinctive contributions. When distinguished *Courier* writer Wendell Smith interviewed various Pittsburgh Pirates about their impressions of Negro League counterparts who worked in the same city, none mentioned Cool Papa's batting average. It was merely incidental.

"I have seen him score from second on just an ordinary fly to the outfield," said Bill Brubaker, an infielder whose best season happened to be 1936. "He musta had wings on his feet. Bell was a big leaguer if there ever was one."

"Bell was one of the fastest men baseball has ever known, and he was a constant worry whenever he got on base," asserted Pie Traynor, the Bucs' manager and Hall of Fame third baseman. "He'd steal a pitcher's pants. I always admired him for his dashing spirit and ability to get the jump on opposing pitchers. And he could go a country mile for a ball. He could have made the grade easily."

Note the past tense. It was 1939 when Traynor made those remarks, and by that time Cool Papa, still in his protracted prime, had been effectively unseen in Pittsburgh or the United States at large for three years, on his way to five. The Crawfords would crumble, and rather than making the grade in the majors, as Traynor affirmed he could have so easily done, Bell would find his homeland roundly unaccommodating and choose to leave it in pursuit of opportunity.

The prevailing agenda was to keep the races apart. On one front, commissioner Landis and Will Harridge, the American League president, troubled by the trend toward black-white exhibitions, did what they could to scale back, if not prohibit, interracial barnstorming. On another, big-league tryouts of black players were called for, scheduled, and canceled, or held and then, absurdly, pronounced unproductive. A few owners—William Benswanger of the Pirates was one—advocated for integration, but most wished the subject would go away. There was preliminary chatter about the top Negro clubs being incorporated into organized ball as a minor league, but it never reached an official meeting.

Meanwhile, black teams kept whipping white teams, more often than not, on the selected occasions when they were permitted to try. Therein lay the wicked irony that Cool Papa Bell could simply not countenance. It became his abiding grievance.

"They always said that blacks couldn't play major-league baseball," he lamented. "They didn't say that blacks were not *allowed* to play. They said we *couldn't* play.

"They were saying, 'We will accept a black man if he is qualified to play. But we can't find one qualified enough to play.'"

It was a theme for his exile, and years beyond. It was, as well, a damnable pretense that oppressed so many of his super-talented, self-respecting teammates and contemporaries—among them Satchel Paige, so adamant about equality that he once threatened not to pitch at Sportsman's Park in St. Louis unless African American fans were permitted to sit in the box seats; Willie Wells, who had to find his freedom and manhood in Mexico; Josh Gibson, whose deadly demons may or may not have been related to the several times Benswanger tried to sign him for the Pirates and was persuaded to back off; Judy Johnson, to whom dignity was a way of life; and Double Duty Radcliffe, who once, in a public setting in Cuba, after beating a team of major leaguers, was asked why he was not one of those himself.

"You'll have to ask the two Grand Dragons of the Ku Klux [Klan]," he replied.

And who would they be?

"J. Edgar Hoover and your Judge Landis."

CHAPTER SIXTEEN

THE DICTATOR'S CAMPAIGN FOR REELECTION

F OR DAYS, OMINOUS MEN IN PANAMA HATS HAD been tracking Satchel Paige around the New Orleans hotel where the Pittsburgh Crawfords had convened for spring training, 1937. Satchel knew full well what they wanted, which was to carry him back to whatever tropical outpost it was where those hats were the fashion and march him to a pitcher's mound. Ordinarily he would judge that as an agreeable arrangement, because of the monetary benefit, but the traveling pea thrower had too-recently jumped the Crawfords for Bismarck, North Dakota, and then Bismarck for the Crawfords, and folks were already fed up with his renegade ways. So he'd steered clear of the skulking figures, ducked out a side door, and rushed to his car for a getaway, except that his pursuers had a car, too, with another distinctively lidded gentleman waiting inside it.

They were from the Dominican Republic, representing its president, Rafael Trujillo, who was associated with a baseball team on which, it appeared, his upcoming reelection might depend. The lead recruiter was Enrique Aybar, dean of the University of Santo Domingo, and his compelling pitch to Paige included the majority share of

$30,000 that investors were earmarking for American players who would enable the Dragones of Ciudad Trujillo (the former and future Santo Domingo, renamed the previous year) to leapfrog the two superior teams whose fortunes were tethered to other candidates.

Once he heard the numbers, Paige set off for the Dominican with his preferred catcher, Bill Perkins. Shortly thereafter, it became evident to the shrewd pitcher that (1) he and Perkins were not nearly enough reinforcement for Ciudad Trujillo to overtake the stiff competition, and (2) failure to win the national championship was an option he would be wise to steer clear of. In consideration of those items, he placed a phone call to his trusted friend back in Pittsburgh, the teammate whose guidance the others would value. Cool Papa was all ears.

It was painfully apparent to Bell that another season with the Crawfords was a dismal prospect. In March, Greenlee had traded Josh Gibson to their nemesis, the Homestead Grays, for $2,500, a corner infielder, and a catcher named Pepper Bassett, whose calling card was the ability to do his job from a rocking chair set up behind home plate. Tin Can Kincannon was sold for a thousand bucks. Jimmie Crutchfield was dealt away. Paige left the country. Players had to cover their own expenses in spring training.

In the face of all that, the Craws opened the season with a doubleheader sweep of the Washington Elite Giants at Greenlee Field. But the next day, at Oriole Park in Baltimore, they lost twice to the same squad, in spite of Bell's homer on the first pitch of the first game. All the while, he was strongly considering a factory job that consisted largely of baseball—perhaps around Pittsburgh and Western Pennsylvania, where steel mills and foundries sponsored hard-core company teams in the industrial leagues.

"Now, I never did jump nowhere unless it was going bad," Cool Papa told Donald Honig in *Baseball When the Grass Was Real*, "and that year it was going bad. The owner of the Crawfords was losing money, and he was giving us ballplayers a tough time, not paying us. Matter of fact, the whole league was going bad at that time. So I was *looking* for somewhere to go when Satchel called.

" 'We're in trouble down here,' he said. 'We're supposed to win this championship. I want you and some of the boys to come down. They'll give you eight hundred dollars, your transportation, and all your expenses for six weeks. Will you do it?'

" 'No,' I said. 'But make it a thousand and I'll say yes.' "

At that point Paige handed the phone to a team official, presumably Aybar, and terms were worked out for each new man to receive $500 at the Miami airport and another $500 at the completion of the short season. Charged with bringing the Dragones up to speed, Bell spirited Leroy Matlock, Sam Bankhead, and infielder Harry Williams from the Crawfords, effectively depleting Greenlee's historic team, which would limp through the summer with a losing record. He also reached across town to reunite with Josh Gibson, who, after a stubborn negotiation, signed on for more than double the standard portion and reported to the capital city a short while later.

Agents of the other two Dominican teams, the Águilas of Santiago and defending champion Estrellas from San Pedro de Macoris, had been working Pittsburgh as well. Greenlee tried to have them arrested and Oscar Charleston got hold of one by the throat, but pitcher Chet Brewer and infielder Pat Patterson were nevertheless persuaded to take up with the Águilas (alongside former Craws pitcher Bertrum Hunter, who found a wife on the island and elected to stay). In all, ten Crawfords would remove to the Caribbean, where the sun beat down so hard that the Americans greased their faces to keep from getting blisters and sirens were set for 1:45 in the afternoon to rouse everyone from their lunchtime siestas.

The defections met with little sympathy back home. The *Pittsburgh Press* was so indignant that it was able to portray Greenlee as a victim of "dastardly piracy":

> President Gus Greenlee of the Negro National Baseball League is going to Washington this week to create a diplomatic rumble that will shake the crease out of every frock coat and striped trouser leg from the State Department to Tanganyika.

What's more, he's enlisted the support of 10 U.S. Senators and 28 Congressmen behind his charge that the Republic of San Domingo has "dealt with, induced and lured away" a score of his league's best athletes, the brightest stars in the Negro baseball firmament.

... It is an open secret that persons anonymously described as "the sugar interests" down there offered enough sugar to lure such stellar performers as Satchel Paige and Cool-Papa Bell from Mr. Greenlee's Pittsburgh Crawfords, one of his principal sources of income.

Trujillo indeed was a sugar magnate, having been instrumental in nationalizing the industry—which amounted to placing it under the auspices of his family—but his clout was military in origin and practice. He'd ascended through the Dominican army, and in his presidency the armed forces were as conspicuous as the oversized electric sign above Ciudad Trujillo that put things in their proper perspective: *Dios y Trujillo* (*God and Trujillo*).

Paige was there to greet Bell and the others when they arrived. So was a squad of soldiers equipped with rifles and bandoliers. The new players were introduced at a press conference in which Aybar, eliciting chuckles and winks among the reporters, explained that, while there was a business component to the acquisition of the Negro Leaguers, "baseball in Trujillo City is not commercial. Money makes no difference. Baseball is spiritual in every aspect, as indulged in by the Latin race. . . . The Americans accepted the terms offered because the pay was much higher than that they were accustomed to receiving in the States. We would have imported white players if the salaries of the white American players had not been such that it was impossible for us to better them."

Afterwards, the military escort delivered Cool Papa's posse to its living quarters, a private club down the coast toward San Pedro de Macoris, where—since the games were played only on Saturdays and Sundays—the imported Dragones would not be distracted during the week by elements of the city. There had been public complaints and critical editorials regarding the conduct of foreign players who'd arrived earlier, and one of the corrective measures was the appointment of a discipline committee to control the situation.

The committee's preference was that the players stay in their pajamas and take their meals in their rooms. More realistically (they didn't all *have* pajamas), they were prohibited from bars, nightclubs (where too many local women had been volunteering to teach the Americans the merengue), and leaving the club without the accompaniment of soldiers. Paige's pal Bill Perkins, a renowned ladies' man, commanded a military detail of five to ward off the temptresses.

The supervision, however, was not unshakable. Drinking buddies Bankhead and Gibson, who would lead the league in hitting, managed to sneak out for beverages now and again, notwithstanding the rumors that anyone selling whiskey to a Dragone would be shot. Prudently, those who painted the town took care to leave their money behind with Bell. He kept thousands of dollars in a suitcase that a valet watched over.

Cool Papa didn't quite know what to make of the armed guards. What was the big deal? He struck up a conversation with one and was told, as he related in *The Pittsburgh Crawfords*, "If you don't win, they're going to kill Trujillo."

"I laughed and said, 'They don't kill people over baseball games.'

"He didn't laugh. He looked me right in the eye and said, 'Down here, they will do it.'"

The isolation, meanwhile, was not without its benefits. The erstwhile Crawfords swam and fished in the ocean—there's a photo of Cool Papa standing on a pier with Leroy Matlock slung over his shoulder and Satchel laughing in the background, all three in swim trunks—and generally enjoyed a level of leisure they'd never known in the course of a baseball season. But Bell's sense of security was compromised by an uneasiness that not infrequently intensified into terror. One such occasion followed a series in which Ciudad Trujillo was bested by San Pedro de Macoris. Upon the players' return to their compound, an army officer, expressing his displeasure on behalf of the president, unholstered his .45 and put several craters in the walls of the courtyard. Those were the times when Clara Belle seemed impossibly far away.

"We all knew the situation was serious," Bell confided to *Sports Illustrated*, "but it wasn't until later that we heard how bad it was. We found out that, as far as Trujillo was concerned, we either won or we were going to lose big. That means he was going to kill us. A very frightening man."

The courtyard walls—to say nothing of the Americans behind them—caught a break when the losing weekend with the Estrellas proved to be an aberration. As the season heated up, San Pedro de Macoris faltered (the Estrellas' best pitcher was suspended for arguing with an umpire), Ciudad Trujillo slipped ahead of Santiago, and the Americans were treated as movie stars. It had been the U.S. Marines who brought baseball to the republic, and the republic was grateful; the shell of the USS *Memphis*, wrecked by a tsunami during the U.S. occupation in 1916, sat imperially beyond the white walls of the municipal stadium, Campo Deportivo. Thousands of fans would turn up when the Dragones practiced and dozens would fall in behind them when they left on foot. The players' pictures were posted in shop windows. Satchel Paige had a blend of rum named after him. (Haitians who shared the island presented Satchel with a charm to ostensibly give him good luck, although it was later understood to bespeak evil intentions.)

The Dragones had assembled a potent roster that, in addition to the Negro Leaguers, included a few capable Cubans, a few mediocre Dominicans, and Perucho Cepeda, a legendary infielder from Puerto Rico who refused to bring his game to the United States as long as the color line went uncrossed. (Twenty-one years later, his son, Orlando—an eventual Hall of Famer—was named National League Rookie of the Year with the San Francisco Giants.) Matlock bolstered Paige on the pitching side, and the Dominican fans were discerning enough to know who was energizing the Ciudad Trujillo lineup.

"It was clear to them," wrote Averell "Ace" Smith in *The Pitcher and the Dictator*, a book about Paige, Trujillo, and the Dragones, "that Josh and Cool Papa were difference makers; in just twelve games Josh was hitting .420 with twenty-one hits, including four doubles, five triples, two home runs with twenty-one RBIs. Cool Papa was batting .323, but even more importantly he was using his great speed to score runs: thirteen in fifteen games."

Playing for Ciudad Trujillo, the pressure was on Gibson, Bell, and the other hired guns from the Negro Leagues.

Cool's locomotion was in fact a wonder to all concerned. The first time he tripled, the game was paused and the opponents argued that, in order to get to third so quickly, he must surely have bypassed second base and cut a more streamlined path across the field. It was a complaint that Bell had heard back home as well, his blurring of the basepaths being so optically irregular. Even umpires had a difficult time sorting through what they'd seen, occasionally calling him out for not touching first base as he turned the corner for second. Unlike other runners, Cool Papa pushed off the bag with his *left* foot while the ump was focused on the right. Once, when Bell protested the decision, the man in blue said, "Didn't I see your right foot go over that base?"

"Well," Papa replied, "I got *two* feet."

In the Negro Leagues, the problem was corrected when Bell began alerting the umpires before the game to his funky footwork. He also advised them that he might not always *step* on the base, per se, but would at least brush it with his toe. For full disclosure, he might have added "usually," but in the spirit of tricky ball he perhaps didn't; having gained the benefit of the doubt, Cool was not above taking competitive advantage. He was not likely, however, to press that advantage in a foreign land, in front of a full house and federal soldiers with rifles angled across their chests.

It was a tense time, and one that the Negro Leaguers, though unaccustomed to an atmosphere of such urgency, didn't shrink from. A month after Bell and his compadres had come to the rescue, by which time only two of the original Dragones remained on the team, San Pedro de Macoris had been eliminated from the title chase and the Dominican Republic was ready for the final phase of the National Baseball Championship for the Reelection of President Trujillo.

THE CHAMPIONSHIP SERIES was preceded by a parade under the swaying palms on Avenida George Washington, alongside the Caribbean, which conveyed ocean breezes to the back of Cool Papa's neck when he defended center field at Campo Deportivo. The familiar soldiers were in the parade, dancing and shooting.

Accounts of the series are neither consistent nor comprehensive, but it appears that the title would not be decided by a simple best-of-seven or the like. Rather, the final games, spread over three weekends, would be tacked onto the season records of the Dragones and the Águilas club from Santiago. Going in, Ciudad Trujillo led by what would equate, in traditional standings, to one game.

Despite the closeness, the Dragones, by the graces of the blackball cavalry, were solid favorites when the playoffs began on a Saturday in late June. That was justified in game one, when Bell and Gibson led an offensive outburst and Matlock would have shut out the Águilas but for Martín Dihigo's harmless homer in the ninth. Paige dominated the Sunday morning game, outpitching Dihigo, and Bob "Schoolboy" Griffith, a towering trombone player by way of Tennessee and the Washington Elite Giants, beat Luis Tiant in the afternoon for the weekend sweep.

Trujillo's team won its fourth straight on the following Saturday, behind Matlock, before the Águilas came to life Sunday in Santiago. They blasted Griffith in the morning affair, and then Chet Brewer—the Crawford who had gotten away from the Dragones—took the measure of Paige, ensuring drama for the final weekend.

There was no game scheduled on July's second Saturday, and that night the English-speaking Dragones were hauled away to the slammer. It was for their protection, they were told. While incarcerated, they enjoyed red wine with their chicken and rice.

There would be a second game the next day only if Santiago won the first, a disquieting possibility that Cool Papa didn't even care to contemplate: he'd heard murmurs that the Americans might never see the mainland again if they didn't wrap things up in the expected fashion. Aybar urged Satchel—according to Satchel, anyway—to please take his advice and win.

On Sunday, July 11, soldiers were ringing the field at Campo Deportivo, knives in their belts, rifles at the ready, by the time the players padded out for warm-ups. Ostensibly they were there to keep the peace and lend a sense of ceremony to the auspicious occasion. To Bell and Paige and the more skittish of their teammates, they were a firing squad just awaiting the word.

Unloosing his famous folksiness and his singular privilege of hyperbole, Paige elaborated in *Pitchin' Man*, a little memoir he wrote in 1948 with Cleveland sportswriter Hal Lebovitz:

> The final—and main game—was played in Trujillo's town. Seven thousand people was in the stands and they all had knives and guns.
>
> I tried to play sick. 'Cause I was sick, believe me. But they stuck a gun at my head and I got well.
>
> The umpires was Trujillo's men, too. I knowed if I threw the ball anywhere it would be a strike 'cause the umpires saw the guns

too, but I was shakin' like a leaf in a high breeze and they had us 5-4 goin' into the seventh. We got two runs that innin' and I said to myself, "L-l-l-listen, S-s-s-atch," (I couldn't talk to myself without stutterin') "pull yourself together before they air-condition you."

Well, we lucked out through the next two innins' and won, 6–5.

The American consul heard what a worrysome situation we was in and they flew us out in a bird that same night.

Not surprisingly, very little of the above checks out, including the implication that Paige was the pitcher of record that day. In fact, he was upset that Matlock got the start.

Through the early innings, however, it looked like an unimpeachable decision. The able lefty kept pace with Chet Brewer, both pitchers posting zeros until the Dragones changed the landscape in the fifth. Two runners were already aboard, including Matlock, when Cool Papa's sacrifice bunt was mishandled, which often happened when fielders were harried by his speed.

Three runs had scored, and the bases had refilled, when Dihigo, the Águilas' outfielder-pitcher-manager, called upon himself to relieve Brewer. Sam Bankhead welcomed the illustrious Cuban with the loveliest grand slam Bell had ever witnessed. Later in the inning, Matlock doubled home the Dragones' eighth run.

It was 8–2 when the ninth inning, and the trouble, started. It was 8–3 when Satchel Paige and his chattering teeth were summoned. And it was 8–6, with two outs and two runners on base, when Satch faced powerful Spoony Palm, Santiago's catcher and Bell's old teammate with the St. Louis Stars. Normal breathing resumed, and paper pesos floated onto the field from the Campo Deportivo grandstand, only through the blessing of a fabulous play by Bankhead at shortstop.

Paige may indeed have caught a flight off the island that night, but Cool Papa, Josh, Bankhead, Matlock, Harry Williams, and Schoolboy Griffith took a day or so to kick back in soldierless safety and sample the Dominican spoils, maybe have a merengue lesson. Between their salaries, bonuses, celebration bounty, and tips for home runs and other

CAMPEONATO REELECCIÓN PRESIDENTE TRUJILLO
1937-1938   1938-1939

The president's recruits won the island championship but lost their taste for
Dominican politics.

heroics, most of them boarded the SS *San Juan* carrying more money—
in excess of $2,000—than they'd ever held or had on American soil.

Three months later Trujillo directed an ethnic cleansing of Haitians living in the Dominican Republic's northwestern sector, whom
he claimed were stealing livestock and crops from the region's farmers.
As many as perhaps twenty thousand Haitians—some estimates ran
as high as thirty thousand or more—were slaughtered by Dominican
soldiers wielding machetes, rifles, knives, and bayonets. Dead bodies were dumped into the sea or gruesome mass graves in numbers
impossible to count.

The international outcry persuaded Trujillo to withdraw his
bid for a third term. He did, however, handpick his successor, who
ran unopposed and saw to it that the *Dios y Trujillo* sign was actually
enlarged. Trujillo returned to office in 1942—the same year Cool Papa
would end his hiatus from the Negro Leagues—lengthening the term
from four years to five and serving two more of them before turning
over the presidency to his brother.

CHAPTER SEVENTEEN

RAILROAD TRACKS
IN THE OUTFIELD

T HEY SAID THAT GUS GREENLEE CRIED WHEN
Cool and the others left the Crawfords to play for Ciudad
Trujillo in 1937. If so, his mood had materially hardened by
the time the *San Juan* docked in New York on July 30.

Big Red's appeal to federal officials had gained the blindsided
owners an audience with the State Department, but the hearing produced no diplomatic redress. Now that the Dominican
season had concluded, their only recourse was to sanction the
outlaws in a Negro League way. And so, at Greenlee's urging,
the AWOL Dragones and other skedaddling ingrates were "banned
for life."

"Life" soon became two years, with a fine attached, for all but
Josh Gibson, whose absence from the Homestead Grays had been
officially excused by Cum Posey. He would be welcomed back. But if
his accomplices wished to keep playing ball and add to their freshly
acquired nest eggs, they'd have to stick together as a collective, market-
able entity—except, maybe, for Satchel Paige, who generally preferred
to keep his sticking to himself.

Paige was nonetheless peeved at the draconian suspensions, and responded under his own byline in the *Baltimore Afro-American*, railing that "I would be willing to go to South America and live in the jungles rather than go back to the league and play ball like I did for ten years.... I find it hard to believe that [people] would turn their backs on me, simply because I wanted to earn more money. If I was such a bad fellow, why did men such as Josh Gibson, Matlock, Bankhead and Cool Papa Bell and others follow me?"

Now, though, the others were actually following Cool Papa. He'd known about the suspensions in advance and made the necessary arrangements. The returning Dragones would be busy and properly accessorized. The jerseys were lettered across the chest with *C. Trujillo.*

"When we come back," reflected Bell, "we toured the United States under the name of the Trujillo All-Stars. They gave me a whole set of uniforms, so I formed a team, although I didn't know nothing about managing. So we made another guy on the team manager, and it seems like that satisfied them. Most people are kind of jealous, you know."

It was a complicated time for Mary Nichols's son. She had passed away in Mississippi while Cool was helping the dictator to his championship. Leaving the island for a visit to Oktibbeha County hadn't been an option—not with Trujillo's title still in the balance—and Clara Belle hadn't been at his side for comfort. He couldn't even mourn with his brothers. Meanwhile his major-league dreams had been fantasies, and now he was unwelcome in his old job as well. With all of that crashing down, the knives and rifles of the Dominican soldiers had made the moment feel existential.

There was a fellow he could turn to, at least, regarding the essential but unfamiliar mechanics of running a ball club. Advisedly, Bell retained the services of Ray Doan—the promoter who represented the House of David team and had put together Dizzy Dean's barnstorming tours—for crucial assistance in scheduling and publicity and the like. For starters, Doan prevailed upon the directors of the *Denver Post* tournament to disregard their prohibition of Negro Leaguers, since, technically, his clients had been stripped of that status. So the Trujillo All-Stars (sometimes referred to as the Santo Domingo All-Stars) made their way to Colorado with an enviable lineup of renegades.

Without Paige at the outset—as usual, he was off turning a buck in parts unknown—and competing in a field of sixteen teams with twenty-four past and future big leaguers, the "chocolate whiz bangs," as one Western pundit labeled them, rolled unchallenged through the early rounds. That set up a high-profile encounter with the Pampa Roadrunners, an unbeaten club representing a Texas oil company, headlined by third baseman Sammy Hale, who had batted over .300 in a long major-league career, and football legend Sammy Baugh, who had just graduated from Texas Christian University. A master quarterback—a prolific, revolutionary passer—Baugh's celebrity was already such that the *Post* arranged for him to put on a passing-punting exhibition on the night before the games began, for which a crowd of twelve thousand showed up.

Prior to embarking on his historic professional football career, Slingin' Sammy, an unvarnished Texan from Sweetwater—home of the world's largest rattlesnake roundup—had taken a summer job with the oil company. He'd played baseball as well at TCU, and while in Denver signed a contract with the St. Louis Cardinals, brokered by Ray Doan on the recommendation of Rogers Hornsby. Among his many talents, Baugh was also a tale spinner of nearly Satchel Paige proportions, and he had one for the eventful ball game against Ciudad Trujillo.

"Hell," he said, "I have to admit, that job was mostly playing semi-pro baseball with the company team going to the *Denver Post* tournament, one of the best damn tournaments in the country. This thing was bigger than most minor leagues and maybe the biggest thing outside of big-league ball. The best talent gathered there each year and scouts were crawling all over the place. You couldn't believe the names: Rogers Hornsby, Grover Cleveland Alexander, Satchel Paige, Cool Papa Bell. . . . And they'd get ten thousand or more people each day at Merchants Park.

"Now, I had played third base all my life. But our team had picked up Sammy Hale, and they wanted him to play third. I had never played shortstop in my life. [The Cardinals, however, must have been impressed by the way he handled the position in Colorado, because they placed him at shortstop as a farmhand in 1938, his only professional baseball season.]

"Cool Papa Bell hit a line drive in the third inning between the left fielder and center fielder [scoring two runs]. The center fielder got over like he was gonna cut it off and Cool Papa rounded first and kinda let up going into second. But that damned center fielder muffed the ball, and God, Cool Papa turned it on and went into third base. He and the ball got there at the same time—*smack!*—and he hit that damned third baseman with his cleats up, cut him on both sides of his face and knocked him back fifteen feet. He was out cold."

The game had been palpably contentious, with hard tags, brushbacks, and snarly rhetoric. Bell's ornery slide was carried out, in all likelihood, with respect to not only the festering antipathy but also to his leadership role with the team he had put together. Perhaps there was even a little pent-up anger concerning the complications of African Americans just trying to make a living playing ball thrown in there. Whatever the impetus, it kicked the intensity up a few notches, to say the least.

"Everybody came running out of those damn dugouts with bats in their hands and arms raised and yelling. I'd never seen anything like that," Baugh recalled, neglecting to mention his good fortune of being moved off of third base. "I couldn't believe it.

"This big black sonofabitch grabbed me by my jersey and I had him by his. We just stood there watching all this going on, kinda holding each other and looking over our shoulders. I got scared and he got scared. There were bats being swung at people's heads, breaking arms. They couldn't stop the goddamn thing. I bet it took them ten minutes to stop it. We didn't have enough police and security. I was never so goddamn scared in my life."

Four of Bell's teammates—Clyde Spearman, George Scales, Showboat Thomas, and Satchel Paige, who had finally arrived—were ejected, though Cool Papa was not. Nor was a single Pampa player. After a half-hour delay to cool off, the Texans' punishment was meted out in the form of a 10–1 shellacking, with Schoolboy Griffith limiting the oilmen to three hits.

Bell claimed that it was the only baseball fight he was ever involved in. A couple of days later he experienced another unprecedented development: the first time he'd lost a tournament game in Denver. It came in the championship round against the Halliburton Cementers of Duncan, Oklahoma, with Paige on the mound amidst rumblings that his teammates didn't really want him there.

The tournament was set up in a double-elimination format, and Halliburton had already lost once, which meant that Cool Papa's team would secure the title with a victory. Sponsors had established a $1,000 bonus for the winning pitcher of the final game, and Bell's banished Negro Leaguers were hoping it would be claimed by Matlock; he, Griffith, and Chet Brewer had thrown consecutive shutouts before Satchel even showed up. For that matter, the outlaws weren't keen on splitting their *regular* shares with their tardy, self-aggrandizing teammate. Nevertheless, for obvious publicity purposes, the promoters insisted that Paige make the featured start.

The favored team's disgruntlement may or may not have affected the outcome, a 6–4 setback. For the record, though, there were three passed balls in the first inning by Spoony Palm, a generally reliable catcher; a ground ball booted by Showboat Thomas, a notably nifty first baseman; and an apparent single that rolled through the legs of Roy Parnell in the outfield. It was an unsightly defeat.

At any rate, the faux Dominicans bounced back in a big way behind Matlock in the ensuing championship match, an 11–1 dismantling for five thousand American dollars, not counting the left-hander's extra grand.

AS IF THE All-Stars hadn't been called enough different things, they now added Satchel Paige's name to their billing. Heading east, Bell's team toured in Lincoln, Kansas City, and Chicago, where most of its members, ordinarily, would have participated a few weeks earlier in the East-West game.

Somehow, catcher Spoony Palm, Cool Papa's old teammate with the St. Louis Stars, let three of Satchel's pitches get away from him that day in Denver.

The suspension stipulated that they not play against Negro League teams or in Negro League stadiums, but that was a fluid proposition, depending on who stood to prosper. It was largely Gus Greenlee's decree, but Greenlee, the king of kickbacks, quietly helped arrange a popular series between the All-Stars and various Negro League clubs, actual or ad hoc. In Cleveland, the All-Stars lined up against the New York Cubans, whose headliner was a slender twenty-one-year-old pitching hotshot named Johnny Taylor. When they moved on to New York for a highly publicized date with the Washington Elite Giants, Taylor was on the mound for Washington, too.

Paige got the ball for the blackballed squad, and with twenty thousand people looking on at the Polo Grounds in upper Manhattan,

Cool Papa worked young Taylor for a leadoff walk. The drop-balling right-hander walked him again in the sixth, and that was the extent of the offense for team Trujillo. In the ninth, Bell grounded out on a sinking curveball, and the kid from Connecticut had completed an unlikely no-hitter.

Paige was humbled and readily agreed to a rematch at Yankee Stadium. The whole scenario was reminiscent of Satchel's two-game showdown three years earlier with precocious Slim Jones, from the venue to the crowd—this time *thirty-five* thousand—to the conclusion. Once again, the wily virtuoso had the final say; it was Taylor's turn to be humbled, 9–4. Joe DiMaggio, the American League home run champion, was on hand that day, and when asked by the press about his impressions of Paige, he was able to say, from winter league experience, that the road-show righty was the best pitcher he'd ever faced. (Of course, the Yankee Clipper was only twenty-two at the time.)

Like Bell and the other Dominican drifters, Satchel was unattached for the foreseeable future, an intriguing circumstance with potentialities not lost on Chester Washington of the *Pittsburgh Courier*. Taking note, also, of the state of the Pittsburgh Pirates—a team with a winning tradition and top-heavy roster, ten years removed from a World Series—the popular sports columnist fired off a Western Union telegram in November to Pie Traynor, the Bucs' progressive-minded manager:

> KNOW YOUR CLUB NEEDS PLAYERS STOP HAVE ANSWER TO YOUR PRAYERS RIGHT HERE IN PITTSBURGH STOP JOSH GIBSON CATCHER FIRST BASE B. LEONARD AND RAY BROWN PITCHER OF HOMESTEAD GRAYS AND S. PAIGE PITCHER COOL PAPA BELL OF PITTSBURGH CRAWFORDS ALL AVAILABLE AT REASONABLE FIGURES STOP WOULD MAKE PIRATES FORMIDABLE PENNANT CONTENDERS STOP WHAT IS YOUR ATTITUDE? STOP WIRE ANSWER

Washington's appeal was published with an accompanying article urging the Pirates to "forget this myth that baseball is different from football and track" (not to mention boxing, in which, that June, Joe Louis had knocked out James Braddock for the heavyweight title that he would successfully defend twenty-five times). The addition of the players in his telegram, he wrote, would electrify 1938 and "make the Pittsburgh owners, players, and fans forget the color of their faces."

There was no reply from Traynor, which implied that he had been advised by higher-ups or knew how they felt about the subject. The Pirates, led by the Waner brothers in the outfield and Arky Vaughan at shortstop, made a spirited run at the pennant in 1938 but again fell short. Traynor lost a considerable amount of weight over the course of the collapse. The following year he confided to Wendell Smith of the *Courier* that, "personally, I don't see why the ban against Negro players exists at all." The great third baseman soon turned from managing to broadcasting, in which position he encouraged the Pirates to integrate in the interest of winning. It would be 1960 before Pittsburgh was treated to another World Series.

Eligible for neither the Negro nor the major leagues, Cool Papa could at least take off-season refuge in the hospitable California Winter League. The money wasn't much, but the Bells didn't need much. They had no children and still lived, presumably, with Clara's extended family on Lawton Avenue in St. Louis. It was not only economical but convenient when Cool was on the road or out of the country.

Bell's paydays were coming gig by gig now, and California was simply the next one. In Los Angeles, in the winter of 1937, he hooked up again with Tom Wilson's commanding Royal Giants. Biz Mackey, the catcher, handled what little managing was required with Cool, Suttles, Matlock, Brewer, Pullman Porter, and Wild Bill Wright on hand. At 21-3, the Royal Giants more than doubled the victories of the second-place club.

Along the way, Bell won match races around the bases, caught his first glimpse of a splintery nineteen-year-old slugger named Ted Williams, and was approached by Tom Wilson about managing and playing for his Baltimore Elite Giants in 1938. It's unclear whether Cool's suspension was about to prematurely run its course or whether Wilson planned to fight it or whether Greenlee was still in a position to enforce it; Greenlee Field was razed that year to make room for a housing project. Nor is it apparent whether an offer was actually extended or whether Bell simply wanted nothing more to do with the Negro Leagues.

The possibility of the latter is raised by the decision he made in the spring to take his game and Clara Belle to Mexico. There, Cool Papa would chase fly balls for the Alijadores of Tampico, a tropical city situated south of Monterrey on the Gulf of Mexico. In that restful locale—and taking advantage of a less demanding schedule than he was accustomed to—Cool would also author a sobering article published by the *St. Louis Argus*.

Writing with a surprising edge, Bell was sharply critical of Negro League owners—he made an exception for Greenlee—who didn't maintain their parks, provide proper equipment, travel appropriately, enforce their rules, or pay their players on schedule. Their shoddy stewardship, he charged, was responsible for a "deplorable lack of interest."

He didn't give the players a pass, either, although he did give them an excuse:

> The average player of today doesn't take his baseball as seriously as the players did years ago. I can never forget the way we would gather in the club houses, hotels and even on the trains studying a way to beat the next team. We kept baseball on our minds. Today the players don't have much time to think. They are playing all the time, day and night, and they can't play their best at all times. And the best is what it takes to keep the fans interested enough to make the game a paying proposition. . . .

They were words that needed to be heard from a man of his stature and credibility. In fundamental ways, working and even living conditions—salary, accommodations, pace, respect—were better on the south side of the border.

On the other hand, the fly chasing in Tampico's center field was complicated by a set of railroad tracks that ran through it.

CHAPTER EIGHTEEN

THE LAND OF OPPORTUNITY

W E CAN ONLY SPECULATE ABOUT THE CON-
versation that lured Cool Papa to Mexico. It may have
been another sales pitch from Satchel Paige, forever
on the leading edge of frontier opportunity. Satch could have been
thinking that, even if they reported to different teams—as they ultimately did, Paige signing with Agrario of Mexico City—they would
be in it together, the first two African American players to cross the
Rio Grande.

The league was ratcheting up. Martín Dihigo, the Cuban icon, had
hustled over to Mexico after the harrowing Dominican campaign of
'37 and won a national championship with the Águila club of Veracruz.
When he returned for the 1938 season, Águila fans met his boat at the
dock and carried the great player to the ballpark on their shoulders.
Águila was Agrario's archrival, and signing Paige for '38 was Agrario's
response. Bell, in turn, was Paige's wingman, his first call for compan-
ionship in foreign adventure.

The other conceivable scenario involves a direct overture to
Cool Papa from Jorge Pasquel or one of his brothers, who were keenly

aware of the impact the Negro Leaguers had made in Ciudad Trujillo the year before. Pasquel, a dashing importer-exporter from Veracruz and baseball's preeminent patron in Mexico, had brazen designs on bringing the major-league game to his country. The strategy was to build the Mexican League's talent and popularity to the point at which he could entice enough big leaguers to threaten the integrity of the majors. Then, at the least, he would leverage a franchise for Mexico City or Monterrey. Along the way, the color line would disappear.

In the modern parlance of moneyball, Negro Leaguers represented Pasquel's market inefficiency. With the exception of Paige, who had methodically nurtured his distinctive brand, they were bargain ballplayers representing optimum bang per buck when compared to American big leaguers. Their recruitment, however, was not a one-sided proposition. On the other end of the equation, Mexico offered an integrated playing field—if not *now*, entirely, definitely in principle and time. That would certainly have appealed to Paige and Cool Papa Bell.

So Satchel, having abandoned a flirtation with the Newark Eagles and their glamorous owner, Effa Manley, signed for $2,000 a month (comparable to what Bobo Newsom made as the ace of the St. Louis Browns), Bell accepted $450 (the approximate going rate for a low-level major leaguer and much more than he'd been making in Pittsburgh), and both, content by their own standards, said adios to the Negro Leagues. In Tampico, with at least three days off every week, Cool and Clara Belle fell into an enchanting routine of dinner and dancing. The sauces were a little peppery, but otherwise life was agreeable. Pasquel even established a relationship with the Cuban Winter League, in which the best of the Mexican League players could supplement their regular-season earnings.

Bell was joined on the Tampico Alijadores by pitching stalwart Chet Brewer, who rolled up an 18-3 record on his way to the Mexican Hall of Fame, and veteran catcher T. J. Young, Brewer's former teammate with the Kansas City Monarchs. Each team was permitted four foreign players, and many of those had followed Dihigo from Cuba. The blackball wave would come rolling in over the next two seasons as the Negro Leagues continued to flounder—an exception being the

Homestead Grays, who would claim nine consecutive pennants—and word got back about the high regard and hospitality extended the African American players in Mexico.

From Pasquel's perspective, the welcoming of Negro Leaguers resonated well beyond the economics. He was of Spanish descent, and his connection with African Americans was forged during his travels in Texas, when he came upon a restaurant sign or two spelling out quite effectively that service did not extend to niggers, Mexicans, or dogs.

Pasquel hunted, dined, and socialized with the players he imported, all the while investing not only in their ballplaying but in their prosperity as well. He intuited that, if their trappings included nice accommodations and cars, they would be held in high esteem by the Mexican fan base. At one point he bought a luxury apartment building and made it available, rent-free, to American players. He considered it a good look, also, if the foreigners had their wives at their sides.

No softie—he would defend the family honor with his fists and once killed an immigration agent who challenged him to a duel in Nuevo Laredo—and not one to scrimp on his personal indulgences, Pasquel was nevertheless an inveterate philanthropist. On his ranches, he built and staffed schools for children of the hired hands. Baseball was not one of his charities, however. It stoked his national pride and competitive fire.

Both would be essential to the challenge ahead. Although it was said that the game had been introduced there by Abner Doubleday himself during the Mexican-American War of the late 1840s, Mexico was a baseball backwater. Only one of the league's stadiums, Delta Park in Mexico City, was equipped with locker rooms and showers. The Tampico railroad tracks, which entered Alijadores Park through a right-field gate and exited in left, were utilized irrespective of the game situation.

Mexican League travel was manageable, with trains taken for the longer trips, but the bus rides for shorter jaunts might be shared with chickens. Some of the American players were uncomfortable with morning games, scheduled so as to leave the afternoons open for bullfights. Others were put off by the whistling of the crowd at times when lustier boos were expected, or by the occasional firecracker pitched into the grass. The flagrant gambling in the grandstands could be unnerving as well, although the money being waved around was also used for tossing at players with whom the fans were particularly pleased. On special occasions they would storm the field, hoist the hero, and transport him royally to the dugout.

Cool Papa, picking up Spanish and playing with his customary panache on both sides of the tracks, batted .356 in his Mexican initiation. He and Brewer, however, lacked the supporting cast to bring down Dihigo and his Águilas. Nor were Paige and Agrario up to the task.

Satchel did beat Dihigo early in the season, before his arm broke down for the first time in his eventful career. He blamed it on the spicy food. Unwilling to quit on his fans or accept the obvious, the one-of-a-kind pitcher tried to soldier on, resorting to off-speed slop and often throwing underhanded, but he was ineffective and inconsolable. A doctor told Paige that his arm might never recover. At the least, his act would no longer play in Mexico.

That winter, Bell and Clara made it back to St. Louis, where Cool peddled his foot remedy and ran into Quincy Trouppe, who was working in a steel plant. Trouppe asked him if any Mexican team might be in the market for a catcher, and a few weeks later he received a telegram from the Carta Blanca club of Monterrey. The 1939 season would be the first of eight in which Trouppe played with distinction across the border. When he returned to Mexico the following year, the former Vashon High School star brought along Theolic Smith, another St. Louisan—and, like Bell, an alum of the Compton Hill Cubs—who would sign with Mexico City and who, too, would log eight stellar seasons in the league.

Other Negro Leaguers were identified and recruited when Mexican Leaguers, attended by club owners, competed against them on a tour of the United States during the autumn of 1938. The best catches from that junket were pitchers Barney Brown, Sug Cornelius, and Pullman Porter, but the top prize was secured independently by Cafeteros de Córdoba, which snagged Schoolboy Johnny Taylor. As a Mexican

In Mexico, a couple of local fishermen shared their expertise with Bell (right) and pitcher Andy "Pullman" Porter.

rookie, the slender right-hander delivered a crisp 11-1 record with a no-hitter tossed in, leading his team to the 1939 league title.

Not ready to cede his office as the ace of the league, Chet Brewer chalked up *two* no-hitters for Tampico that year. Bell, meanwhile, scarcely slowing down at age thirty-seven, produced a cool .354 batting average for the Alijadores, but his second Tampico season would be his last.

Jorge Pasquel, whose stake in the Mexican League had never involved ownership, was founding the Azules of Veracruz—the Veracruz Blues—and reserving center field for Cool Papa, with not a single rail or tie in the kindly veteran's path.

VERACRUZ, OF COURSE, already had a team. However, at the tail end of the 1939 season, the Águilas' owners had been expelled from the league for blowing off the final series against Córdoba, since Córdoba had already pocketed the championship. Pasquel was quick to fill the void, but rather than inherit the Águilas' baggage, he started up his own franchise.

As might be expected, it wasn't quite that simple. Politics made an appearance, a fracture ensued, and suddenly Mexico had *two* baseball leagues for 1940. That magnified the demand for talent, which resulted in sixty-three African Americans playing ball that year before the Sunday bullfights. Pasquel's customs operation had an office in Nuevo Laredo and its company cars were kept busy scooting over the border with Negro Leaguers in the trunk, smuggled like contraband.

The best of them, not surprisingly, were carried to Veracruz, although that was not so simple, either. The roster rules were fresh and fluid (with the foreigner quota raised to seven), teams came and went, and players did the same. Cool Papa played in some games for Torreón, in the state of Coahuila, in addition to Veracruz, but it's hard to say when or how many. For that matter, playing for the Blues didn't actually mean playing in Veracruz (where Cortés landed from Spain in 1519). Early in the season, the Veracruz newspaper determined that it would recognize Águila—which was still kicking, in spite of the ownership problem—as the hometown franchise, so Pasquel, leaving Veracruz in his team's name, shifted the Blues to Mexico City, which meant that the players no longer had to sleep under the mosquito nets required in the old harbor settlement. Pasquel even bought Delta Park, the stadium out of which the club operated after the move.

The Blues might just as well have hung out their shingle in Cooperstown, given the eventual Hall of Famers they collected. There

were an astonishing six at various times: Bell, his old buddy Willie
Wells, Dihigo, Leon Day, Ray Dandridge (the stocky third baseman, a
bullfight fan, struck a matador pose after making signature defensive
plays), and, for the final month of the season, Josh Gibson.

Dihigo was charged with managing the team, Wells took over
when Pasquel was dissatisfied, and Pasquel himself took over when
he was *still* dissatisfied. Gibson made him look smart with a mon-
strous month that put the Blues over the top for good, finishing with
a presumably suitable record of 61-30. Mexico's greatest team, as it's
been called, also received winning contributions from Double Duty
Radcliffe and pitchers Roy Partlow (another late addition), Cuban
luminary Ramón "El Profesor" Bragaña, and Schoolboy Johnny Taylor,
who was gifted a new suit by Pasquel every time he threw a shutout,
ending up with one for each day of the week and a spare in case tomato
sauce dripped onto his lapel.

It was Cool Papa, though, who put up the shiniest numbers of
1940. At thirty-eight, the wandering blackballer became the first
Mexican League player to win the Triple Crown, leading the circuit in
batting average (.437), home runs (12), and RBIs (79), as well as triples
(15) and runs scored (119). Taking advantage of fenceless ballparks,
eight of his homers had to be legged out, like mega-triples—quadruples,
if you will. Two of those occurred in one game, earning him a shower
of pesos.

Bell, of course, would have made good use of a few nice suits or
whatever flourish Pasquel might have spontaneously presented from
his pocket or person—watch, tiepin, you name it—as he was wont to do,
but there's no further record of financial gain from the center fielder's
historic season. For what it's worth, however, there was a Cool Papa
postcard in circulation that year describing him as "the Great Batter
of the Mexican League."

BELL'S LAST SEASON in Mexico was anticlimactic. He spent it
in Monterrey, swatting another dozen homers, with Sam Bankhead
and Quincy Trouppe as teammates. Afterwards, Trouppe rounded

JAMES
BELL
DEL EQUIPO
UNION-LAGNNA
Y GRAN BATEADOR DE LA LIGA
MEXICANA

If he wished to drop a line to his brothers from Mexico,
Cool Papa could put it on his own postcard.

up an auspicious contingent that included Cool, Bankhead, Gibson
(draining Mexican beer bottles along the way, Josh clobbered thirty-
three homers that year for Veracruz and one more in Puerto Rico that
knocked a fan out of a tree), Wells, Dandridge, Leroy Matlock, and
Schoolboy Johnny Taylor for a tour of the United States. Sanctions
precluded any games against Negro League teams, but the alternatives
succumbed in ten matches out of ten.

Bell and Clara Belle were home in St. Louis, living now on the
4200 block of West Belle Place, when the Japanese bombed Pearl
Harbor. He was too old for the draft, but many of his baseball friends
were not. Some of them remained in Mexico.

The avoidance of military duty, however, was not the only rationale for that decision. It was common for Negro Leaguers—especially
those reared in the Southern states—to cherish the unfettered citizen-
ship that Mexico offered them. Its perks were famously articulated by

Wells, the Devil himself (fondly regarded across the Spanish-speaking nation as El Diablo, which is inscribed on his Texas tombstone), who observed to Wendell Smith of the *Pittsburgh Courier* that "we live in the best hotels, eat in the best restaurants, and can go anyplace we care to. We don't enjoy such privileges in the United States. Players on teams in the Mexican League live just like big leaguers. We have everything first-class, plus the fact that the people here are much more considerate than the American baseball fan."

El Diablo was hardly the only blackballer to rhapsodize about Mexican living. It was a proposition rife with self-respect, bolstered not only by a reasonable salary, comparative comforts, and Pasquel's egalitarianism but also by local folks who didn't give a hoot about the pigmentation of a lady an African American talked to. The welcome went a step or two beyond tolerance. Mexican fans wouldn't permit even average players to walk to the ballpark (drivers would wait in front of the hotel to provide free rides) or pay for enchiladas.

Monte Irvin, the future Hall of Famer, played only one season in Mexico before he was called away to World War II, but that season made a profound impression. "It was the first time in my life that I felt free," he said.

"You know how it is when the sun comes up after night?" remarked Max Manning, an extremely nearsighted pitcher from Georgia known as Dr. Cyclops. "That's pretty much what it was like."

"Mexico," stated Schoolboy Johnny Taylor to John Holway, "was the savior of black baseball."

More than 150 African Americans, including fourteen Hall of Famers, would find work and dignity in the Mexican League. Pasquel went to great lengths to make that happen. In 1942, after Cum Posey offered Josh Gibson $6,000 to play for the Homestead Grays, Pasquel outbid him with $6,400 plus lodging and living expenses. In 1943, when Trouppe and Theolic Smith reported to their draft board and were assigned to work in a defense plant, Pasquel struck a remarkable deal with the U.S. government: If Trouppe and Smith were allowed to play ball in Mexico City, he would make *eighty thousand* Mexicans available to wartime factories in the States.

Pasquel was nearly as resourceful, though less effective, in enticing white Americans to Mexico. In 1944 he brought Rogers Hornsby down to manage Veracruz. In 1945 he met Danny Gardella, an outfielder with the New York Giants and off-season trainer at a health club that Pasquel frequented when he was in New York. (Such was his clout that, on one of those visits, Pasquel prevailed upon Saks Fifth Avenue to open the store on a Sunday so that his lady friend, Mexican movie star María Félix, could do a little shopping.) Gardella's recruitment signaled the start of Pasquel's concerted raid on the major leagues. In 1946—the first full season after V-J Day and the centennial anniversary of the start of the Mexican-American War—the ranks of the Mexican League included, among other major leaguers, Gardella, pitchers Sal Maglie and Max Lanier, and catcher Mickey Owen. On the Blues, white players answered to a black manager, Ramón Bragaña.

His ambitions unchecked and his wealth seemingly unlimited, Pasquel was eager to capitalize on the uncertainties involved with players returning from the battlefronts. He zeroed in on the biggest names in the game—Ted Williams, Stan Musial, Joe DiMaggio, Bob Feller, Phil Rizzuto, and Enos Slaughter among them—and tendered aggressive offers not likely to be matched, in some cases blank contracts. Victory in that theater, which was not forthcoming, would have recast not only the geography of big-time baseball but its complexion.

As it happened, though, the race question was at last being addressed at the major-league level. Commissioner Landis had died, replaced by a junior senator from Kentucky named A. B. "Happy" Chandler, and late in 1945 the Brooklyn Dodgers did the deed, snapping the color line with the signing of former UCLA football star Jackie Robinson. To ease him into the system, the Dodgers assigned the intrepid African American to their minor-league affiliate in Montreal for the 1946 season.

Robinson's contract was both a momentous milestone and a cruel irony. During the war, when depleted major-league teams were so desperate for players that they took on a fifteen-year-old pitcher and a one-armed outfielder, no genuine interest was shown in the richly seasoned services of Josh Gibson, Satchel Paige, Willie Wells,

Leroy Matlock, Chet Brewer, Buck Leonard, Ray Dandridge, Wild Bill Wright, or Cool Papa Bell. Now, with the stroke of a pen, the landscape had shifted.

Understanding the jeopardy in which his dream had been put, Pasquel made Robinson a lucrative pitch. The rugged Californian let it go by.

Fatefully, Robinson was promoted to Brooklyn in 1947, whereupon talented young black players would no longer set their sights on either the Negro Leagues or Mexico.

CHAPTER NINETEEN

FISHING ON THE FOURTH OF JULY

I F WRITTEN OR ORAL HISTORIES DON'T TELL US much about the state of Cool Papa Bell in 1942, Candy Jim Taylor does. By that time Cool's old manager in St. Louis was holding down the same job for the Chicago American Giants, and when the Giants made their way north to start the '42 season, Candy Jim had the aging speedster, finally back in the Negro Leagues after his four years in Mexico, playing first base.

In baseball custom, first base is the place for players whose bat is an asset to the lineup but whose mobility and dexterity are not up to the challenge of spatially rigorous defensive positions, such as center field. Bell was forty, and his knees were failing him.

His eyes weren't so nimble, either, but through the benefits of his switch-hitting, his improvisational skills, and his indispensable glasses, he still managed to make himself useful in the batter's box. In that respect, signing with Chicago was invigorating. It took Cool Papa twenty years back—exactly half his life ago—to his first career-changing brush with the American Giants' revolutionary manager,

Rube Foster, and their speeding, bunting outfielder, Jimmie Lyons; to his unforgettable introduction to the artful, strategic, captivating wonders of tricky ball. He'd always wanted to be the exemplar of that brand of baseball. To be an American Giant.

The first time he saw a Rube Foster team, it became Bell's dream to play for the Chicago American Giants. He would be forty years old when it happened.

The 1942 edition was not a vintage Chicago team. It featured few players in their primes, and the best thing Candy Jim could say about it was "Never before in the history of the Giants have older men and younger ones worked together with such perfect harmony." That was, in great part, a nod to the ripened Mississippian whom he'd long ago instructed in the nuances of switch-hitting. It should be noted, however, that perfect harmony, while generally beating the alternative, does not always beat the baseball team in the opposite dugout, which the American Giants demonstrated at a convincing rate.

Bell's knees were not to blame, however. Over the years he'd learned how to nurse and coax them through a season. His home remedies, in fact, had become so familiar that he served his various teams as the de facto trainer, administering salves and moral support as needed. His products were recommended by his resilience. To wit, when Chicago's official season began at Comiskey Park in early May, Cool Papa was somehow back in center field, flanked by his old pal Jimmie Crutchfield and Art Pennington, an athletic but less experienced player from Memphis.

"That Cool Papa Bell," recalled Pennington, speaking to Brent Kelley in *Voices from the Negro Leagues*, "I thought I could outrun him. I was young [Bell's junior by twenty-one years], and Taylor would have us get out and run the hundred-yard dash. We would run, but all at once Cool Papa would walk on by me. And I thought I could fly in those days."

At that stage of his career—though only two years removed from his Triple Crown for the Veracruz Blues—Bell found it difficult to maintain his top speed on a daily basis. He required recovery time. But if he paced himself and picked his spots, his could trick his legs into thinking they were still in their mid-twenties.

"He was the sensation of great spectacular running catches in their opening game at Chicago," reported the *Atlanta Daily World*, taking the opportunity to add, incidentally, that Bell was one of the best bunters in the Negro Leagues.

True to the spirit of tricky ball and his mandate as a leadoff man—and long before the rise of on-base percentage and protracted at-bats as indicators of hitting worth—Cool Papa was a leading practitioner in the unrelenting pursuit of first base. It was a matter of resourcefulness. While his quickness obviously abetted his bunting, Bell, moreover, paid homage to the art of placing the ball in an indefensible spot. Crediting such predecessors as Lyons and Bingo DeMoss, he perfected both the drag bunt, in which he kissed the ball toward one of the baselines as he initiated his sprint to first, and the push bunt, a generally right-handed device by which he shoved the ball between the helpless pitcher and first baseman. To discourage corner infielders from invading his bunting space, he also refined the skill of chopping and slashing balls in their general direction. Line drives were welcome to the game's fastest player—especially those that found an alley and *rolled*—but largely collateral. Hilton Smith, a Hall of Fame pitcher, remembered seeing Bell generate four hits one day without sending a ball to the outfield.

It was all a practiced, purposeful exercise in what a modern analyst might call avoiding outs. That meant adjusting his swing, managing the count, protecting the plate, even fouling off the baseball—he claimed he would often slap fifteen or twenty strikes into foul territory—in the hope of precipitating a fat pitch or an errant one. As

By spreading his hands and choking up on the bat, Cool Papa was able to control it, send the ball in a chosen direction, and take full advantage of his speed.

Bell described in an interview recorded by the Society for American Baseball Research, "If I got two balls on me, I move up to the front of the plate and everything they throw I just foul it off until I got a walk. When we were behind, they'd tell me, 'We want you on base.' I said, 'That's all I wanted to know.' With two balls on me, I take care of everything."

The various estimates have him batting as high as .373 in 1942, without a noticeable drop in defense. In July, Cool Papa saved one of Chicago's rare victories, a 2–1 affair against the Homestead/Washington Grays, by robbing Chester Williams of a ninth-inning home run. "In all probability," gushed the *Chicago Defender*, "there will never be another baseball game better." But there was another still to play that day, and the old man had plenty left for it: "Bell was the star of the second game by hitting three singles out of three times at bat, driving in four of the Giants' eight runs."

Cool Papa's singles, of course—his walks as well—paved the way for the essence of his game. Stealing bases was the most conspicuous component of his legwork but hardly the extent of it. "Then," he said, on the subject of singles and walks, "if I start running and the man behind me bunts the ball, I go all the way to third base."

PURPOSEFULLY OR NOT, Bell's return to the States coincided with the nation's entrance into the war and the latest round of baseball's integration rumors, which were not unrelated. Duty-bound Red Sox and Dodgers et al. left craters on major-league rosters, and it stood to reason that those holes could be neatly filled by Negro Leaguers who hadn't volunteered for military service or been selected in the draft lottery.

On that subject, of course, reason was not a strong suit for big-league baseball executives. At the same time, however, the black population's employment rate was sharply boosted by the labor requirements of wartime industry, which, putting dollars in pockets, led to an uptick in Negro League attendance. Suddenly it was good—*comparatively* good, at any rate—to be a black ballplayer in America.

Even so, that consolation was not enough to silence the resistance to baseball's institutionalized segregation. The *Daily Worker*, a Communist Party publication, was a chief agitator for the obliteration of the color line. It quoted Leo Durocher, the Dodgers' manager, saying, "I'll play colored boys on my team if the big shots give the OK. Hell, I've seen a million good ones." For his efforts, Durocher received a dressing-down from Commissioner Landis.

The episode also spawned a flurry of interviews between black newspapers and other major-league figures. "I am sure," declared Gabby Hartnett, manager of the Chicago Cubs, to Wendell Smith of the *Pittsburgh Courier*, "that if we were given permission to use [black players], there would be a mad scramble between managers to sign them."

Bill Benswanger, owner of the Pittsburgh Pirates, said to the *Courier*, "I know there are many problems connected with the question, but after all, somebody has to make the first move."

One of those many problems was the unwillingness of some major leaguers to accept Negro Leaguers as teammates. At the East-West All-Star Game—where Cool Papa, returning to familiar ground (doubly so, since Comiskey Park was now his home field) after five years abroad, went one for two—a solution to that prickly complication was suggested by Satchel Paige. The theatrical pitcher climbed up to the press box, took over the public address system, and declared that if white players refused to share their dugouts and locker rooms with blacks, he had no problem with placing an all-Negro team in one of the leagues.

There was, in fact—if you believe the story—a fellow prepared to make the all-important first move on roughly that basis. In his 1962 autobiography, *Veeck—As in Wreck*, Bill Veeck narrated a scenario in which he'd intended to purchase the downtrodden Philadelphia Phillies and fill the roster predominantly, if not entirely, with African Americans, competing in the National League in 1943 (although he mistakenly wrote 1944).

At the time, Veeck was still a year away from joining the Marines for a hitch that led him to a remote Pacific Island where he would lose his right leg, to be replaced by a wooden one into which he cut a hole for an ashtray. A former popcorn vendor for the Chicago Cubs and future maverick owner of the Cleveland Indians, St. Louis Browns, and Chicago White Sox, the baseball-loving son of a sportswriter was then the maverick owner of the minor-league Milwaukee Brewers, on the prowl for a bigger stage and, as always, an edgy concept. Perhaps Veeck's idea sprang from Paige's remarks at the East-West Game, where major-league scouts were on the scene. Perhaps it sprang from the general knowledge that the failing Phillies were for sale and crying out for drastic reconfiguration. Or perhaps it sprang from his fertile imagination as Veeck worked on his memoir twenty years later, which was the likeliest conclusion to be drawn from a 1998 report in *The National Pastime* that impugned the whole episode, citing the absence of contemporaneous and third-person corroboration.

That study has since been mitigated by subsequent findings (including those referenced in a SABR *Baseball Research Journal* article by author/professor Jules Tygiel), the upshot being that while Veeck's style involved a fair amount of carnival barking and his account is certainly sketchy on the particulars of late 1942 and early 1943, it was not fabricated to peddle a book. Cool Papa believed it to be true, in some fashion—most significantly, the one that would have had him playing the Cardinals and Pirates four years before Jackie Robinson did.

"Let me make it plain that my Philadelphia adventure was no idle dream," wrote the puckish, shirtsleeved executive. With that, Veeck began his tale, asserting that he made an offer to Phillies owner Gerry Nugent and Nugent "expressed a willingness to accept it. As far as I knew, I was the only bidder."

In the controversial passage, Veeck made no mention of revealing his revolutionary plans to Nugent. He noted, however, that Negro League players would be rounded up by Harlem Globetrotters honcho Abe Saperstein (who was also involved with blackball) and sportswriter Doc Young (he meant Fay Young, a different fellow) of the *Chicago Defender*. As for the matter of baseball's unyielding aversion to black players, he'd reasoned that a continuance of their exclusion would be unthinkable at a time when African Americans were fighting and dying for democracy in the epic struggle against history's most infamous bigot.

Out of respect, Veeck claimed, he took his designs to Landis, a decision he regarded as his "one bad mistake . . . The next thing I knew, I was informed that Nugent, being in bankruptcy, had turned the team back to the league and that I would therefore have to deal with the National League president, Ford Frick. Frick promptly informed me that the club had already been sold to William Cox, a lumber dealer . . . for about half what I had been willing to pay."

While Veeck's scheme was not reported in real time, it was periodically alluded to in the forties and fifties. In 1954, Saperstein disclosed to the *Philadelphia Independent* that the players he and Fay Young recruited would have trained secretly in the spring of 1943 while the incumbent Phillies went through their customary paces in Florida. The same old Phils would then be dismissed on opening day, with the former Negro Leaguers taking the field in their stead.

Some of the names involved were shared by Veeck in a 1978 interview with the *Black Diamonds* audio series. "I planned to sign a considerable number of black ballplayers," he said. "There was Josh Gibson, there was Satchel Paige, there was Luke Easter [which seems unlikely, since Easter was in the Army at the time and his Negro League career wouldn't begin until 1947], a fellow by the name of Artie Wilson, Roy Campanella, and Cool Papa Bell, who was at the end of the road." Other sources included Buck Leonard, Monte Irvin, and Theolic Smith among the would-be Phillies.

"So I got on the train [after meeting with Landis] figuring I had not only a major-league ballclub but I was almost a virtual cinch to win the pennant the next year. Because this was really the only untapped reservoir of playing talent. And you had one thing going for you, that you could justify this on the grounds of the shortage of manpower. I figured I could stretch that a considerable distance to quell some of these screams I knew would occur."

Bell provided another detail during an interview in 1974 with the Center for Oral History and Cultural Heritage at the University of Southern Mississippi. The Phillies' manager, he said, would have been Winfield Welch, the skipper of the Birmingham Black Barons and an associate of Saperstein with the Globetrotters.

The grandiose plan was not only authentic to Cool Papa but so heartening—and ultimately so heart*breaking*—that over the years he retained a special regard for Veeck and Saperstein. "In my mind, I believe they were fair men," he said, and consequently a far cry from the baseball bosses who once more took their cue from Jim Crow.

"I was told," confided Bell, "that they said, no, we can't put a black team in there, because the Fourth of July, they'd be the ones telling you they're going fishing.

"They thought the black man was going to get in there and be fighting and do all this rough stuff, you know. They just thought it was that way."

CHAPTER TWENTY

SLUGGER IN A STRAITJACKET

F OR A SHORT WHILE, IN THE SPRING OF 1943, Cool Papa considered himself traded. As the season lurched ahead, there would be a ruckus over the validity of that transaction, but as he pulled out of St. Louis heading south toward Memphis, rather than north to Chicago, Bell presumed he'd be playing ball that year for a Tennessee outfit owned by three Martin brothers, two of whom were dentists.

The swap was Cool Papa for an outfielder, Ducky Davenport, and the popular pitcher-catcher Double Duty Radcliffe, who would also manage the American Giants. Cool was led to believe he would be reimbursed for his travel expenses—presumably train fare—but when he arrived in Memphis, he was told no, that wasn't the policy. Also, the remuneration for ballplaying would involve dental work. As he explained to John Holway, "I didn't have a toothache and I wasn't about to pay a man to fix what didn't need fixing." One of the Martins also owned a funeral home, and while Bell was getting along in years, he was not in the market for those services, either. "So I just turned around and went home."

It was just as well, because the Negro American League, in which Memphis and Chicago participated, was quite at odds with the Negro National League, the more eastern association whose membership was dominated by the Homestead/Washington Grays. At the heart of the squabbling was the National's contention that Chicago had illegally signed Cool Papa the *previous* season. Prior to that point Bell's last Negro League affiliation had been with the Pittsburgh Crawfords of the NNL, whom he'd left five years earlier without being officially waived. Consequently—in the considered opinion of the Negro National League—his contract with the American Giants had violated an agreement that no player could move between the NNL and NAL without first clearing waivers. By that convoluted interpretation, Cool Papa was ineligible to play for either Chicago or Memphis.

The complaint was aggressively pushed by Grays executive Cumberland Posey, who still ran the team—although, to keep it afloat during the Depression, he had ceded principal ownership to racketeer and socialite Sonnyman Jackson, proprietor of the popular Sky Rocket Café. By subjugating his pride in such a way, Posey had outlasted Gus Greenlee in their bareknuckle battle for the Pittsburgh market. In turn, his distinguished tenure had earned him substantial influence in league affairs, and heading his agenda for 1943 was enforcement of the waiver rule. That meant relocating relevant players from the Negro American League to his Negro National . . . starting with Cool Papa Bell.

The Grays signed Bell shortly after the great center fielder had exercised his freedom of dentistry. Even after six consecutive league championships, the addition of Cool Papa put a bounce in Homestead's step as Posey's ball club—now managed by Candy Jim Taylor, accompanying Bell in his circuitous move from Chicago—took its spring training at home in Pittsburgh, due to wartime travel restrictions. (The same restrictions forbade Negro League clubs from traveling during the season by private buses, all of which had been appropriated by the Office of Defense Transportation. The consequences were severe for NAL teams, whose league opponents, situated in the Midwest and South, were too distant to reach affordably by train. The NNL, on the other hand, was conveniently clustered on the East Coast, from New York to Washington.)

Bell's assets on the field were a luxury for a franchise that already dominated its league, and his popularity would be a boon at the turnstile as well. All things considered, the acquisition was sufficiently newsworthy to attract the attention of even the mainstream *Pittsburgh Press*:

> The morale of the Homestead Grays baseball squad conditioning indoors at the Homestead Junior High School gymnasium was enhanced yesterday with the arrival of "Cool Papa" Bell, along with holdover Jud ["Boojum"] Wilson, both of whom were signed.
>
> Owner Cum Posey maintains that with Bell in the fold, the Grays can point with justifiable pride to having the fastest outfield in the Negro National circuit. Bell will be in the outer pasture along with Sammy Bankhead and Jerry Benjamin.
>
> Cool Papa is one of the Negro baseball's most dangerous batsmen, being a switch hitter. He also rates among the fleetest base runners, his stolen base record being almost double that of any other baserunner in the Negro National loop.

The deal, however, did not go unchallenged by the Negro American League. At a joint league meeting in early June, it was ostensibly nullified by a ruling that ten players who had moved from NAL teams to NNL teams would have to be returned to the former. Defiant, the Grays refused to send Cool Papa back—Posey was described in the *Chicago Defender* as being "on the warpath"—and a month later they reached a settlement with the NAL. Bell would remain with Homestead.

Although their roots were in that steelmaking borough on the Monongahela River, the Grays now divided their home games between Forbes Field in Pittsburgh, where the Pirates played, and Griffith Stadium in Washington, D.C., where the neighborhood (at the edge of historically black Howard University) was largely African American, the seating was segregated, and Posey's perennial champs regularly outdrew the Washington Senators. Their dynasty itself was an attraction, and the Grays provided star power as well: the assault on the Negro National League had been famously driven by the so-called Ruth and Gehrig of Negro baseball, Josh Gibson and first baseman Buck Leonard.

Bell's meandering journey to Homestead had brought about an agreeable reunion with Gibson, who'd returned to the Grays in 1942 after his pair of bottoms-up seasons in Mexico. At thirty-one, the powerhouse catcher was at the apex of his acclaim in 1943, even profiled in *Time* magazine. Despite the vast reaches of both home ballparks—Forbes's center field, dubbed Death Valley, stretched an extraordinary 462 feet from home plate, and the daunting configuration of Griffith made it impossible to clear a fence that wasn't more than 400 feet away or 30 feet high—Gibson easily led the league in home runs again, many of them rhapsodized in the press for their magnificence. A multidimensional hitter, he also set a league record for doubles and batted far upwards of .400. It was all a wonder, because the withering of his burly body was well under way.

Josh Gibson didn't have to cover much of cavernous Forbes Field,
but he had no trouble hitting the ball out of it.

On New Year's Day, after a long night of overindulgence at the Crawford Grill, Gibson had gone home to Hattie, his common-law wife—there were reports that they had been married on the road the season before, after nearly a decade together—and lost consciousness. He spent ten days at a Pittsburgh hospital, some of them in a strait-jacket. The episode was variously ascribed to exhaustion, a seizure, a nervous breakdown, and a brain tumor.

He returned to the hospital throughout the 1943 season, and every time, immediately upon his release, the Negro Leagues' greatest batsman would reassume his place in the Homestead lineup. As he settled in at the plate, eyes fixed forward, hands held low, big bat pointing to the sky, there was less bulge in the biceps under his rolled-up left sleeve. Unable to crouch, he caught practically standing up. He mumbled to himself and occasionally to visions of Babe Ruth or Joe DiMaggio.

Some blamed his deterioration on the epic drinking that Gibson and Sam Bankhead had perpetrated in Mexico. Some blamed his new female companion, Grace Fournier, who, while her husband was soldiering overseas, was suspected of introducing Josh to narcotics. Some blamed heredity, his mother having been an alcoholic. Some blamed the devastating loss of Gibson's teenaged first wife, who died giving birth to twins he dearly wished he could be more involved with. And some blamed the failure of Bill Veeck's desegregation gambit, the infertile flirtations by Bill Benswanger of the Pirates and Clark Griffith of the Senators (who had become close to Josh through the games the Grays played at Griffith Stadium), and Gibson's ultimate realization that, in the baseball hierarchy and national consciousness, he would never stand with Ruth and DiMaggio.

Whatever the nature and number of his debilitating troubles, when Josh made it to the ballpark, even wasted or hungover, he still brought the prodigious power that set him apart. That season he cranked ten home runs into the faraway Griffith Stadium bleachers, eight more than the Senators and the rest of the American League combined. One of those, a 440-foot swat, was described by the *Baltimore Afro-American* as "a rare treat." At Forbes Field, where the

Grays played fewer games, a writer for the daily *Pittsburgh Post-Gazette* was awed by the strongman's "bullet-like shot over the left-field scoreboard."

Gibson's maladies, unfortunately, were not the type that Cool Papa could soothe with a concocted salve. Bell, meanwhile, ten years older than his ravaged teammate, had his own ailments to play through, which received no sympathy from the seemingly boundless square footage he had to negotiate at Forbes and Griffith. (As if the amount of pastureland itself wasn't challenging enough, both outfields presented architectural peculiarities. Forbes featured a batting cage in center field, presumably too distant for a fly ball to encounter. And Griffith's deepest fence pinched inward a bit where, on the street beyond, the Senators had been unable to acquire five houses and a sizable tree.)

It fell upon Buck Leonard, Cool's roommate with the Grays and eventually his fellow Hall of Famer, to dispense collegial health care for the teammate who did it for all the rest. Leonard wasn't sure if it was arthritis or neuritis or too much sliding or too much ballpark that Bell suffered from, but he knew for certain that the ancient outfielder was in a bad way on the day after a hard game and a *really* bad way after two of them. On such occasions, Bell "could barely get out of bed the next morning," the sturdy first baseman told John Holway. One particular morning, after a lively doubleheader in Cleveland the day before, Cool Papa was immobilized by the pain and stiffness until Leonard ran hot water in the bathtub, carried his slender friend to it, and gently lowered him in. "He had to get good and warm before he could move."

As a mitigator if not a remedy, "he started drinking gin and lemon," Leonard said. "He'd put the peel and everything in there, cut it up, add about two teaspoons of sugar, shake it, and have about three swallows every night before he went to bed. In the morning, three more swallows.

"Cool Papa was in better shape if he just played occasionally, but he could still fly, he could still run those bases like no one else and catch balls all over the outfield. He would get all tuckered out after a doubleheader, but he would recover fast and fly some more. The best baserunner I ever saw was Cool Papa Bell. He knew how to slide so well, he could find his way around any throw that was slightly off. Had a beautiful 'swan slide,' he called it."

The presence of Gibson and Leonard in the middle of the Homestead lineup was a blessing for Bell, and so was the company of Jerry Benjamin at the top. A switch-hitting outfielder from Alabama who resembled Cool in size and speed, Benjamin was able to give Papa some welcome relief in center field, often nudging him over to left. The benefits were mutual, as Benjamin bounced back vigorously from a couple of subpar seasons.

Both players were practitioners of tricky ball, and their symbiotic styles played to stunning effect. Bell and Benjamin piled up the hits that year—Cool had six in a game against the Newark Eagles—and

Switching to left or right field was no problem for Cool Papa when he played for the Homestead Grays, because he'd been catching fly balls in both places for two decades.

the league was crushed by the run production that followed. It was demoralizing excess.

"In our league," said Philadelphia Stars catcher Bill "Ready" Cash, as quoted in *Shades of Glory*, by Lawrence D. Hogan, "all we needed was one run. Lots of times I tell people when we played the Homestead Grays and Cool Papa gets on second base and Jerry Benjamin comes up and lays a bunt down the third-base line that's all you need 'cause Cool gonna dust off at home plate. That ain't no lie."

"He set us catchers crazy," added James Dudley of the Baltimore Elite Giants, speaking to Brent Kelley for *The Negro Leagues Revisited*. Cool Papa would say, " 'You ain't got no trouble today. Those bones have got the old man,' and you squat down there and stay down and give the signal and when you look he's standing on first base. No play, the old man's safe. And he'd do the same thing when he got on third base. You better keep your eyes open 'cause he'd run right over top of you."

One bone-aching, swan-sliding, catcher-slamming, tricky kind of run may have been all the Grays *needed* on a given day—Johnny Wright and Ray Brown were a pair of ace pitchers—but it was seldom all they got. Not with Gibson, Leonard, and significant others yet to come after Bell and Benjamin. The result was a runaway title in the NNL, the Grays' seventh straight pennant, and a preposterous overall record of 78-23 (or 95-25; take your pick).

An imposing contingent of eight represented the Grays at the East-West game: Bell, Gibson, Leonard, Benjamin, Wright, Sammy Bankhead, third baseman Howard Easterling, and veteran Vic Harris, who served as manager. Bell, wearing uniform number 1, was the first batter of the game and remained in it for the duration, manning left field.

More than fifty-one thousand fans, a record crowd for the late-summer classic—less than three weeks earlier the major-league counterpart had drawn thirty-two thousand to Shibe Park in Philadelphia—brought high fashion and ready rolls of cash to Comiskey Park. The game itself, however, was more understated. Like most of the East players, Cool Papa went hitless—Satchel Paige pitched the first three innings for the other side, allowing only a walk to Gibson—but was deprived of at least a single when right fielder Ducky Davenport, who'd been on the other end of the preseason trade that Bell had walked away from, made an acrobatic catch of his line drive in the ninth inning. Had the ball fallen safely, Leonard's two-out home run would have tied a contest that the West held on to win 2–1.

A month later Cool was again conspiring with stars, joining a team of Negro Leaguers from St. Louis for an exhibition against an outfit put together by Honus Wagner and headlined by Dizzy Dean, whose best days were now far behind. The outcome of the game was not a matter of record, but we know that Bell was clocked circling the bases in fifteen seconds, roughly two seconds behind his best reported time (although he claimed to have once completed the circuit in twelve seconds flat) and perhaps the clearest sign yet that he was seriously slowing down.

THE NEGRO WORLD Series commenced in late September. It had been played off and on in recent years and was loosely structured this time around, with the Grays and Birmingham Black Barons meeting eight times in a best-of-seven format (there was a tie involved) covering seven cities.

Opening at Griffith Stadium, where Bell tripled but Birmingham won, the series then slid over to Baltimore, where it ran afoul of the midnight curfew after twelve inconclusive innings. So it was back to Washington the following day for a makeup game. Clark Griffith, the Senators' owner, shuffled their schedule to make it work. Such was the importance of Homestead crowds to the Washington club's revenue.

For reasons we can only suspect, Josh Gibson didn't start that day. But Cool Papa did, in spite of the arthritis and chilly air, doubling in a couple of runs early, making a sterling catch to enable extra innings, and coming to bat with the bases loaded in the bottom of the eleventh. His crisp single to right field knotted the series at a game apiece.

Game four, at Comiskey Park, was an easier proposition for the Grays, a 9–0 whitewashing behind Johnny "Needle Nose" Wright. Bell contributed three hits, and in the bottom of the third inning, when the game was still close, he supported Wright with a play that Fay Young described in the *Chicago Defender*:

> [Felix] McLaurin waded into one which looked like a double and perhaps a triple. Over raced "Cool Papa" Bell, who took the ball while running at top speed, turned and threw to second to double up Radcliffe who couldn't get even halfway back from third. Bell's throw wasn't so accurate as it went to Easterling on the first base side of the bag and Bankhead moved over to take Easterling's toss for the out.

Gibson was back in business for game five, played in Columbus, Ohio, and true to form the ailing star came through with a grand slam. His heroics, however, went for naught, as Homestead came up a run short.

Johnny Wright's, on the other hand, were put to good advantage in Indianapolis. The polished right-hander, who led the NNL in wins that season, notched his second straight shutout in an 8–0 romp. A New Orleans native, Wright would spend the following year and most of the next in the Navy. But he had made an impression, and in 1946 he joined Jackie Robinson in the Brooklyn Dodgers' spring training camp, although he would never reach the big leagues.

In Birmingham, W. C. Handy, the blues and ragtime virtuoso, delivered a speech in advance of game seven and the Grays responded with banjo hitting, blanked 1–0 by Johnny Markham in eleven innings. With that, the arduous series was even at three wins apiece, the title to be resolved with a final match in Montgomery.

But not until the eighth inning. Homestead trailed 4–2 before rallying for four runs in the eighth and two more in the ninth, certifying its rank as the preeminent team in blackball. Gibson, surmounting whatever still weakened him, bore the brunt of the hitting burden, mustering two singles and a double.

Great as they were, though, the Grays may not have been the best team Cool Papa played for in 1943. At Hollywood Baseball Park, new home of the California Winter League, he lined up with Leonard,

Bankhead, Easterling, Double Duty Radcliffe, and a pitching staff featuring Markham, submariner Porter Moss, and living legend Satchel Paige. Gibson was also expected but instead stayed back in Pittsburgh, in the grip of Grace Fournier, whom he entertained in a two-story house he evidently bought for that purpose. Not to worry: His absence was offset, and then some, by Paige, whose "aging but highly valuable bones" bedazzled the *Los Angeles Times*. The paper submitted that Satchel mixed his irresistible slowballs with "fast ones that literally smoked."

The Elite Giants' principal opponent, Joe Pirrone's All-Stars, that year sported such major leaguers as Peanuts Lowrey, Andy Pafko, and Lou Novikoff of the Chicago Cubs, Roy Partee and Catfish Metkovich of the Boston Red Sox, Babe Dahlgren of the Pittsburgh Pirates, and veteran pitcher Bobo Newsom, a twenty-game winner on three occasions. A South Carolinian who would make the American League all-star team the following season for the Philadelphia A's, Newsom had played in the CWL only once before, ten years earlier, and it hadn't gone well for him. After the Elite Giants had pummeled him for the fourth or fifth time, he'd finally confronted his tormenters and declared, "I'm not going back to the major leagues until I can beat you niggers!" As might be imagined, Newsom's remark was a topic of conversation when the Negro Leaguers reached the locker room, where Willie Wells expressed his displeasure and Cool Papa suggested, "Well, let's keep him out here about two more years."

While he took his medicine more graciously this time around, Newsom found the going no easier, particularly when his counterpart was Paige. But he was not lacking for company. In the majority of matchups, the white All-Stars had the worst of the rivalry.

It was all quite informal and rather friendly, however, until the resolute Commissioner Landis lowered the boom once again, ordering the major leaguers—there were nineteen of them altogether—to cease and desist. He declared them in violation of a policy prohibiting their participation in exhibition games more than ten days removed from the conclusion of the major-league season.

Meanwhile, in the European theater, the Allies were in the process of deciding on Normandy in northern France as the landing point for the D-Day invasion, half a year away. In the interim, Landis would double down on the Winter League ban, launching an investigation to reveal the scandal's magnitude.

As might be expected, the league fizzled out a little early that year. Cool and Clara Belle were standing outside their Los Angeles hotel, waiting for a taxi to the bus depot, when Paige approached, keys in hand, and asked if they'd like to drive his car back to St. Louis, then keep it. "It was a bright green Packard convertible that had belonged to some movie star. Bette Davis, I think," Bell recalled to author James Bankes. "Anyway, it cost a whole lot of money.

"Well, neither of us drove. We always used public transportation. So, I said no thanks. He just dropped the keys in the front seat and walked away. 'I'm sure somebody will appreciate it,' he said."

CHAPTER TWENTY-ONE

GROUND BALLS TO JACKIE'S BACKHAND

H AD COOL PAPA'S RECOLLECTION OF NEGRO
League events not been so relatively dependable—not
impeccable, mind you, but more verifiable than the garden
variety—his version of the 1944 batting race would be disregarded
here. The published numbers don't support it and there's a scarcity
of corroboration. But the man deserves to be heard.

Unquestionably, Bell came out swinging that year. A month into
the season, the fastest forty-two-year-old in baggy pants, unstiffened
by salves and steaming baths, had hit safely in every game, including
a four-for-four against Baltimore. The Grays had played at Yankee
Stadium and Ebbets Field in Brooklyn—where Branch Rickey, the
Dodgers' opportunistic general manager, might have taken a peek—and
Bell, well served by the exposure, had made headlines for leading the
league with an improbable .515 batting average.

In spite of another stint in the hospital for Josh Gibson, this one
prompted by what was described as disorderly conduct, the Grays
were setting the pace in the standings as well. When the season's first
half was wrapping up, Homestead thought it had clinched the title with

a doubleheader split against Newark; but the Eagles protested, claiming that the Grays' winning pitcher, Roy Partlow, was actually under contract with the Philadelphia Stars. The league upheld the complaint and ordered the game to be replayed, with the winner awarded a place in the postseason playoff. In the do-over, Homestead prevailed again, powered by two home runs from Buck Leonard.

Soon the Grays were forging ahead toward the *second*-half crown, benefiting from Gibson's return. They didn't blink when their manager, Vic Harris, was called off to a Defense Department job, replaced by the usual suspect, old reliable Candy Jim Taylor, who became Bell's boss for the fifth time (the second with Homestead).

The league season was interrupted in mid-August by Cool Papa's final East-West game. Leading off again for the East team, he went the distance, and hitless, in a Chicago swelter that registered 98 degrees. The heat, however, had no effect on Satchel Paige, who sat out the big event after the promoters denied his demand that a percentage of the gate be donated to the war effort.

A month later the Grays found themselves involved in yet another title protest. They lost an end-of-season doubleheader to the New York Cubans in Detroit, but only one of those games was counted as a league match. By that peculiar stroke, Homestead would hold on, narrowly edging out the Philadelphia Stars for the second-half Negro National championship. Not surprisingly, the Stars challenged the convenient outcome, claiming that both games had originally been scheduled as league affairs. This time, though, the protest was not upheld. And so, by virtue of the same team winning each of the season's halves, an NNL playoff was averted and the dynastic Grays, with their eighth straight league title in hand, advanced straight to the Negro World Series against the Birmingham Black Barons.

As if that was not sufficient confusion, there was also the matter of the regular-season batting title to be worked out. The various tabulations have steered clear of unanimity in regard to the champion—Bob Harvey? Sam Jethroe? Frank Austin? Shifty Jim West?—but none shows Bell in the immediate vicinity of the leader. His own memory placed the title in the lap of Austin, a diminutive infielder from Panama with the Philadelphia Stars. That recollection, in fact, was firsthand, because Austin's crown required Cool Papa's cooperation.

At the time, the collapse of the color line was looking increasingly inevitable; tantalizing, even. Public pressures were escalating. Black journalists such as Sam Lacy of the *Chicago Defender* and *Baltimore Afro-American* kept the heat on Commissioner Landis and big-league ball clubs. The great Paul Robeson—actor, singer, athlete, civil rights activist, and Communist Party member—addressed the major-league owners' annual meeting, although Landis instructed the owners not to engage the outspoken African American in discussion.

All the while, tryouts of Negro Leaguers, genuine or farcical, were taking place—or being called off—in Cleveland, Pittsburgh, Philadelphia, Boston, and Bear Mountain, New York, where the Dodgers trained. And the war was hacking away at the major leagues. The Cincinnati Reds had trotted out a locally raised, fifteen-year-old pitcher named Joe Nuxhall. The St. Louis Browns were about to employ outfielder Pete Gray, who did the best he could in the absence of a right arm.

Against that backdrop there was an operative theory that if desegregation were at last to happen, it would likely seek out young, trainable Negro Leaguers. Austin—they called him Pee Wee—was twenty-two and fundamentally sound.

"See," Cool Papa said, "we had to have a good record in our league in order for them to try us out. So, the way they did it, they had to do a lot of maneuvering. In order to get our young boys in that had a chance, we had to sit back from the old boys, move their records back, and move the young boys' records in front. We did that in our league just to maneuver."

When the numbers had been crunched and mangled, Austin—who would later spend some years in the minor leagues but never see the majors—was declared the batting champ with a .390 average, although subsequent research has not been as generous. Bell remembered his own figure as .407 initially, but, for the good of the cause, he granted permission for that percentage to be shaved—hits removed, totals tinkered with—until Pee Wee emerged at the top of the heap. After a look at the final tallies, the kindly quadragenarian's only objection was "Why'd you take off that many points?"

It's the bottom line, sure enough, that casts doubt on Cool Papa's account. His batting average for 1944 has been reported as low as .274 and as high as .373. On the other hand, his credibility squarely outranks Negro League bookkeeping's. Moreover, Bell's story is consistent with his character and was circumstantially supported by Satchel Paige.

"Cool Papa? The man had no selfishness or jealousy in him," the great pitcher testified. "He knew he was too old to do a job in the majors and he knew it was important for our boys to do a good job when they got the chance."

In any event, Bell didn't go home without a title that year. The Negro World Series began in Birmingham, just after four Black Barons were injured in an auto accident. The Grays won all three games played in the South—the last of those on a one-hit shutout by Ray Brown—dropped the only one held in Pittsburgh, and wrapped things up with a 4–2 triumph at Griffith Stadium in Washington.

The Homestead Grays' 1944 title was their eighth straight. Note the *W* on the sleeves, representing Washington, where they played roughly half of their home games. Left to right: Jelly Jackson, Ray Battle, Booker Robinson, Sam Bankhead, Josh Gibson, Buck Leonard, Dave Hoskins, Jerry Benjamin, and Cool Papa

It was Cool Papa's seventh championship (four in St. Louis, one with the Pittsburgh Crawfords, and two now with Homestead) in seventeen Negro League seasons. They seemed to track him around the league and even the continent, for that matter, counting the crowns in the Dominican Republic and Mexico.

Of course, not much was made of that when the decorated veteran arrived back home in St. Louis before catching a bus to California for one more Winter League season. The city was preoccupied not only with the national defense work going on at the ammunition plant, the aircraft factory, the chemical facility, and the powder company but also with the Browns—whose history began the year James Nichols was born in rural Mississippi—playing in their first and last World Series. And losing it. To the Cardinals.

The following month Judge Landis died.

BY 1945, BRANCH Rickey was making news. The Brooklyn mastermind knew that the passing of Landis—which was immediately followed by the commissioner's special election into the Hall of Fame—might crack open a door to the black ballplayers whose talents so intrigued him. Then, in January, the United States League was conceived in a meeting hosted by Gus Greenlee at the Crawford Grill in Pittsburgh.

Greenlee had been away from the Negro National League for six years, and Cumberland Posey did his best to keep him away. When the NNL denied Greenlee's application for a 1945 franchise—among other indiscretions, he had pilfered NNL players for his independent team the season before—Gasoline Gus had trained his sights on an alternative league. It's unclear whether Rickey also played a role in the initial planning for the United States League, but the calculating former catcher was soon involved, stepping up to sponsor a member team that he named the Brooklyn Brown Dodgers.

The Brown Dodgers would play at Ebbets Field, and when a headline in the *New York Times* announced their formation on May 8— Victory in Europe Day, eight days after Hitler shot himself in an air-raid shelter—Rickey had his cover. Now, under the pretense that players were being eyeballed for the *Brown* Dodgers, he could send his scouts around the established Negro Leagues in search of a proper candidate—"the right man," as he put it—to integrate the *Brooklyn* Dodgers. It was additionally fortuitous when the new commissioner, Happy Chandler, answered questions for a crowd of writers from black newspapers and made clear his support for the desegregation of the major leagues.

Although it hung around for two years, the USL, situated in six cities, never played much of a schedule or attracted much established talent. Its aim was to prepare young players for graduation to the big leagues if the opportunity finally arose. Bell was contacted as a prospective coach or instructor, and with his playing days nearing an end the position had some appeal, even though he'd already declined an opportunity to be a player-manager for the Memphis Red Sox.

"They said, we want to hire some experienced older ballplayers to train these younger fellows and call it the black farm," Cool Papa recalled in his oral history interview with the University of Missouri–St. Louis. "But they didn't want to pay them anything. They had a meeting. I didn't go to the meeting because they wanted to pay a hundred and twenty-five dollars a month. And you couldn't hardly get jobs after the baseball season was over [because the off-season] was only for five months. I wouldn't mind sacrificing for the future of blacks in baseball, but how was I gonna live?"

There were still no kids to care for, and Clara Belle wasn't an expensive wife, aside from a few nice things to wear. (Cool's cousins in Mississippi tried to keep a straight face one late September when she showed up in a fur coat, sweating and not about to take it off.) Even so, Bell needed all the work he could get and would continue to play ball year-round for as long as he could—or not play at all, giving up the game for full-time employment. That prospect was beginning to make its case. The winter between the '44 and '45 seasons had taken a toll.

"I was sick. I had a stiff arm. I couldn't throw. I couldn't run. I lost about twenty pounds."

Cool Papa missed most of May and half of June as the Grays took up the pursuit of another postseason. He had been back on the field for a little over a week when Homestead played three games on the East Coast against the Kansas City Monarchs, who featured Satchel Paige and a rugged rookie shortstop named Jackie Robinson. At least, the young man *thought* he was a shortstop.

Robinson's name was not unfamiliar to Bell. A second lieutenant in the Army, the fiery Californian (though born in Georgia) had initially made his reputation at UCLA, where he was the first athlete to letter in four sports. As a collegian, he'd been best known for football and track, but Robinson was hitting well for the Monarchs and was thought to be among a number of Negro League players whom Rickey's scouts were discreetly keeping an eye on. Buck Leonard and even Cool Papa were rumored to be on that list also, along with others that included Sam "the Jet" Jethroe, a switch-hitting outfielder who would win the Negro League batting title that year, and slugging catcher Roy Campanella.

Understanding that his own candidacy was no longer realistic, Bell, like some of his fellow Negro League elders, was hopeful that the player chosen to shatter the color line would be Monte Irvin, a power-hitting star for the Newark Eagles before he was drafted into military service in 1943. Beyond reproach in talent and character, the handsome slugger would surely do blackball proud in that historic role. But Irvin wasn't home yet from the war; and besides, it was now grimly apparent that the course to integration would not be guided by Negro League interests.

Curious about all the noise surrounding the subject, the mayor of New York, Fiorello La Guardia, had requested a report on it from Yankees president Larry MacPhail. The response wasn't released to the public at the time—fear of looking nonsensical wouldn't have been unfounded—but it revealed a lot about baseball's racial disposition over the previous half century. "There are few, if any, negro players who could qualify for play in the major leagues at this time," wrote MacPhail, tapping into themes that would be expanded in a more formal dissertation he would oversee a year later for major-league owners.

"A major league player must have something besides natural ability. . . . In conclusion: I have no hesitancy in saying that the Yankees have no intention of signing negro players under contract or reservation to negro clubs."

Neither, evidently, did the Boston Red Sox. In late April, Robinson had been one of three players—the others were Jethroe and a young infielder from Texas named Marvin Williams—whom the Red Sox, in the face of political coercion, had hosted for a tryout at Fenway Park; a city councilman had threatened to withhold a license for Sunday games if an audition wasn't arranged. In advance of the intriguing session, Bell had been alerted by a Grays official to expect an invitation. "I told him no, I was just about as old as baseball," he recounted decades later to *Black Sports* magazine. He was also still recovering from the overexertion of his extended previous season. "I said, 'Well, I can hit, but if I triple or hit a home run inside the park, I would just about be through for that day, as far as running.'"

He didn't miss much. Dutifully, and perhaps disingenuously, the Red Sox put Robinson, Jethroe, and Williams through some paces and wished them well. The specific knock on Robinson, not without merit, was that he lacked the skill to play shortstop. Of course, the same could be said for the vast majority of major leaguers, including most of the all-stars.

Among Negro Leaguers, the Boston misadventure was common knowledge by the time the Grays and Monarchs got together a couple days after the summer solstice. It was Bell's introduction to Robinson and an afternoon of which he often spoke in later years, memorable not only for the spirited young Kansas City infielder but also for his own personal contribution to American history and a precious cause. His accounts of that day were included in an interview with author John Holway, another with Chester Morgan for the oral history program at the University of Southern Mississippi, and a panel discussion moderated by Hall of Fame historian Cliff Kachline, from all of which the following chronicle is a composite.

"In 1945," Cool Papa recalled, "we played the Kansas City Monarchs in Wilmington, Delaware, and the secretary of the team [Dizzy

Dismukes, the former pitcher, manager, coach, and columnist], he come to me and he said, 'I want you to do a little favor.' I said, 'Yeah, what is it?' He said, 'Well, I'm telling you that after the season's over, maybe before the season's over, Jackie Robinson's gonna be signed into organized baseball.'

"He said, 'He want to play shortstop, except for we don't want him to play shortstop.' You see, if Robinson missed his chance, I don't know how long we'd go before we'd get another chance. They said Boston had turned him down. Said he couldn't play. That's what had been happening all the time. They'd have a tryout and then say, 'We didn't see anybody worthwhile.' Well, we wanted to show Jackie that he should try out at another position.

"Dizzy Dismukes and Frank Duncan, the Monarchs' manager— he was there, too—they told me, 'Jackie Robinson is a major-league ballplayer, but his best position is second base. But he won't *play* second base.' And so they told me, 'Now, we want you to hit the ball to Jackie's right.' I'm the type of hitter that nine times out of ten I could hit the ball to any field I want. Not that I would get a hit every time, but I could hit it where I wanted to. And so, they was trying to confuse Jackie out of that position.

"He couldn't play shortstop," Bell said. "He couldn't backhand the ball. He couldn't go into the hole toward third base and throw anyone out. Well, I was leadoff and the first time up I hit the ball so Jackie could catch it, but he couldn't get in front of the ball and he couldn't backhand it. He caught the ball all right, but you've got to catch it and throw in one motion. Jackie was chasin' and had to make two extra steps. He couldn't backhand and pivot. He couldn't throw me out.

"The first two times up I did that and beat the ball out. And I stole second base with a trick slide. And the next two times I walked and I stole two more bases. I'd step right over his hand or slide past him and reach back and touch the base. They never did get me out. And I told him, 'In the major leagues, Jackie, they've got tricky guys like that.' He came to me [later] and said, 'I want to know how to run the bases and I want to know how to hit the ball the way you hit it.' Jackie could only hit the ball to left field. He could only hit the ball one way. I told him if they throw it out here, hit it to right field.

"Jackie wasn't our greatest ballplayer. Monte Irvin was our first choice because we wanted somebody to go in there as a long-ball hitter. But Jackie was smart. He was fast, too. We played back on him anyway because we just wanted to see him run. Sam Jethroe could outrace him, but Robinson would steal more bases."

Jackie Robinson played out of position at shortstop for the Kansas City Monarchs in 1945, his only Negro League season.

It was two months later when Branch Rickey called Robinson into his office on Montague Street in Brooklyn for what would become a famous three-hour lecture and cross-examination. Robinson assumed he'd been summoned to sign with the Brooklyn *Brown* Dodgers, but Rickey swiftly unfurled his grander design. He then proceeded to blister his prospective "right man" with slurs, insults, challenges, and explosive scenarios—at the plate, on the bases, in the field, in the dugout, in the grandstand, in the clubhouse, in a hotel, in a restaurant, on a street—that he knew could not discourage, unnerve, or most of all incite the smasher of baseball's long-standing color line.

Rickey had done his diligence on Robinson. He knew that the collegiate star was educated, proud, principled, and feisty. He knew that, as a soldier, a month after D-Day, Robinson had been court-martialed at Fort Hood in Texas for boarding a bus, sitting next to a light-skinned black woman (the wife of a friend), and refusing the driver's order to move to the back. He was subsequently acquitted, but his resistance was on the record and Rickey was heartened by it. Defiance was a vital asset for the racial pioneer he was about to designate. Temper, however, was positively not.

"Do you want a ballplayer who's afraid to fight back?" Robinson asked.

"I want a ballplayer with guts enough *not* to fight back," Rickey replied. "Above all, you cannot fight back. That's the only way this experiment will succeed."

The formal signing was announced in October. Robinson would spend a minor-league season in Montreal and debut for the Dodgers on opening day 1947 in front of fourteen thousand black fans and twelve thousand white ones at Ebbets Field. Playing first base that season next to veteran Eddie Stanky, he would be named Rookie of the Year in the National League, which he led in stolen bases. The following year he settled in at second base for the long haul. The year after that he was the National League's MVP and batting champion. In 1953, the fifth of Robinson's six straight all-star seasons, he made his only big-league appearance at shortstop. And in 1962 he became the first African American inducted into baseball's Hall of Fame.

"Jackie Robinson surprised me," Cool Papa said. "He played better in the majors than I thought he would."

CHAPTER TWENTY-TWO

STEPPING ASIDE

HOMESTEAD SWEPT THAT MEMORABLE SERIES with the Monarchs, roughing up Satchel Paige in the process. Having exploited Jackie Robinson for a pair of hits, Cool Papa did the same, when the time came, to his dear old friend on the mound. But it was a pace he couldn't keep up at the age of forty-three. The 1945 all-star game was played without him.

The Negro World Series, however, was not. Bell did his part in seeing to that, surmounting his late-season creakiness in a double-header sweep of the Newark Eagles that clinched the Grays' ninth consecutive Negro National League title. He took personal charge of the twin bill's first game, smacking three hits and exacting some revenge on capacious Forbes Field with an inside-the-park home run that made excellent use of the gratuitous acreage. For about fifteen seconds the breathless dash might have helped Cool Papa forget that he was actually forty-three, but probably not. Fortunately, the second game was handled nicely by curveball artist Ray Brown, a Hall of Famer in progress. Brown, the husband of Cum Posey's oldest daughter, Ethel—they were married at home plate on the Fourth of July ten years prior—had thrown a perfect game against Chicago in August.

Homestead was heavily favored in its World Series against the Cleveland Buckeyes, who featured the blazing Sam Jethroe. Born the year Bell broke into the Negro Leagues and raised in East St. Louis, the Jet once prevailed in a race against Olympic gold-medal sprinter Barney Ewell. The Buckeyes, moreover, were managed by Quincy Trouppe, Cool Papa's former protégé from the Stars Park neighborhood in midtown St. Louis. It shaped up as a chummy series.

But Cleveland was not visitor-friendly that week. At Municipal Stadium on Lake Erie, only Josh Gibson could drive in a run for the Grays in a 2–1 opening defeat. Nor were Homestead's hitting troubles relieved by skipping over to League Park, with its forty-five-foot-high (but very close) right-field fence, for game two, a 3–2 setback.

The end of the era, though, was played out back east. In a futile surrender of their preeminence, the Grays were shut out at Griffith Stadium by George Jefferson, the younger brother of co-ace Willie Jefferson—the first time they'd been blanked in three years—and shut out again at Shibe Park in Philadelphia by an otherwise unaccomplished right-hander named Frank "Big Pitch" Carswell. Wendell Smith of the *Pittsburgh Courier* ranked the unforeseeable sweep as one of the most stunning upsets in blackball history.

Retrospect, of course, would see it differently, noting the physical attrition of Gibson and Bell, for much different reasons. There was also the tectonic cracking of the color line, not yet shaking up the respective rosters but in the process of rearranging baseball's continents in a way that unsteadied the Negro Leagues. The old world was on its way out.

One of Cleveland's hitting heroes that series, outfielder Willie Grace, reflected years later on the magnitude of the Buckeyes' triumph. "Me and Sam Jethroe was talkin' about it," he told Brent Kelley in *Voices from the Negro Leagues*. "He couldn't understand what I was saying. I said, 'Sam, can't you understand what I'm saying? No other ballclub you know of had four guys in the Hall of Fame on the same team at the same time.' He said, 'Oh no. There's plenty of teams got four guys in the Hall of Fame.' I said, 'Sure it is, but the Homestead Grays had Buck Leonard, they had Cool Papa Bell, they had Josh Gibson, and they had [Ray Brown]. You can't think of no other team that had those same type of guys on the same ballclub.' "

Before the Grays could regroup in the spring of '46, their avuncular owner, Negro League champion Cum Posey, had died of lung cancer in a Homestead hospital. A week later, as Jackie Robinson trained with other Brooklyn farmhands, the Dodgers signed Roy Campanella, the burly, brilliant catcher of the Baltimore Elite Giants, and fearsome pitcher Don Newcombe from the Newark Eagles.

THE REST OF organized baseball was now on high alert. Vexed by "the race question" and particularly troubled by the implications of Branch Rickey's so-called experiment, major-league executives established a six-man committee of owners and league presidents to compile what came to be known as the MacPhail Report. While the document also addressed labor issues and the Mexican League challenge, it was destined to be remembered primarily as a working statement of Major League Baseball's position on desegregation. It would be, in effect, a defensive response to "the people who charge that baseball is flying a Jim Crow flag at its masthead—or think that racial discrimination is the basic reason for failure of the major leagues to give employment to Negroes."

MacPhail's task force reported back before the season was out, although the communiqué would not be released to the public for five years—and then, only because a copy was brought to light by a congressional committee. That was an awkward moment. Noting that professional baseball is fundamentally a business enterprise, MacPhail and his cronies had articulated a stance—a rationale for excluding dark-skinned athletes from their clubs—that barely outlasted a loaf of white bread.

After some hollow verbiage about honoring Negro League contracts, the study alluded to the major leagues' vested interest in preserving blackball. "The Negro leagues," it pointed out, "rent their parks in many cities from clubs in Organized Baseball. Many major and minor league clubs derive substantial revenue from these rentals. . . . Club owners in the major leagues are reluctant to give up revenues amounting to hundreds of thousands of dollars every year. They naturally want the Negro leagues to continue."

In its representation of the owners, for the owners, the MacPhail Report formalized many of the familiar talking points that irritated Cool Papa. One in particular was MLB's insistence that black players, regardless of their experience or abilities or domination of interracial games, would require minor-league training before competing in the big leagues. "A major league player must have something besides great natural ability," the paper said, with chilling transparency. "He must possess the technique, the coordination, the competitive attitude, and the discipline, which is usually acquired only after years of seasoning in the minor leagues. The minor league experience of players on the major league rosters, for instance, averages 7 years. The young Negro player never has had a good chance in baseball. Comparatively few good young Negro players are being developed. This is the reason there are not more players who meet major league standards in the Negro Leagues."

For all the posturing and hooey, snatches of candor could also be found in the major-league manifesto, including some language that touched upon organized baseball's socioeconomic concerns. There was, for example, the dark warning that "a situation might be presented, if Negroes participate in Major League games, in which the preponderance of Negro attendance in parks such as the Yankee Stadium, the Polo Grounds, and Comiskey Park could conceivably threaten the value of Major League franchises owned by these clubs."

In other words, too many black folks in the house could ruin everything.

HOMESTEAD WAS DOWN a Hall of Famer in 1946; down *two*, counting Posey. Ray Brown, no longer beholden to his father-in-law, terminated his fourteen-year association with Posey's team by answering Jorge Pasquel's call to Mexico, a decision that earned him, along with Ray Dandridge and others, a five-year suspension from the Negro Leagues. Gibson and Leonard were poised to go as well, until the financial incentive for staying reached a suitable level.

More, of course, than their less compensated teammates, the graying Grays—the staunch Leonard, at age thirty-eight, and the declining icons, Gibson and Bell—were entrusted with carrying on the Homestead tradition. Although they didn't have another pennant in them, there was no shirking from the veteran leaders. Leonard was an all-star again. Gibson missed out on plenty of doubles by stopping at first base, daunted by the next ninety feet, but the strength he summoned at home plate left witnesses agape in some of the nation's biggest ballparks—gargantuan clouts at Forbes Field and Yankee Stadium, breathtaking blows into the upper deck of the Polo Grounds and over the roof of Shibe Park, a whistling missile of more than five hundred feet at Sportsman's Park in St. Louis.

Bell, meanwhile, was able to shake out his infirmities of 1945, subdue his jealousy of youthful comrades with seminal opportunities, and actually contend for a batting title in his twenty-fifth year of professional baseball. But wear and tear—and perhaps a little collusion—reduced him to only six games over July and August.

The Grays were playing out their season—and Bell his career—as the Newark Eagles, led by Larry Doby, Monte Irvin, and the two-way stalwart Leon Day, made their way to the Negro World Series, where they would turn back the Kansas City Monarchs. In decisive game seven, the Monarchs would have given the ball to their meal ticket, Satchel Paige, if they could have located him.

From where Cool Papa stood, the unfamiliar absence of pennant tension, along with the uncharacteristic days off, provided an ample opportunity to step back and think things over. The decision wasn't difficult. He knew it was time to excuse himself when his sharp ground balls became unaccustomed double plays now and again.

With the retirement of Boojum Wilson, who'd persevered through epilepsy his last few years, Bell had outlasted every player, save a pair of savvy catchers, who'd been in the league when he signed up in 1922. Both of the catchers—Biz Mackey, like Cool a man manifestly bereft of vices, and Frank Duncan, who'd spent a partial year in the Army during World War II and set a marksmanship record—had extended their careers as player-managers. The abiding leadoff man, on the other hand, for all of his playing career, had been all *player*, forever and seemingly ever. Through his full-length, first-person, documentary tour of the blackball experience, Cool Papa Bell had matured into the virtual embodiment of the Negro Leagues.

And now, at forty-four, picking his spots, he was still churning out base hits, an intriguing story line that prompted some dialogue with league officials. The resulting agreement was this: If Bell, as a final gesture in a legendary quarter century of fabulous outfielding and classic tricky ball, would cede his potential batting title to a younger player with prospects—preferably Monte Irvin—the league or the Grays or somebody would find him $200 for his sacrifice, that being the sum earmarked for the leading hitter. He might well have done the deal without the $200, but guaranteed cash sounded pretty good, not knowing where his next paycheck was coming from.

The plan didn't involve tanking in the batter's box but rather avoiding it altogether, accumulating too few at-bats to qualify as the batting champ. Bell, in fact, finished strong, piling up five hits in a late-September doubleheader against the New York Cubans to finish with a batting average computed variously as .447, .402, .393, and .368. But he also did more than his share of sitting out down the stretch—nobody could question that, given the miles on his legs—and his 87 at-bats (counted elsewhere as 137) kept him well shy of the cutoff for official league leaders. When all was said and done, Irvin, with an average ranging between .370 and .398, was indeed awarded a batting crown, and signed eventually—many would say belatedly—with the New York Giants.

"I gave up my title so Monte would have a better chance at the majors," Cool Papa told Mark Kram for *Sports Illustrated*, a narrative quite like his yielding of the batting honors to Pee Wee Austin two years earlier. "We'd do anythin' to get a player up there. The fans were mad, but they didn't know what we were trying to do. After the season I was supposed to get the $200 for the title anyway, but my owner, he say, 'Well look, Cool, Irvin won it, didn't he?' They wouldn't give me the $200. Baseball was never much for me makin' money."

It was a poignant farewell to playing the game, but not so sad as Josh Gibson's. If the long seasons were hard on Gibson's mind and body, a bitter winter, lacking the gratification of adulation and royal home runs, might have been too much to bear. Or, given his escalating headaches and other maladies, perhaps that better describes his physical condition. No one knows for certain.

We do know that the best-hitting catcher of any league at any time—the best pure hitter, period, some would argue—had foregone his customary off-season gig in Puerto Rico; passed, also, on the lucrative, coast-to-coast airplane tour with Satchel Paige's black team and Bob Feller's high-profile white one; and was sticking around Pittsburgh in January 1947. Josh's former Crawford teammate Ted Page came upon his once-jolly friend in a bar one night, shaking another patron in his crushing hands. When he recognized Page, Gibson demanded that his old buddy set the fellow straight as to who hit the longest home run ever.

On January 19, Gibson had a few drinks at the Crawford Grill and then slipped into a movie theater, perhaps thinking that the darkness would assuage his headache. Later, as the theater emptied, he was found unresponsive in his seat. A doctor was called, and Josh was taken to his mother's home, where, according to one account, he briefly awakened an hour or so after midnight, asked for his trophies, then fell back and expired at the age of thirty-five.

The cause was never officially declared, although Ted Page was convinced of it. He often said that Josh Gibson, spurned by the major leagues, had died of a broken heart.

CHAPTER TWENTY-THREE

A BASKET OF FRUIT

H AVING DEBUTED TWO YEARS BEFORE COOL Papa, the Negro Leagues outlasted him by roughly the same negligible duration. They straggled on, significantly diminished, into the early fifties, but the passage over the color line, for all practical purposes, left their dated world behind.

The same year Jackie Robinson broke in with the Dodgers—and Larry Doby integrated the American League after Bill Veeck, the ringmaster who'd finally found a big-league team to buy, brought him straight from the Newark Eagles to the Cleveland Indians (just ahead of Hank Thompson and Willard Brown catching on with the St. Louis Browns)—Bell went to work with Robinson's old blackball team, the Kansas City Monarchs. His job was developing players for the promised land that, as it turned out, lay just beyond the end of the road he'd raced along for a generation.

More than any other Negro League franchise, the Monarchs, at that point, placed a premium on development, making prospects salable to their new clients, the major-league organizations. Thompson and Brown began the 1947 season in Kansas City before crossing

Missouri and assimilating into the mainstream, although Cool Papa had nothing to do with their graduations. He was involved only with the Monarchs' so-called B team, a separate squad of mostly greener players who weren't quite as ready for the big time as Robinson, Thompson, Brown, or, for that matter, Buck O'Neil, Hilton Smith, and, when the spirit moved him, Satchel Paige.

Kansas City's official Negro American League entry—the A team, as it were—was managed by Cool Papa's contemporary, the longtime catcher Frank Duncan, a wise mentor who knew his way around racial nuance. His wife, Julia Lee, a popular blues singer, often performed in whites-only establishments. To attend her shows, Duncan had to pose as a musician and sit with the band.

Bell managed the junior club and helped in the outfield more often than he'd bargained for, which enabled the promoters to use his name on posters and placards. It was employment close to his heart but admittedly not his first choice. "I was looking for a job, but I couldn't find one," he told interviewer Arthur Shaffer for the Missouri–St. Louis oral history project. "A regular job, that is. I stayed thirteen years longer than I intended to play."

To the public, the distinction between Duncan's league team and Cool Papa's developmental outfit was not always apparent—especially after the mercurial Paige showed up at his old roomie's side in 1948, slumming with the B team.

The confusion was not discouraged by the Kansas City organization. When Bell's charges played in the vicinity of home, where the Monarchs were well-known, they went by the name of the Kansas City Stars with Satchel Paige; but when they ventured afar, they swapped out the identifying panel on the side of the bus and presented themselves, for marketing purposes, as the Kansas City *Monarchs* with Satchel Paige. There was no ambiguity, however, when one of Cool Papa's farm-team players signed with a major-league organization, as about twenty of them ultimately did (although most never made it to the parent club): the sale was credited to the Monarchs.

Paige himself, after six weeks of riding with kids half his age in a coach bus with his name on the side, proceeded directly from Bell's

Bell didn't aspire to be a manager, but there were bills to pay.

club to Cleveland, where Larry Doby was playing center field. Abe Saperstein, seeking a recommendation for a Negro Leaguer to sign, had approached Cool on behalf of Bill Veeck. When Bell touted Paige, Saperstein of course brought up the great pitcher's age, which was well north of forty. No worries, Cool Papa said; Satchel's sizzle might have cooled down a little over the years, but his control is now the best in the business. Paige left the Stars/Monarchs in Sioux City, Iowa, and the signing was orchestrated on July 7, his alleged forty-second birthday. It was theater befitting both him and Veeck.

Cynics belittled the move as a promotional stunt by an owner characteristically inclined toward such a thing. But the Indians were in a heated battle with the Red Sox and Yankees for the American League pennant. And Veeck, who maintained that his conceptual, segregation-busting 1943 Phillies would've been "almost a virtual cinch to win the pennant," had demonstrated his faith in the competitive merits of black players, of whom Paige was the most celebrated.

Satch didn't let him down. Pitching mostly in relief—his curriculum vitae, of course, included a long history of abbreviated appearances, day after day—the wily Alabaman charmed the skeptics and believers alike with a 6-1 record and 2.48 earned run average that year (accentuated by an exceptional 165 ERA+: ERA adjusted for the pitcher's ballpark and league), even spinning two shutouts among his seven starts. Paige contributed mightily to Cleveland's pennant, and in game five of a World Series that the Indians would win in six, he became the first African American to pitch on that stage, retiring the only two Boston Braves he faced. Even without his famous fastball, relying instead on impeccable control, occasional trickery, and outrageous confidence, the old master would ultimately appear in two all-star games, at the ages of forty-five and forty-six. The former came in 1952 when, pitching for the St. Louis Browns, Paige remarkably led all American League relievers with a 3.5 WAR (wins above replacement-level player).

Meanwhile, as the unlikeliest rookie was making organized baseball wonder what it had been missing all those years, Bell had his eye on quite another kind of newbie. He'd happened upon "a boy down in Birmingham," raw, dynamic, and seventeen, in whom he recognized special qualities that he was uniquely equipped to appreciate. With the type of training the Monarchs were featuring, which he would personally oversee, Cool Papa could envision a wonderful center fielder. The kid, he thought, just might be his ticket out of baseball.

"Our owner," Cool recalled, "was told that there was a great ballplayer down there. He couldn't hit the ball, but he swings level, and he could run and throw. All you would have to do was just bring him up.

"He was supposed to be the understudy for me, because I was going to quit as soon as I got a job. But they wouldn't take the chance on Willie Mays."

NO SOONER HAD Cleveland won the World Series than Paige was arranging for his new best friends to meet him in California for some interracial games and extracurricular cash. Bob Lemon, a twenty-game winner that year—plus two in the Series, including the clincher—assembled some major leaguers and Satchel rounded up a mostly youthful Negro League contingent to play them.

It was not merely coincidence that Bell's team of prospects was out there at the same time. A few of the fellows were filling in for Paige's group as needed, hoping to get the attention of a scout; but there was one more player, less inexperienced, whom Satch was itching to lure for an upcoming game at Wrigley Field in Los Angeles. It was a tough sell, as Bell explained for the Missouri historical records.

"I said, 'No, sir, I'm not in condition. I'm just about halfway in condition. I don't play every day; I'm just training these boys.'

"He said, 'Well, I'll tell you what. You just come on out and you just play five innings. I'm going to pitch five innings and then I'm going out and then you can go out.'

"Well, he wanted Bob Lemon to see me. He had told Bob Lemon different things I did in baseball. Lemon would say, 'Oh, he can't do that,' and Satchel said, 'He did it against major leagues or anybody.'"

The fact was, Paige didn't want Lemon to just *see* Cool Papa. He'd been boasting and exaggerating about his pal as only Satch could do, taunting the Indians' star about Bell being forty-five years old—he was actually forty-six, contrary to most reports—and how his legs were shot and his joints were stiff and his eyes were going, but no matter, he'd *still* make Lemon look silly. Paige wanted Cool Papa to *humiliate* Bob Lemon. All in good fun, of course.

Bell wasn't playing along with that particular angle, but he was resigned to the inevitability that Satchel would moan and persist until he had his way. The best deal Cool could get was an assurance that he wouldn't have to lead off. To minimize his exposure, he could bat eighth in the order.

"So anyway," Bell said, omitting the part in which, by way of introduction, Lemon buzzed him with a fastball under the chin, "I had watched Bob Lemon pitch. If he got a man on base, he'll look around and he'll never look back again. So I got on base the first time; I got a double off of Lemon. And I knew his moves. He looked back and he turned his head and I went to third base. They didn't even throw it."

In retrospect, the double and steal by a middle-aged, semi-retired Negro Leaguer might have been enough to constitute proper humiliation for a World Series hero in his prime. It may have been sufficient to validate Paige's reputation as a prophet and Cool Papa's as an otherworldly phantom of the basepath. But Bell would come to bat once more, with Paige right behind him.

"So I got on base again and Satchel sacrifices me to second."

It was, in fact, an unusually good bunt that Paige laid down, between home plate and the pitcher's mound, skewed slightly left, causing the first and third basemen to charge in to field it and the catcher to hustle out for the same purpose and the second baseman to cover first and the shortstop to cover second.

"Well, now they left third base open and I went to third," Cool Papa recalled. "The catcher was [Roy] Partee—he was the catcher with the Browns—and he happened to see me running to third and he was out there in front of home plate to pick up the ball and he was going to beat me to third and I beat him there and there was nobody at home plate and I just came running and he hollered, 'Time! Time!'"

One would expect that either the first or third baseman, in that suddenly urgent scenario, would think to cover home plate, or perhaps Lemon himself would do it—*especially* Lemon himself—but there was no precedent for such an unscripted occurrence, no moment's pause in which wits might be gathered, no instinct quite as fast as the old man now headed for home.

"The umpire said, 'I can't call time—the ball is in play.'"

"So I scored from first base on a sacrifice and people didn't believe me. But I been doing that a lot of times."

IT WOULD BE poetically satisfying to say that Cool Papa's shenanigans in Los Angeles were the capstone of a singular career, a dramatic display of hanging up his spikes while they were still ablaze.

Close enough. There are vague glimpses of him going through the motions of ballplaying in succeeding years—listed as the right fielder against the East Helena Smelterites in Montana; pinch-hitting in

Lethbridge, Alberta; showing up in Kansas City with one of Satch's all-star teams—but the end of his era was nonetheless conspicuous to the Negro League community. "I'm sick of all this talk about the speed of Robinson and Doby," wrote a correspondent from Cleveland, as published in Wendell Smith's *Pittsburgh Courier* column. "In comparison with James (Cool Papa) Bell, ex-Homestead Grays' star, they look like snails. Bell would have stolen 100 bases per season in the majors had he been given the chance."

As a mentor, though, he had plenty to offer, and not all of it pertained to the playing field. Papa's personalized lessons involved both game situations and life situations, the likes of drag bunting and dignity. Bell knew well that, beyond the baseball—and even within it—the Negro Leagues presented unremitting challenges in conducting oneself. What to make, for instance, of the "famous pepper ball act" (per the advertisements) that his up-and-comers engaged in as warm-ups, a hardball version of the sleight of hand performed by the Harlem Globetrotters to the tune of "Sweet Georgia Brown"? Like the donkey baseball that Cool Papa disdained, was it harmless entertainment or racial clowning? In that and countless other circumstances, there was no undisputed right, wrong, or recommended; only personal choice as to what was appropriate. As the B team toured the towns and country, the players were schooled daily by mid-American scenarios. What should be said or done, Cool must have wondered, when rolling through Oklahoma past the road sign for the Grand Café, featuring "nigger chicken"? As a rule, he searched for the intersection of pride and decorum.

"When we went to Memphis," wrote Dennis Biddle in his memoir, *Secrets of the Negro Baseball League*, "the players would head to Beale Street, where they had a lot of nightclubs. Cool Papa Bell would always make us wear a tie and a suit whenever we went out. He would say, 'You're professionals and you're gonna act like it.' I liked that about him. He felt that acting in a professional manner was important no matter where you played or who you played for.

"Many times, though, I would sit in a hotel room and listen to the stories that the elders told me about the Negro League. Cool Papa

Bell—I called him Mr. Bell—didn't smoke or drink, so he would stay back in the room at the hotel and tell me about the true history of the Negro Leagues and tell me about players that would have been in the Hall of Fame if they had the opportunity to play in the major leagues. . . . He mentored me, but also any young person who had enough talent to make it to the majors.

"As far as I knew," Biddle added, "he was just one of the trainers. He never talked much about himself. Later, I learned he was the fastest man ever to play the game."

It was a conflicted period for Cool Papa. His dream had been unfairly, irrationally deferred. For twenty-five years he had stooped in the hot sun to plant the seeds of desegregation and lesser players had climbed on his back to snatch the fruits. And yet, he didn't ache to be where they were. Not *now*. His pride wouldn't permit him to perform in the big leagues as a mockery of the player he'd been, to so discredit the legacy of the Negro Leagues.

He had a chance or two. At some unspecified point, after Veeck bought the St. Louis Browns in 1951 and signed Satchel Paige, Cool brought a copy of Satchel's birth certificate or some other pertinent document to the Browns' offices to clear up the popular confusion about Paige's age. He spoke to the general manager, Bill DeWitt, and was advised that they weren't the least bit interested in solving the Satchel mystery and in fact didn't want to *know* when he was actually born. But they *were* interested in Cool Papa putting on a Browns uniform. Paige had been talking it up, and Veeck was a fan.

"You want to play ball?" DeWitt asked him, according to Bell in his interview with Chester Morgan for the Southern Mississippi oral history archive.

"No," Cool answered, "I don't want to play out there. I quit playing ball."

"Can you hit?"

"Yes, that's about all I can do now is hit. My leg is bad and I can't catch the balls that the other guys hit."

"Well," said DeWitt, "I will let you sign a contract and have you on the field tomorrow."

"No. I just come out here to bring Satchel up his papers that had his age in there. I just don't want to play."

It wasn't the first dialogue of that nature. Dennis Biddle recalled Bell's account of being approached by Branch Rickey about playing for the Dodgers and replying, with uncharacteristic rancor, "Why didn't you ask me twenty years ago?"

Had Rickey instead offered a job as a scout or coach or instructor—or if the Browns had desired him as one of the above instead of a broken-down outfielder—Cool would have been both satisfied and suitably employed. He didn't conceal his ambition along those lines. But time and again, it seemed, some or another baseball agenda played out to his detriment. In the Browns' office, Bell had the distinct impression that Veeck's staff was keeping him from seeing the boss, and vice versa, lest Veeck hire him on the spot to do whatever he wished. Professionally, that was crushing. Cool Papa sorely needed full-time work, and he couldn't get it training prospects for the Monarchs.

What he *could* get from that position, however, was an enduring, auxiliary level of satisfaction. He was able to play a supporting role, at least, in the obliteration of the color line, the better day that his mother had insisted he be ready for. Bell's vicarious contentment attached not only to those who finally broke through and assumed their rightful places in the profession but especially to the younger men and boys of color for whom stable, properly recognized, adequately rewarded, top-level baseball was now an inspiring possibility.

"When they said we couldn't play . . . There were more guys before me who didn't have a chance," Cool told John Holway, "and I wanted us to prove it to them all, black and white alike."

In that quest, the Monarchs contributed bountifully, ultimately forwarding twenty-seven players to the majors. It was a mission that Bell conspicuously embraced. "Cool Papa Bell has the knack of getting all the talent out of young players," reported the *Helena Independent Record*. "Since the majors are now open to them, his yearlings hustle from the start."

The hustle was heartening, but the actual currency in play was the talent itself. Bell was constantly on the lookout for it and therefore quick to follow up on the recommendation of a St. Louis acquaintance concerning a polite, solidly built, all-around athlete named Elston Howard. While attending Vashon High School, Quincy Trouppe's old stomping ground, Howard had attracted a number of Big Ten offers for football and various others for track and basketball but after a tryout had been passed over by the Cardinals, whose roster wouldn't be integrated until 1954.

Cool referred Howard to Buck O'Neil, who was now managing the Monarchs, and thereafter kept the Browns apprised of the prospect's progress with Kansas City. He was doing all he could for a deserving young fellow, of course, and was also hoping for an eventual bonus from the Monarchs—Bell's arrangement with the club called for a third of the sale price when a player he developed was signed by a major-league organization—or perhaps, now that he had the Browns' attention, an overture from them that might bring him back home.

In the meantime the Stars were on a Southern tour when Cool Papa took notice of a slender high school shortstop with a lovely swing and matching demeanor. Introducing himself to Ernie Banks of Dallas, Texas, Bell promised the smiling teenager that if he finished high school the following year, he'd have a place with the Monarchs. "Cool Papa Bell was the first one who impressed me," Banks reminisced to author Lew Freedman in *Game of My Life: Chicago Cubs*.

When Cool had the follow-up conversation with O'Neil, however, the skipper pointed out that, in a promising Iowan named Gene Baker, he already had a fine shortstop. They reprised the discussion another time or two—Bell was quite persistent—until, fortunately for all concerned, Baker was signed by the Chicago Cubs in the spring of 1950. That cleared the way, finally, for Banks to report to Kansas City, where he roomed with Elston Howard.

Now Bell was touting both to his big-league contacts. "But the Browns didn't want them," he recounted, with timeworn disbelief, to Mark Kram of *Sports Illustrated*. "I then went to the Cardinals, and they say they don't care, either, and I think to myself, 'My, if they don't want *these* boys, they don't want *nobody.*' "

Howard and Banks, though, were less disillusioned. They vowed that whichever of them made the majors first—a *big-league* club, not an affiliated farm team—would call the other and tell him what it was like. That distinction would ultimately belong to Banks, in spite of Howard's head start.

Around mid-season 1950, Howard was signed not by the home-town Browns or Cardinals but by the New York Yankees, whose scout, Tom Greenwade, had come to Kansas City to check on another player and was pointed in Howard's direction by Buck O'Neil. After being folded into New York's farm system, Howard took a two-year detour into military service, which consisted almost entirely of playing base-ball, and returned to the minor leagues in 1954, when Yankees legend Bill Dickey tutored him in the art of catching. In the second game of the Bronx Bombers' 1955 season, Howard, prized for his gentlemanly manner as well as his brawn and versatility, substituted in left field, singled home a run in his only at-bat, and so became the mighty Yan-kees' first black player. As a vital component of the pinstriped dynasty for thirteen years, the quiet St. Louisan, primarily but not always a catcher, would be a nine-time all-star, a four-time World Series champion, and the American League MVP for 1963.

Shortly after Howard moved on from Kansas City, Banks was summoned into the Army and dispatched to Germany for two years, reconnecting with the Monarchs in 1953 but not staying long. Sitting next to Banks on the bus one day, "I told him he was going to be sold," Cool Papa said. "He was a little timid, but I told him, 'Don't be afraid.' I told him nobody was going to beat him out at shortstop."

The Chicago Cubs—the same team that had signed his predeces-sor, Gene Baker, who hadn't yet reached the majors but was projected to become the Cubs' future shortstop and pioneer black player—paid the Monarchs $20,000 for Banks and a pitcher who didn't pan out. There was no report of O'Neil being financially rewarded for the Banks transaction, but in a subsequent, perhaps related event—long before

A thin Texas teenager when Cool Papa discovered him, Ernie Banks served two stints with the Monarchs, separated by two years in the Army.

he became the beloved spokesman for Negro League nostalgia—the former first baseman was hired by the Cubs as a coach, the first African American to serve in that capacity at the major-league level.

"I didn't get anything," Bell told anybody who asked and at least a few who didn't. The Monarchs maintained that there was no contract involving a third of the player's sale price or any other portion for Cool Papa. No contract, no commission. "They gave me a basket of fruit."

Banks never played an inning of minor-league ball, proceeding straight to the big leagues on the same day as Gene Baker. It was September 17, 1953, when the sunny slugger made his major-league debut, starting at shortstop and abolishing the Cubs' color line. As Bell had assured, he remained a fixture at that position for more than eight years before crossing the diamond to first base. When Baker finally cracked the Chicago lineup, three days after Banks's first appearance, he was playing second base, where he would operate exclusively for four seasons. Though an item of considerable note, Baker's long-awaited introduction was eclipsed by his keystone partner's first home run and two other hits.

Ernie Banks, of course, became Mr. Cub—or Mr. Fruit Basket, depending on the perspective—a figure and player so admired that he won back-to-back MVP awards for losing teams. Had he been born a generation or so earlier, needless to say, he would have played no part in major-league history. And yet, when he retired in 1971 after his nineteen-year Chicago honeymoon, Banks stood tied with Eddie Mathews for eighth place all-time in home runs, trailing only Babe Ruth, Hank Aaron, Willie Mays, Harmon Killebrew, Mickey Mantle, Jimmie Foxx, and Ted Williams. He was a first-ballot Hall of Famer and the first player to have his uniform number retired by the Cubs, who'd been around longer than uniform numbers.

Cool Papa may or may not have foreseen the greatness of the graceful infielder for whom he had lobbied so hard, but the basket of fruit told him all he needed to know about his own future in baseball. Clara Belle deserved better.

The transition, however, wasn't as simple as seeking it. Bell was job hunting in a nation whose unemployment rate for blacks doubled the percentage for whites, and that didn't even speak to the matter of wages: African Americans with college degrees earned less—about 25 percent less on average—than white folks *without* them. Then there was James Bell, with a stellar batting average but no high school diploma. For all of his good cheer and critically acclaimed baseball, Cool Papa's résumé didn't play particularly well in a segregated city where lunch counters and certain movie theaters were off-limits to black people and the local economy was dominated by such corporate goliaths as Monsanto, Anheuser-Busch, and McDonnell Aircraft, who had their standards. His search had pressed off and on for seven years, to no avail.

Less than a month after the Banks premiere in Chicago, with nothing else in the works, Bell gimped onto the field for an indulgent game celebrating Satchel Paige Day in Kansas City, joining, among others, Paige, Banks, Howard, and Quincy Trouppe, who was now a scout for the Cardinals. The following year, unemployed and doing what he could, he put together his own team for one last barnstorming junket.

The traveling opponent was a club led by Ned Garver, a former twenty-game winner for the Browns who was now pitching for the Detroit Tigers. Bell's recruits included Banks, Baker, and Paige. The papers did their part, spreading the news, but the going was rougher than expected. Players were fickle about showing up, and the fans responded in kind. A game was canceled in Colorado. Cool was back in St. Louis sooner than he'd planned to be.

It was there and then that the old center fielder's persistence paid off and he finally received a reliable, full-time offer he couldn't pass up. It came from City Hall.

Cool Papa Bell was now a janitor.

CHAPTER TWENTY-FOUR

OBSCURITY

F ROM THE REDBRICK, TWO-STORY DUPLEX ON Dickson Street where Bell and Clara Belle had recently moved, City Hall was a two-mile walk, southeast, in the direction of downtown and the meandering Mississippi, although the world's best-dressed custodian—the old Negro Leaguer emptied waste baskets in business attire, flourishes added—must have made at least occasional use of the buses, streetcars, or automobiles of friends and relatives when the weather didn't match his ensemble, especially in the summer, with perspiration going undefeated in the infamous St. Louis humidity.

Dickson was a sociable street in those times, the congeniality unmitigated by the presence of a funeral parlor a few doors down from the duplex at 3034. Cool and Clara lived on the left side of the building, built in 1896, and the right was occupied by her sister, Mary, and three children. One of them, Ken Webb—who had often looked in on Clara when her husband was away doing baseball—became a local radio personality, and on a subsequent Sunday night, in a community setting that included neighbors and wine, conducted a live interview with his uncle Bell from the funeral home.

The other nephew, Norman Seay, was at Vashon High School—when the Bells moved next door, working toward a career as a college administrator and apprenticing as an activist. He was among a midsize group of Congress of Racial Equality (CORE) members who met once a week to picnic, play bridge, study Gandhi, and game-plan the peaceable infiltration of local lunch counters and the like, aspiring to spare black St. Louisans from having to pack sandwiches and eat them in restrooms when they shopped downtown. It was a city in which segregation was systemized by zoning laws and whose leading institution of higher learning, Washington University, had excluded African Americans until 1952.

The lunch counter sit-ins, pulled off by protestors who typically outdressed the white customers, were some of the first in the country, well in advance of the more celebrated events at Woolworth's in Greensboro, North Carolina. But Seay was still at it in the sixties, serving ninety days in jail for his part in the 1963 demonstrations against Jefferson Bank and Trust for its unfair hiring practices. Of all the discriminatory employers in St. Louis, Jefferson was singled out for its response to CORE's request that the bank hire four blacks for clerical jobs: there weren't "four blacks in the city" qualified for that kind of work, the company asserted. The protest carried on for seven months—during which JFK was assassinated—representing the largest, angriest civil rights uprising in St. Louis history until, perhaps, the Ferguson riots of 2014, set off by the fatal police shooting of African American teenager Michael Brown. (The Ferguson incident occurred less than a year after Seay had visited the White House to meet and present a medallion to President Obama.)

By the time of his nephew's incarceration, City Hall had promoted Bell to night watchman. It was a job that better suited his wardrobe, now accessorized with a firearm. Clara was proud of her man, fussing meticulously over his scrapbooks, but sometimes wondered aloud why he couldn't be more like Norman. Her brand of resistance was more public than Cool Papa's.

Wherever he went—even to City Hall to mop floors or check doorknobs—
Cool Papa looked good.

These, though, were not public times for Bell. Ironically, the decorated outfielder was fading from society's view just as his young relatives were marching into it and his professional descendants were standing front and center in major-league baseball.

After Jackie Robinson crashed the party, it was no time at all until the tacit ban on black players had been exposed as not merely un-American but utterly ridiculous. In the fifties, the first full decade of African American inclusion in organized ball, eight of the ten Most Valuable Players in the National League—the American was more sluggish about integrating, the Boston Red Sox being the last team to do so in 1959—were former Negro Leaguers, with Roy Campanella winning the honor three times, Ernie Banks twice, and Willie Mays, Don Newcombe, and Hank Aaron once apiece. Black players collectively batted .280, white players .261. For every twenty home runs a black hitter hit, a white one, in the same number of at-bats, managed thirteen. The pro-rated advantage in stolen bases—Cool Papa's specialty—was an overwhelming ten to four.

In the sixties, by which time African Americans made up 23 percent of major-league rosters and Latin Americans another 14, seven of the National League's batting champs were one or the other. The same minorities provided *all ten* of the players who finished first in home runs—and, just in case the point was missed, all ten who finished second.

Given the surpassing performances of black superstars at the earliest opportunity, there was simply no enduring logic in presuming that Willie Wells could not be credibly likened to Honus Wagner, Buck Leonard to Lou Gehrig, Satchel Paige to Walter Johnson, Mule Suttles to Jimmie Foxx, Willie Foster to Warren Spahn, Boojum Wilson to Rogers Hornsby, Wild Bill Wright to Mickey Mantle, Biz Mackey to Bill Dickey, or Turkey Stearnes to Ted Williams. And who in mainstream baseball could even approximate the singular talents of Josh Gibson, Martín Dihigo, Bullet Joe Rogan, or Cool Papa Bell? In spectacular, incontrovertible terms, the Negro Leagues had been validated.

And yet, the more celebrity the black ballplayers acquired in the present, the deeper Cool Papa slipped into obscurity.

WITH A LIFETIME of Cool's persistent, modest earnings, the Bells were able to pay off their half of the house soon enough and appoint it with such touches as a china closet, a crystal chandelier, and a living room picture of Jesus, which waited patiently until portraits of JFK and Martin Luther King took up space nearby.

They were homebodies. Clara Belle, an ardent Catholic, went to church and bingo. James, a casual Baptist, went to work and ball games. Otherwise they stuck around Dickson Street, she in her housedress, he in his brown and red checkered robe, and pretended not to get along. A foot shorter than her husband, Clara still managed to get in his face. She called him Bell in phrases such as, "Bell, you low-down skunk . . ." He enjoyed it. As he explained to the Associated Press,

"People think we fight, but we don't fight. I wouldn't want to marry a person if I had to fight her."

At Busch Stadium—Sportsman's Park had been renamed in 1953, just before the Browns moved to Baltimore and became the Orioles—familiar regulars referred to him more respectfully as *Mister* Bell, the night watchman. The grandstands were no longer separated by race, but Cool Papa still favored the cheap seats, occasionally watching with an old friend or two from the packing plant, maybe a brother. How special it would have been, as a lover of baseball lore, to find oneself sitting, unwittingly, next to Cool Papa Bell at the ballpark, engaging politely, eyes adjusting to a dimly lit, captivating universe, courtesy of its most courteous survivor.

Bell, however, was not easily distracted in that setting. He liked to arrive early, study the big leaguers in their warm-ups, and, as the game assumed its course, focus on its subtleties. From time to time they compelled him to approach a player with whom he closely identified.

In the early sixties, his attention turned, not surprisingly, to Maury Wills, the Dodgers' shortstop and whizbang base thief. At the urging of some of Wills's black teammates, Junior Gilliam and John Roseboro among them, Bell made his way to the players' gate one day and introduced himself to the slender switch-hitter.

"Maybe you heard of me, maybe not. It don't matter," he said. "But I'd like to help you. When you're on base, get those hitters of yours to stand deep in the box, close to the plate, and hold their bat back. That way, the catcher, he got to back up. That way, you goin' to get an extra step all the time."

"I hadn't thought of that," replied Wills, who led the National League in stolen bases for six consecutive years and in 1962 broke Ty Cobb's single-season record with 104.

"Well, that's the kind of ball we played in our league. Be seein' you, Mr. Wills. Didn't mean to bother you."

Cool saw much more of Wills's successor as the game's preeminent base stealer, the irrepressible Lou Brock, who became a Cardinal in 1964 by virtue of a famously fortuitous trade with the Cubs. By that time Bell had already singled him out.

It must have been 1962 or '63, with Brock's base-running skills and especially his sliding still conspicuously unrefined—to Bell, anyway—when the night watchman ventured down the stands to the edge of foul territory as the Cubs were loosening up before a game at Busch Stadium. "Hey, young man," he called softly. "Can I see you for a second?"

Bell offered his name and Brock, a student of the game—also a friend of Ernie Banks, who'd no doubt done some talking about the Kansas City Monarchs and associated people of interest—hit the pause button. "Don't move!" he said. "Stay right here." He then scurried about gathering up Cubs and brought them over to meet the man who, it turned out, was not just a myth after all. The session ended with Brock telling Cool Papa to please stay in touch, which Cool did as the fleet outfielder from Arkansas, leading off for St. Louis over the Cardinals' championship stretch and beyond, led the National League in steals eight times, breaking Wills's record with 118 of them in 1974. "Over the years," Brock would later say, "I learned more about stealing bases from talking with him than with anyone else."

Although he lived just over a mile from the stadium, Bell's visits there were less frequent after Brock's arrival. Discretionary walking was discouraged by the crippling arthritis in his left hip and leg. Clara, watching him struggle up from his favorite chair and set out haltingly across the room, would shake her head and say, "There he goes, the fastest mouse in Mex-ee-co."

But he managed to make it to work every evening, where he was more of an honoree than a security officer. It was he whom the vagrants would ask to open the door and let them in on cold winter nights, and it was they who broke his heart when he had to say he was sorry. In warmer weather he sat by the big window above the lobby and listened to Cardinals games—Brock, Gibson, Flood, Cepeda, Javier. . . .

His gun, however, came in handy at home. The neighborhood was now in rapid decline, and he kept the weapon in his robe. His nephew, Ken Webb, remembered visiting one day and Uncle Bell's pistol falling out of his pocket and clattering on the floor as he unlocked and opened the door.

It should be pointed out that Ken Webb, the son of Clara's sister, is no relation to Tweed Webb, Cool's best friend and most frequent visitor in those years. Tweed made his living as a sign painter and his reputation as an unceasing advocate for African American baseball. For decades he was instrumental in the operation of the Tandy League—he was, in fact, known as Mr. Tandy—a semipro St. Louis circuit that turned out numerous Negro Leaguers and linked Webb to such future *big* leaguers as Sam Jethroe, Luke Easter, Nate Colbert, and Elston Howard. Unable to get his fill of the game, he was also a longtime baseball columnist for the weekly *St. Louis Argus* and the foremost living authority on the Negro Leagues, with the scorebooks, scrapbooks, and memories to confirm it. In a front window of his home on Enright Avenue, there was a sign—painted by the owner, no doubt—identifying the place as the Tweed Webb Library. "Tweed Webb," declared Bob Burnes, venerable sports editor of the *St. Louis Globe-Democrat*, "has done more in bringing recognition to the black player than anyone else."

Webb's real name was Normal, the nickname deriving from his affinity for being nicely turned out. It was one of several organic commonalities he shared with Cool Papa, going back to when Webb was a pint-sized shortstop whose local team, the St. Louis Black Sox, managed by his father, took its lumps from the Bell-laden Compton Hill Cubs.

Tweed, like Cool, was a deep-seated Rube Foster man. When he was twelve, he'd been hired by the Negro League father figure as the batboy—at the time, they called it a mascot—for Foster's Chicago American Giants when they took on the St. Louis Giants at Kuebler's Park.

This was 1917, when the Negro National League was three years away and James Nichols was still back in Oktibbeha County, getting his baseball education under the pecan tree from Cousin Dave. Normal's father brought him often and usually early to the Giants' park because the first kid there could be the one to stand on the platform by the right-field scoreboard and put up the numbers every half inning. Folks at Kuebler's came to know the little fellow, and that included

Rube Foster, who one day asked Normal if he'd like to make twenty-five cents helping the Chicago side with its bats and whatnot.

It became a semi-regular gig for a few years, wherein young Webb, while tending to the visitors' equipment needs, was incidentally schooled by Foster in such important studies as gentlemanly dressing, applications of bunting, and the strategic powers of a corncob pipe. He was, consequently, on the scene when the Negro Leagues were conceived, and remained ever after in their closest negotiable proximity.

A slick fielder himself, Tweed actually played in 1926 for an associate Negro National League team out of Fort Wayne, Indiana. "I was five-foot-three, 140 pounds, little bitty guy, but I stood ten feet tall," he told Jay Feldman for the *Baseball Research Journal*. "Littlest man out there, with the biggest mouth. I was a hustler. But to tell the truth, I didn't like that life. Bad traveling conditions, bad accommodations. The professional players were a rough bunch. I didn't drink or smoke,

Tweed Webb, Bell's best friend over the second half of his life, was a mite of a young shortstop but a giant among Negro League historians.

and I didn't like the women that hung around the players. And the pay was low, twenty-five dollars a week."

The modest wages helped him see the merits of painting signs for grocery stores. Sign painting, on the other hand, couldn't keep him away from baseball. Nor could raising eight kids. In 1932, the year after Bell left the St. Louis Stars, Webb became their official scorekeeper, then parlayed that position into his chattery "Hot Stove League" column, which endured until 1971.

Through its latter years, a fair amount of his material resembled recent conversation in Cool Papa's living room. There was always something to get them started: another shutout from Bob Gibson, a baseball signed by Josh Gibson, the ground covered by Curt Flood, a Mule Suttles story, things Satchel said, the season Hank Aaron was having, the contents of Rube Foster's pockets, one of Cool's scrapbooks, or one of Tweed's.

Visits with Bell were recurring reminders to Tweed of his mission. Everything in that house—the mementos, the humor, the struggle, the dialogue, the dignity—and certainly the encroaching decay outside it impressed upon him that his beloved Negro Leagues weren't getting their due. Proper homage was not being paid to either the institution or its neglected representatives. History was being defrauded.

He wrote about it passionately, to negligible avail. The little painter dreamt of a day when Rube Foster, Satchel Paige, Josh Gibson, and his dear pal Cool Papa would take their rightful places in the literature and pantheon of the game, followed by no shortage of others.

From time to time a progressive columnist at one of the metropolitan dailies, such as Shirley Povich of the *Washington Post*, would take up the cause, pointing out the absurdity that was the absence of Negro Leaguers in the Hall of Fame, but the leaders of the game were unmoved. And then, on July 25, 1966, Ted Williams stepped up to a microphone in Cooperstown, New York, for his Hall of Fame induction speech.

Williams was the only man elected that year, and the audience was all his. Not that his remarks would be taken casually in any scenario. The classic left-handed hitter, hero of two wars and man of conviction, had been less than voluble over his closely watched career, snapping at reporters and withholding tips of his cap to cheering fans. But he was noted, at the same time, for his considered perspective on anything pertaining to fishing or baseball. When Ted Williams spoke, people perked up.

Growing up in Southern California, the Splendid Splinter had observed and competed against Negro Leaguers in the California Winter League. He had also matched up with the original black players of the American League—although the Red Sox themselves were colorless for seventeen of his nineteen seasons with the club—and had taken a number of turns at the plate against Satchel Paige. In 1951, when the Alabama sage was forty-five and scuffling through his worst major-league season, he struck out Williams on a change of pace, so infuriating the Boston slugger that he slammed his bat on the dugout railing and broke it in two places. The bat somehow made its way to the Hall of Fame, where, fifteen years after its demolition, Teddy Ballgame solemnly stood on a memorable midsummer Sunday.

Near the end of what is roundly regarded as the greatest of Hall of Fame acceptance speeches, Williams took an unprecedented detour from his concise remarks. "I hope someday," he said, "that the names of Satchel Paige and Josh Gibson in some way could be added as a symbol of the great Negro players that are not here only because they were not given the chance."

From that day forward, there was substantially more to talk about at 3034 Dickson Street.

CHAPTER TWENTY-FIVE

THE CALL THAT CHANGED EVERYTHING

A T THE TIME OF TED WILLIAMS'S HISTORIC speech, baseball's commissioner was a retired Air Force lieutenant general named William Eckert who had not been to a ball game in more than a decade and apparently hadn't read about one, either. He was well acquainted with racquet sports, golf, and equestrian events, but he somehow missed the Dodgers' move to Los Angeles. Eckert understood that Cincinnati had a team and there was one called the Cardinals but didn't quite puzzle out the distinction. Tone-deaf and tentative, he was seemingly untouched by Williams's stirring call to action concerning Negro Leaguers and the Hall of Fame.

Eckert's inactivity, however, didn't stop Tweed Webb from researching and writing religiously about Negro Leaguers who belonged in the Hall of Fame. As a matter of course, he bounced it all off Cool Papa Bell, and there was no ambiguity, nor dissent, in the central dialogue. Of his own accord—it's preposterous to think that Bell would solicit or even discuss such a thing—Webb would do all he could to get his friend to Cooperstown on some distant, dreamy day, but first things first: Rube Foster.

Cool was the choir Tweed preached to. They both knew that if the Hall ever set its cap for a Negro Leaguer, all eyes would be on Satchel Paige. For starters, Paige had been legitimized by his major-league adventure. And for more than a generation, in patented, legendary style, he'd been the face, mouth, superstar, epitome, and caricature of blackball. To the nostalgic old-timers on Dickson Street, the official immortalization of Satchel, should it occur, was intuitive and fine so long as it wasn't *final*, in terms of Negro Leaguers. So long as it wasn't conferred at Rube Foster's expense.

Paige, as it happened, showed up at Cool Papa's door from time to time. They'd also caught up with each other in September 1965, when Satch was invited by Charlie Finley, owner and barker of the downtrodden Kansas City Athletics, to sign a one-day contract, pitch a little, and become the oldest fellow—it was a couple of months past his fifty-ninth birthday—to ever do so in the major leagues.

Paige lived in Kansas City with his family and a bluetick hound. There he tinkered with his cars and musical instruments—the ukulele and bongo drums were put to good use—and when dinner was being made, he'd repair to the kitchen, beat a pot with a spoon, and get the children to fill out the rhythm. Baseball friends came over to the rambling house for dominoes. His wife, Lahoma, would accompany him fishing in his flashy boat, throw out a line on a cane pole, sing to the fish, and fill the bucket while Satch would set up a column of high-tech rods, reel them in empty, and grumble that something was wrong.

In a purposely peripatetic career, Paige had played longer for the Kansas City Monarchs than any other team. He was an icon in that city, which Finley translated as gate attraction. To embellish the cameo appearance, the controversial owner encouraged Satch to bring along a few old Negro League cronies. Bell was delighted to join Buck O'Neil, Hilton Smith, and Bullet Joe Rogan for pregame showmanship, a matter of sitting with Satchel while a nurse rubbed liniment into his bony pitching arm and he poured them coffee from a rocking chair.

The crowd of roughly 9,300 might not sound like much but for the fact that the A's had drawn only 690 souls two nights before. The curious fans got more than they bargained for. Paige started the game and pitched three remarkable, scoreless innings against the Boston Red Sox, flaunting his famous hesitation pitch and surrendering but one hit, a double by Carl Yastrzemski.

Satch remarked later that the affair had particularly tickled Cool Papa. Bell seemed to thrive in settings of Negro League fellowship, a commodity in short supply. Three months later, attending Branch Rickey's funeral in St. Louis, he expected he might fall in warmly with former colleagues paying their respects to the architect of baseball's desegregation, but the only other Negro Leaguers on the scene were Jackie Robinson (one and done in 1945) and Cool's contemporary, Frank Duncan.

Bell's funeral going was restricted by his lack of a driver's license or car—by this time his fading eyesight, impaired by glaucoma, might have made it a moot point anyway—but he felt duty-bound and kindly disposed toward memorial services, and sorry when he missed one within his baseball circles. A former catcher named Nish Williams died in 1968 in Atlanta, where he ran a restaurant at which blackballers gathered, and Cool was still thinking of him two years later when Williams's stepson, Donn Clendenon, put together a strong season for the New York Mets. Bell was moved to phone Clendenon with his congratulations and an emotional apology for missing Nish's funeral. Clendenon returned the courtesy by inviting Cool Papa to the Mets' clubhouse, where folklore's fastest player soaked in the big-league atmosphere and enchanted the defending world champs with tales from another time.

They were memories that he was loath to lose—for blackball's sake as much as his own. Fortunately, Tweed Webb, with his mobile archives and Hall of Fame campaigns, wasn't about to let that happen. And every month or so, it was story time when Double Duty Radcliffe and Lester Lockett, an old Birmingham Baron, motored down from Chicago and stayed the night, making sure to check out the suits that hung in the guest room where they slept upstairs.

All the while, as he flipped through the pages of his precious past, it was important to Bell that he also mingle with assimilated modern baseball, which he held sacred. To that end he enjoyed the company of

Bob Broeg, the longtime, bow-tied sports editor and columnist for the *St. Louis Post-Dispatch*—soon to assume a spot on the Hall of Fame's board of directors—who occasionally joined Cool and Tweed at their spontaneous Dickson Street baseball conferences. But Bell's escort at Busch Stadium was most often the Cardinal idol and harmonica buff, Stan the Man (the famous nickname was Broeg's doing) Musial. In sweetness, Musial was the Cool Papa Bell of organized ball.

Busch was relocated downtown, out of reasonable walking range from Cool Papa's house, in 1966, the year before the Gateway Arch opened on the St. Louis riverfront. Bell's night schedule also limited the number of Cardinal games he could attend, but he filled the void happily by working with youngsters at the Mathews-Dickey Boys' Club. One of them, a strapping athlete named Nate Colbert, matured into a three-time National League all-star, the San Diego Padres' first and foremost power hitter, twice clubbing thirty-eight home runs and in 1972 tying a record—set by Musial in 1954—with five homers in a doubleheader. Eight years old at the time, Colbert had been at Busch Stadium with his father on the day Stan the Man did the deed.

"He was helpful in pushing Nate Colbert along," said the club's cofounder Martin Mathews of Cool Papa. "He was always willing to do something for somebody. He was a person you could trust. He never complained. He was denied a lot of things in his life, but he didn't complain."

That was Clara's department. She was indignant that her humble man was denied the credit and dollars he deserved over a lifetime well played. And when, in the privacy of home, he softly groused about the objects of his ointments and salves—the aches in his knees and the itching of his skin—she groused about his grousing. Then they giggled.

Baseball broadcaster George Grande had occasion to be in St. Louis in the late sixties and was advised by Roy Campanella that he should go see Cool and Clara while he was there. He was entertained. "They were like a comedy act," he recalled. "He'd say, 'Well, I got to go to work,' and she'd say, 'What do you mean? You never worked a day in your life.' She would hold him to the fire."

Bell's working days were truly over in 1970, when he retired from City Hall. Life became decidedly more sedentary at that point, a far cry from his days of blistering base circling and folkloric fly chasing. Clara Belle rarely left the house, nestling in the comfort of the French Provincial couch under the brass-framed mirror, and Cool would pass hours sitting in the reclining chair that City Hall gave him for his retirement, a shotgun in his lap, listening to ball games and watching Dickson Street crumble around him. One particular evening, with no game going on, he was tuned into a local sports talk show when a caller asked the host if he'd ever seen a player score from first base on a sacrifice bunt. The host said no, that couldn't be done. Cool Papa dialed the number and informed the gentleman that, yes, it could, because he had done it.

Behind his Dickson Street house in his old St. Louis Stars getup, ready to lay one down.

It was a satisfactory existence. There was no money for indulgence or travel, but no lament along those lines—at least, from Cool—because there were *people*. Now and then Bell paid a visit to a brother over by old Stars Park. He kept in touch with Brock and Musial and the citizenry of Busch Stadium. There was always a kid to counsel at the boys club. He saw a little of Broeg, who called him Jim, and a lot of Tweed. His nephew, Ken Webb, also came by frequently, on one occasion bearing deceased furry mammals.

"I'd gone hunting with a bunch of older men early in the morning, around four-thirty or five. The sun wasn't up yet," Webb remembered, "and as I was getting out of the car I heard a noise, a couple sounds, and saw something in a tree. I took my shotgun and aimed between two sounds and with one shot I brought down two coons. I didn't know what to do with them, because we were rabbit hunting. They weren't dead yet, so I had to shoot them with a pistol. Then I brought them home and showed them to Uncle Bell and he was excited as he could be.

"I can still see Cool Papa Bell in his kitchen cooking coons, that tall guy with a long apron hanging from his neck."

BOWIE KUHN, A seasoned, deep-voiced attorney for the National League, replaced General Eckert as commissioner in 1969 and by 1971 had persuaded the Hall of Fame to appoint a committee that would select a few former Negro Leaguers to be recognized in its shrine. Ted Williams had been heard but not really understood.

"It hit a little note," Williams told Bob Costas in a subsequent television interview, "and they came out with, I have to say, a half-assed program for the black players to get into the Hall of Fame."

The plan called for the ten-man committee, which included five former Negro Leaguers—Campanella, Judy Johnson, Bill Yancey, Frank Forbes, and chairman Monte Irvin—to meet every year for the purpose of choosing at least one blackballer to be "part of a new exhibit commemorating the contributions of the Negro Leagues to baseball."

In other words, the Negro Leaguers would not be actual Hall of Famers. They would not be honored like Rogers Hornsby, Babe Ruth, Bob Feller, and Ted Williams in the gallery of plaques but acknowledged, exhibit-like, as personalities of interest. A sideshow. Separate, not equal. Restricted to the colored-only section.

The pretext for that cockamamie scheme—some referred to it as a compromise—was the traditional Hall of Fame criterion that a player required ten years of major-league service to be eligible for induction. "I wouldn't call it a compromise," said Kuhn, as reported by Joseph Durso in the *New York Times*. "The rules for the Hall of Fame are very strict, and through no fault of their own these stars of the Negro Leagues didn't have major-league exposure.

"The Hall of Fame is not segregated. The two greatest Negro stars eligible [Jackie Robinson and Campanella] are already there, and they will soon be joined by the Willie Mayses, Henry Aarons, Ernie Bankses and other major leaguers. Guys like Lefty O'Doul, who hit .349, can't get into the Hall of Fame because he played only nine years in the major leagues."

Plenty of people were having none of that, including Satchel Paige—even after Satchel was the only man selected by the committee in its initial meeting. (Durso had noted him, Josh Gibson, and Bell as potential honorees.)

"I was just as good as the white boys," Paige stated flatly. "I ain't going in the back door to the Hall of Fame."

Before the formal induction that summer, the Hall had reconsidered its position, deciding that ten years of major-league service was perhaps not an appropriate standard for players to whom the major leagues, like a St. Louis lunch counter, did not offer service. Satch was properly enshrined with the class of 1971.

The following year the committee anointed both Gibson and Buck Leonard. In 1973, committee chair Monte Irvin, twenty-seven years removed from the Negro League batting title that Bell gifted him, became a Hall of Famer.

And on a refreshingly warm Wednesday in February 1974, the telephone rang at 3034 Dickson Street with a call from New York. It was Joe Reichler of the commissioner's office, breaking the glorious news to Cool Papa that he was invited to Cooperstown in August for official entry into the pantheon of baseball's greatest players.

"Yeah, that's okay," replied Bell.

Reichler paused. He had never received such a tepid response to his message from on high, and was compelled to clarify. "You don't understand. . . ."

From the couch, Clara Belle heard her husband say, "Yes, I do. I knew it was going to come eventually."

BELL UNDERSTOOD, ALSO, that things would be different thereafter. His cover of obscurity was blown. No more tranquil anonymity. And that, too, was okay.

Sports Illustrated, anticipating his selection, had been to the house in late 1973, meeting Tweed and Clara. Webb was so certain about the call from the Hall that he was already reveling in the prospect, as the *SI* story described:

> "Can't believe it," says Tweed. "Can you, Papa? Papa Bell in the Hall
> of Fame. The fastest man who ever played the game."
>
> "Ain't happened yet," cautions Papa, adjusting his tall and
> lean figure in his chair.
>
> "Tell me, Papa," says Tweed. "How's it goin' to feel? The Hall
> of Fame . . . mmm, mmm."
>
> "Knew a fella blowed the horn once," says Papa. "He told me,
> he say, 'Ya got to take the gigs as they come.'"

Mainstream local media, longtime confederates in Bell's privacy, now played their parts in his unveiling, as did publications aimed at African American markets. Oral historians acquired an interest in Cool Papa. Baseball historians came knocking. He was on Joe Garagiola's NBC baseball show, along with Paige and Tweed. He overdressed many times for radio.

In April, *Black Sports* magazine paid Papa's way to Atlanta to see Hank Aaron break Babe Ruth's career record for home runs. It was the kind of occasion—an incidental tribute to integration—that he would have attended anyway if he'd had the funds. There was even a Negro League connection. In 1952, Aaron, eighteen at the time, had received a signing bonus of two shirts, plus a suit for his father, to join the Indianapolis Clowns, with whom he remained for half a season, playing shortstop, batting cross-handed, and listening to Josh Gibson stories. The Boston Braves purchased his contract in June. The bonus that time was a cardboard suitcase to put the shirts in.

Tracking Aaron's pursuit of Ruth, Bell of course thought often of Gibson, although Mule Suttles and especially Turkey Stearnes were closer matches. Like Aaron, Stearnes was a long-lasting, unflagging, understated home run hitter whose lifetime totals testified to that prolific consistency. As opposed to the popular presumption, Cool Papa suspected that it had been Stearnes, not Gibson, who piled up the most home runs among all Negro Leaguers.

But the Aaron comparisons didn't apply only to power hitters. "You know," Bell told the magazine, "he reminds me of myself. They used to call me Cool, you know, and he's the same way. The same type of temperament. What he do, he do it and that's all. He don't seem like he might be doing much. That's the way I played ball."

By summer, Bell's preoccupation was Cooperstown. A St. Louis contingent of black businessmen was making arrangements to be there for Cool's crowning moment, allowing extra room in the budget to cover expenses for Tweed Webb and friends. Tweed would be honored the following year with a tribute in the *Congressional Record*, but he would still refer to Cool Papa's induction as the highlight of his career, even if it wasn't Rube Foster's. Webb's party would join Bell's on a bus to upstate New York.

In the meantime Cool Papa's preparation revolved around his ensembles, as usual, and of all things his handwriting. Between arthritis and fuzzy eyesight, he felt that autographing a baseball or even a piece of paper—a rite of Cooperstown—was an exercise that didn't become him. What's more, an unrefined signature, he thought, didn't embarrass just him but the Negro Leagues altogether. So he sat at the kitchen table with a spiral notebook and practiced. *James "Cool Papa" Bell.* Filled the whole book, two columns a page, front and back.

Any remaining anxieties would be relieved, theoretically, with an orientation visit to the Hall of Fame that Cool took as the main event drew near. It didn't unfold exactly as he imagined. "Upon returning," reported relative Ken Webb, "Bell indicated they were walking around to acquaint him with Cooperstown, were on the first level, and he started ascending the stairs. When they reached the second level, he overheard one of the attendants saying to somebody, 'Don't worry about it. I guess it's a day for the niggers.'

"When he got back, we were all talking about it. He was supposed to appear on the radio in St. Louis, and the broadcaster told him he shouldn't mention what happened. He was really hit hard by that incident. I strongly suggested that he should say something about it in his public appearances, but he felt that it might hurt the chances of other blacks being nominated into the Hall of Fame."

Instead, he talked about Lou Brock. Like most of the greater baseball community, Cool Papa was watching closely as Brock, at age thirty-four, having won seven of the previous eight stolen base titles in the National League, took off running that year as never before, bearing down on Maury Wills's single-season record for steals. A column by Bob Broeg in the *Sporting News* examined how Brock's thieving prowess and durability derived in large part from his use of the pop-up slide, which was not a style passed along by Bell but reflected an emphasis on sliding technique that the old tricky baller had underscored since their first meeting. The Cardinals' dynamic left fielder was in range of the record when Cool Papa packed his finery and set off to be formally immortalized.

"He talked a lot about preparing for Cooperstown," said Ken Webb. "He'd go to one of the better men's fashion stores and get ties and things together. Bell was always very debonair, very up-to-date, very well-organized.

"He had his own travel arrangements, and on our way to Cooperstown my daughter and I ran into him in Utica. He told us his luggage had not arrived. The mayor of Cooperstown picked him up in Utica and took him to a tailor in Cooperstown to get more clothes."

Yankee pals Mickey Mantle and Whitey Ford were also inducted that year, along with umpire Jocko Conlan, who couldn't understand why Oscar Charleston, Bullet Joe Rogan, and Rube Foster hadn't yet been enshrined. Bell showed up at the pre-ceremony press conference wearing a gold bow tie that matched his gold teeth. Bowie Kuhn introduced him as "the fastest man ever to play the game." Since nobody asked about Willie Wells or Turkey Stearnes, Cool Papa talked about Brock.

The luggage having finally arrived, he reprised the gold theme for the festivities on the lawn: tan suit, gold shirt, gold, blue, lavender tie. "I'm standing here now to receive the greatest honor a ballplayer can receive," Bell told the world in a self-abnegating acceptance speech. "But if it hadn't been for the equal opportunity and the concern and the kindness of the commissioner and great research by many writers, my baseball career would have been in vain."

He thanked the committee and the Hall of Fame for allowing him to "smell the roses while yet living" but neglected to mention Ted Williams, whom he later recognized "for starting it all with his kind words." He acknowledged Tweed, Broeg, and some of the St. Louis businessmen, but forgot Clara Belle, which prompted him later to ask Kuhn if he would apologize for him at next year's ceremony.

Other than that, James Bell was cool indeed in front of the Cooperstown crowd. Paige, Musial, Gibson, Dean, DiMaggio—he knew he belonged in those galleries, and knew, unreservedly, that so did plenty more from his time and circumstances. To Cool Papa, the Hall of Fame was home, not to be confused with heaven.

"It's the biggest honor I've ever gotten," he often said of his induction, "but it's not the biggest thrill. The biggest thrill was when they opened the doors to the major leagues."

CHAPTER TWENTY-SIX

COOL PAPA BELL AVENUE

I T WOULD TAKE COOL PAPA THE REST OF HIS LIFE, and then some, to complete his victory lap.

First on the agenda was Lou Brock's big day. The fleet Cardinal, whose acquisition ten years earlier had been precipitated by the retirement of Stan Musial and the club's subsequent need for a left fielder, swiped second base twice on the evening of September 10, 1974, tying and breaking Maury Wills's record. Upon the latter, the Cards and Philadelphia Phillies stopped what they were doing so that the historic feat—and Brock's historic feet—could be properly observed. Bell, still in his first month as a Hall of Famer, made his way carefully to the Busch Stadium infield and presented the man of the hour with the corresponding prop.

"We decided to give him his 105th base," he told the appreciative audience, "because if we didn't, he was going to steal it anyway."

It was a moment that, among other things, validated a decision Cool Papa made before he got to Cooperstown. When a player enters the Hall of Fame, he does so representing the "primary team" with which he is, or elects to be, most closely associated. In Bell's case an argument could have been made for the St. Louis Stars, the Pittsburgh Crawfords, or to a lesser extent the Homestead Grays, all of which prospered famously when he flashed their colors. He chose St. Louis, where he started as a player and remained as a citizen.

At that point, roughly, St. Louis chose to associate with him as well. His relationships with Brock, Musial, and Broeg helped a little in that regard. Noted sportscaster Bob Costas, his career getting started at KMOX Radio in St. Louis, cultivated a relationship with the old center fielder and included Dickson Street on his rounds. Broeg's counterpart at the *St. Louis Globe-Democrat*, Bob Burnes, was an admirer of both the Negro Leagues and Cool Papa, whom he had watched play in the 1930s, and over the years he was impressed equally by two of Bell's special attributes: his locomotion, of course, and his "quiet dignity."

In 1975 the James "Cool Papa" Bell Baseball League opened at Fairground Park in St. Louis. Cool's adopted hometown marked the center of his retirement world, but certainly not the circumference. In short order he was named to the Missouri Sports Hall Fame, another in Pittsburgh, and another in New York City—everywhere, it seemed, but Mississippi, from which he was the only delegate to Cooperstown.

Traveling without Clara—the second time their home was broken into while they were away, they decided that one of them should always stay put—Bell joined Satchel Paige and Musial for an event in New Orleans. He signed autographs in Las Vegas. Walking with a cane now and wearing a bow tie as usual, he was honored in Chicago for contributions to baseball, sportsmanship, and community. "People look at me now and say, 'There goes a Hall of Famer,'" he told the Chicago crowd. "I prefer them calling me a child of God."

In 1979, Cool met Negro League friends in Ashland, Kentucky, to celebrate the birthday of Clint "Hawk" Thomas, an outstanding former outfielder who once homered against Fidel Castro in Cuba. The gathering included Buck Leonard, Monte Irvin, Buck O'Neil, Turkey Stearnes, Ray Dandridge, and Judy Johnson, who reminisced about the year he batted .392 and earned a $10 raise. Before it was over, the gray-haired gentlemen had decided to do it again the next year,

referring to the event as a Negro League reunion. In the third iteration Bell and Paige were honored, and in front of his peers Cool Papa
pronounced the official version of the light switch story (described
in chapter thirteen).

Willie Mays, Hank Aaron, Bob Feller, former Newark owner Effa
Manley, and former commissioner Happy Chandler, among distinguished others, ultimately found their way to Ashland. A short-lived
attempt was even made to establish a Negro League Hall of Fame in
the stately house where they met, to which cause Papa donated an
old, beaten-up pair of his baseball shoes.

All the while, after first manufacturing a pile of signatures and
cutting them out to hand to autograph seekers—thereby avoiding the
humiliation of struggling spontaneously with a ball and pen—Bell
trekked every summer to Cooperstown for the Hall of Fame induction
weekend. He became a familiar figure at the Otesaga Hotel, settled into
a comfortable lobby chair, chatting warmly with whoever approached.
He was on hand for Judy Johnson's enshrinement in 1975, Oscar
Charleston's in 1976, and those of two old foes in 1977, Pop Lloyd and
Martín Dihigo.

At that point the Negro League committee was disbanded and the
selection of blackballers turned over to the Hall of Fame's Veterans
Committee. It troubled Cool Papa when, under the new format, no
Negro Leaguers were named in 1978. The election of Willie Mays in
1979—which no doubt would soon be followed by that of Aaron, Banks,
and others from the major leagues' spectacular second wave of African
American superstars—made him wonder if the door had been quietly
shut on the rest of his exceptional contemporaries.

Then, in 1981, the veterans committee showed its mettle and
Rube Foster was at last admitted to the Hall. Bell was doubly gratified,
thankful on behalf of the man who had fathered and defined the Negro
Leagues and also of the fellow, his own best buddy, whose relentless
stumping had won the day. Cool and Tweed had much to celebrate on
Dickson Street. There might have been some pent-up venting as well.

In his interview with Jay Feldman for SABR's *Baseball Research
Journal*, Webb offered up a sample of the latter. "Everybody talks

about how I campaigned for Cool Papa Bell and Rube Foster for the Hall of Fame," he said, "but I shouldn't have *had* to campaign for Rube Foster; he should have been the first. There wasn't anybody did more for black baseball than Rube Foster. And they waited until 1981 to put him in. That was nothing but a joke."

For Bell, nevertheless, Foster's induction added a layer of snugness to those easy chairs at the Otesaga. Papa loved Cooperstown, and now he could feel good about it—the feel of reparations received after all those hardscrabble decades of dismissal; of a collegial, inclusive community after a monochrome career of division. His eyes twinkled under his thick glasses when Ernie Banks walked him out to the rocking chairs on the back porch or when Stan Musial introduced him to the likes of Pee Wee Reese and Yogi Berra.

"Stan was almost like his receptionist," recalled sportscaster George Grande, for many years the Hall of Fame's master of ceremonies. "Stan Musial loved Cool Papa."

It was a popular sentiment. Grande would play word association with Buck O'Neil, "and I'd say 'Cool Papa' and a big smile would come to Buck's face, his eyes would well up, and he'd say, 'Yes, he had the greatest speed, but also the biggest heart. He was the most gentle man I knew from the Negro Leagues.'"

Bell's gentility, however, and especially his Cooperstown bonhomie, ought not have been confused with total contentment. It ate at him, even after Foster was given his due, that Willie Wells was not sitting in the next easy chair and Turkey Stearnes hadn't had the pleasure before he died in 1979. Cool, in fact, would have given up *his* chair for either. Of course, he had no way of knowing that both would be inducted after he was gone: Wells in 1997 and Stearnes in 2000.

"Turkey Stearnes," he said more than once in those days, "is the man who should be in the Hall of Fame. If he isn't in, no one should be in. Take me out and put Turkey in."

In Wells's biography, written by Bob Luke, there's an account of a phone call Cool Papa made, on the occasion of his old friend's death in 1989, to the daughter of the greatest shortstop he ever saw. "Stella," Bell said, "this is Cool Papa Bell. I remember you as a baby and I am going to make them take me out of the Hall of Fame and put your daddy in." She told the story during the Hall of Fame speech she made on her father's behalf.

"I said, 'Oh no, no, no, don't do that. Because he wouldn't want you to do that and I wouldn't, either.'

"And he said to me, 'Well, okay, but I'm just letting you know, I'll do that.'"

HALL OF FAMERS from the Negro Leagues were invited to the White House in 1981, but Bell found it necessary to cancel his trip due to shortness of breath, equilibrium issues, nerve troubles, itching all over, and not feeling too well. A short while later he did make it to Hollywood, sporting a sharp bow tie, for the premiere of the TV movie *Don't Look Back: The Story of Leroy "Satchel" Paige*, with Lou Gossett as Paige and Clifton Davis playing Cool Papa. He caught up with President Reagan the following year when the chief executive, with soft spots for kids and baseball, came to St. Louis and dropped by the fast-growing, good-doing Mathews-Dickey Boys' Club, whose teams were named for African tribes.

With no presidents or movie stars involved, St. Louis aldermen took it upon themselves in early 1983 to officially change the name of Dickson Street. It would henceforth be known as James "Cool Papa" Bell Avenue.

The turf in question, about a mile north of old Stars Park, was a stretch of five blocks of vacant lots, peeling paint, window bars, corner drug deals, and occasional dead bodies found in front of houses like James and Clara Belle's. A man was shot in the head on Cool Papa's block. A woman was raped outside his front door. When the weather warmed up that year and two locals took up an argument farther down the avenue, one pulled a rifle out of his gym bag and blasted the other four times in the chest. (Through all of that somehow Cool maintained his tranquility. A friend reported that once, when Bell phoned him, he could hear Brahms's Symphony no. 4 playing in the background.)

The recognition of one of their own was not lost on the neighbors. It encouraged a community revitalization project in which trees were planted and houses painted along those five blighted blocks, culminating in a day of music, softball, and magic tricks. Among the dignitaries in attendance were Musial, Brock, Broeg, and Cool's activist nephew, Norman Seay, in whose name a new park would open nearby. The civic improvements were all Bell needed out of the whole affair . . . well, that and one of the James "Cool Papa" Bell Avenue banners that hung over the street. It went into his living room, where the pictures of Kennedy, Jesus, and Martin Luther King had now been joined by one of Cool and Bowie Kuhn in Cooperstown, which sat on the television alongside a model of Bell's Hall of Fame plaque. (Another benefit of having his name on the avenue: letters addressed simply to Cool Papa Bell, St. Louis, Mo., would find their way to his mailbox.)

A few months after the street was rechristened, Cool Papa was the guest of honor at a luncheon thrown by the Cardinals at Busch Stadium. Stan Musial then escorted him onto the field to lob a ceremonial pitch that marked the start of construction for a compact lighted ballpark to be built by Mathews-Dickey. Neighborhood kids would play the game at Cool Papa Bell Stadium.

Come midsummer, Bell found himself at a much roomier, quite familiar stadium. Comiskey Park was hosting the 1983 all-star game, fifty years after the very first one had been staged there. Of course, the old Chicago site had also been the setting, the same year, for the Negro League's inaugural East-West extravaganza, starring Mule Suttles.

As part of the anniversary celebration, an old-timers' exhibition was scheduled for the day before the main event. It featured the likes of Joe DiMaggio, Warren Spahn, Bob Feller, Brooks Robinson, Ernie Banks, and Billy Williams (who would club a sizable home run). Veterans of the East-West game were too old to take part—Bell was now eighty-one—but as the show was about to begin, three of its most exemplary alums strode in unison to the home plate area. From there Willie Wells proceeded on to the mound to throw out the first pitch. Standing arm in arm, Judy Johnson and Cool Papa Bell held back and soaked in the scene.

Imagine their thoughts at that moment. Their pride.

Buck Leonard, with whom Papa still exchanged Christmas cards, was also on hand, and a photo taken that day shows him and Johnson both outfitted in the full uniform of the Homestead Grays. Wells wore a sweater and a porkpie hat, and Bell, the tallest of the lot, a plaid sport coat, white tie, and Grays cap; he'd recently sold the rest of his Homestead uniform to a collector for $2,000.

As fellow Hall of Famers bustled about, Cool Papa watched the old-timers' game from a folding chair in front of the dugout, responding to autograph requests by handing out pre-signed cards and apologizing that his eyesight prevented him from complying in the moment.

Proud old buddies were special guests at Comiskey Park for the fifty-year anniversary of both the major-league all-star game and the Negro Leagues' East-West showcase. Left to right: Buck Leonard, Judy Johnson, Willie Wells, Cool Papa.

BELL HAD COME late and reluctantly to the memorabilia trade. He preferred to keep his keepsakes or give them away. Clara, who stashed various small treasures behind a brick wall in a hidden compartment that was discovered years after they were both gone, rarely agreed with the latter practice. She distrusted most of the dealers who came around.

Others, like Barry Krizan and Dave Jackson, became welcome guests, though not immediately. Their initial visit had been encouraged by a mutual friend, Lou Dials, a former Negro Leaguer with whom Bell had frequently traveled to Mexico—not to be confused with Lewis Dial, the *New York Age* columnist (after baseball, Lou Dials worked as an electrician for the Lockheed Aircraft Corporation)—and while that connection was enough for Bell, it didn't take the edge off *Mrs.* Bell.

For the most part, Clara kept her distance from Cool's baseball company. Larry Lester, a leading Negro Leagues authority and author, made numerous visits to the house on Cool Papa Bell Avenue and periodically heard Bell's feisty wife but never laid eyes on her. She was holed up in the bedroom. But if a purveyor of memorabilia dropped by, even a keen collector, she was on the scene.

"When we came to the door the first time, Clara was very protective of him," Krizan recalled. "She was leery of him being taken advantage of and was pretty well snippy with us the whole time. She just stared at us. After an hour or so we asked Mr. Bell if it would be okay if we came again, and he said, 'That would be nice, boys.' We said, 'Mrs. Bell, can we bring anything?' Her response was sarcastic. She said, 'Quail on toast.'

"Dave had noticed Mr. Bell drinking 7 Up and eating bananas, so we knocked on the door a month later—we always called before we came over—gave Mr. Bell some 7 Up and bananas, handed Mrs. Bell a couple frozen quail and pheasant and a loaf of bread, and said, 'Ma'am, you'll have to make your own toast.' She said, 'I've never even eaten quail!'

"Later, Dave's wife would make little Cornish hens and we'd bring them over. When they found out we had access to rabbit—a friend of mine had a game farm in Illinois and would have the rabbits cleaned and frozen for us—they were happy to see us. They would put the rabbits in coffee cans to keep them frozen, because you never know when you might have a special guest for dinner—maybe Lester Lockett or Double Duty Radcliffe." It no doubt reminded Cool of those delicious days in Mississippi when he disobeyed his mother by sneaking out to go rabbit hunting with her no-good brother.

The relationship prospered, and the Bells prospered by it. Cool had been offered a thousand dollars for a baseball of his that Josh Gibson and other Negro Leaguers had autographed, and when he finally decided to sell it—he might have been emboldened when he heard that a memorabilia dealer collected $1,500 for a contract signed in Cuba by a certain James Bell—he asked his collector friends to see what they could do. They found an auction house in New York that purchased it for nearly $8,000 and waived its commission, instead sending along two bats for Cool Papa to sign. By then Clara Belle was so appeased that she urged Krizan and Jackson to share in the proceeds, which they declined to do. They did, however, agree to handle the cashing of the check, for which they enlisted Broeg and a police captain to accompany them to the bank as witnesses.

"We became really close," said Krizan. "Clara was gruff on the outside, but once you got to know her, she was a real sweetheart, a kind and loving person. We always got a hug when we left. I've still got a cloth valentine she gave us once on Valentine's Day. I think more about them as a pair than I do about Mr. Bell. Sometimes we'd split up and one of us would talk to Mr. Bell, the other to Mrs. Bell, and then we'd change over. We'd do odd jobs when we were there. I don't know how many times Dave relit their pilot light. He also called the power company about a problem, and when he was told there were a lot of James Bells in the phone book, Mr. Bell responded in the background, 'But there's only one Cool Papa.' Dave's sister-in-law did their income tax, and she had Mr. Bell declared legally blind."

The taxes weren't complicated. Between them, the Bells received $275 a month from Social Security. For a time, Major League Baseball sent Cool Papa $500 a month for assistance, then had it reclassified as a gift. It was enough that they—at least he—didn't feel indigent. When he was handed a personal check for $300 by Willie McGee, the Cardinals' speedy center fielder and National League MVP when St. Louis won the pennant in 1985, Cool thanked him and handed it back, insisting he didn't need it.

That year a *Post-Dispatch* reporter visiting the house on Cool Papa Bell Avenue, taking note of its modesty and all too aware of its surroundings, remarked about the material difference it would have made for Cool if only he'd been fortunate enough to come along a little later.

"A lot of people tell me I was born too soon," Bell replied. "I wasn't born too soon. They just opened the door too late for the black ballplayer.

"What do I need money for? I got a roof over my head and I can eat whatever I want," he graciously added. (That said, he was plenty steamed that City Hall, from which he'd been retired for fifteen years, still owed him two weeks of overtime pay.) "If I found a million dollars now, I wouldn't keep it. I'd give it away to somebody who needs it."

After all, he had no children to pass it down to.

Or did he?

THE *POST-DISPATCH* INTERVIEW occurred around the time a middle-aged woman, a Pennsylvania native, became prominent in Bell's affairs. Connie Brooks referred to herself as Cool Papa's daughter, which was highly peculiar, inasmuch as there'd been no previous mention of a child in the Bell family and no record of one in census data. And yet, nobody seems to recall him contradicting her claim. Nor did he—or she—explain it.

The operative theory is that the Bells, or perhaps just Cool, adopted Brooks as an adult. She denied that to a reputable SABR historian, which only confused the situation. Either way, it was speculated that perhaps Brooks and Bell met and forged a bond at one of the Ashland reunions, where she might have accompanied her aunt, legendary Newark Eagles owner Effa Manley.

Brooks and Manley indeed were close, at least for a while. According to Jim Overmyer, Manley's biographer, Brooks was listed as Manley's next of kin by the cemetery in New Jersey where Effa's husband was buried and Effa likely would have been also if she hadn't scurried off to Los Angeles after the Negro Leagues faded away. Her relocation was evidently a sore point for Brooks, as was the custody of Manley's baseball files—which Brooks expected to inherit—being awarded to the Newark Public Library. Ultimately, there was a falling-out between them. Nevertheless, it was Brooks who, on behalf of the family, accepted Manley's Hall of Fame plaque at her 2006 induction.

At least one of Papa's friends suspected that, rather than the biological daughter of Manley's brother, Connie had been the result of a dalliance between Bell and the glamorous grande dame of blackball herself, who was somewhat well-known for the amorous interest she took in Negro Leaguers from time to time. But Overmyer found no evidence of that and it seems inconsistent with Cool Papa's character. Then again, standards for character itself can be inconsistent from circle to circle.

Effa Manley, the only woman in the Baseball Hall of Fame, co-owned the Newark Eagles with her husband, Abe, and was the aunt of the mysterious Connie Brooks, who claimed to be Cool Papa's daughter.

At any rate Brooks called him Pop, and Cool Papa—as noted by Chuck Bolton, a North Carolina college professor who, during that period, spent considerable time researching Bell's life for a prospective biography—was known to speak of her as his daughter. He appeared to tolerate and even encourage her active participation in his goings-on. Clara, however, was not so indulgent. She was suspicious of a con afoot.

Like Clara, Brooks took a wary view of memorabilia collectors and dealers. Unlike Clara, her attitude left no room for adjustment. When she questioned Jackson and Krizan, Bell interceded and smoothed it out. But when she took a more aggressive approach with opportunistic strangers, he got out of the way, willing to credit her with looking after his best interests. Third parties tended to be less willing in that regard.

It was quite apparent, however, that Cool Papa was vulnerable to those who came knocking. He invariably let them in, told them stories, showed them his scrapbooks and souvenirs and heavy flannel uniforms, and signed stuff. To put his signature on a baseball, Bell would place the pen in one unsteady hand, start with the *J* for "James," and slowly turn the ball with the other unsteady hand he until he'd completed the last *l*.

"He always had all of this memorabilia," Norman Seay said to Charles Pierce for a thoughtful article in the *National Sports Daily*. "People came from everywhere, from Timbuktu, to get autographs from Uncle Bell. It was a normal occurrence around that house."

But there was nothing normal about the visit he received in March 1990 from a dealer—actually, a dealer and his uncle—who drove seventeen hours from New Castle, Pennsylvania, to see what Bell had and leave with some of it. Robert Retort was thirty-eight, Ed Grybowski was sixty-five, Cool Papa was eighty-seven, and the session went on for three or four long days.

Slowly, methodically, memento by memento, Bell dragged out the vestiges of his thirty-year career in baseball's shadows. The dealers filled a suitcase and several boxes with rare Americana, including Cool's old uniforms from the St. Louis Stars, Kansas City Monarchs, and Trujillo All-Stars. Reportedly, some of the loot was merely swept off the kitchen table with a forearm, taking with it wedding pictures, unopened mail, and a utility bill. Bell waved as the Pennsylvanians drove away. A few days later, on the phone, he told Connie Brooks all about it.

She flew in from New York, where she lived near Chinatown, and later remarked that Bell was shaking when she got there. She called the police. The police called the FBI.

The investigation was assigned to the FBI office in Pittsburgh, where Bell had been a favorite Crawford and Gray. Retort, owner of the collectibles company R.D. Retort Enterprises, said that he paid $500 for the relics and Cool had been thankful. Cool said that he and Clara Belle had felt trapped.

The agent in charge, Bob Reutter, was a fascinated baseball fan who perceived that, over the many years, this obliging man and wonderful player had already been shorted of more than enough. For the *National* article, he told Pierce, "I did a lot of work on this out of loyalty to Cool Papa. I heard that he wasn't doing too well and I wanted to get that stuff back for him."

Reutter's determination quickened when a stroke put Bell in the hospital for a short while. Soon after, by dint of a sting operation that sent in an ostensible buyer with $40,000 in marked bills, Retort was busted trying to sell the Trujillo uniform and indicted for transporting stolen property across state lines. The FBI report charged that he had given Bell $100 for merchandise worth an estimated $300,000.

"I couldn't believe it when they said that," marveled Seay. "All that stuff he had, I thought its real value was intrinsic. It's funny—all those years growing up next door to him, I didn't realize that he was a celebrity. He was just Uncle Bell. I never realized how great he really was. You know, as an African American athlete, he never got the respect he should have. It was kind of a second-class identity for him."

The case was heard over four days in St. Louis and a mistrial declared when, owing to one dissenter, jurors were unable to reach a verdict after seven hours. A retrial was ruled out because Bell was too ill and unclear to provide a suitable deposition, and the parties eventually agreed to a settlement: All the items that could be accounted for would be returned. The estimated value was revised downward to $77,000.

That was the day before Thanksgiving in 1990. Clara Belle died in January.

Bell was able to take care of the necessary arrangements, with help from others. After the service, Bob Burnes, his friend from the *Globe-Democrat,* stopped by the house and whispered, "We lost a great one, Papa." Then, with nothing more to say, he held the old center fielder's trembling hand, knowing they were not likely to see each other again.

Cool Papa's heart gave out about six weeks later.

THE *NEW YORK Times* ran an obit. The *Post-Dispatch* placed the story of Bell's death at the top of page one. It quoted Bob Broeg, who had written of him so often and warmly:

"Cool Papa Bell was a noble man, an elegant man."

Broeg authored his own column the next day. The service was still a week away—there would be folks coming from Mississippi and elsewhere, and the former Jamie Nichols had wanted to allow them travel time—but the avuncular writer already knew one poetic detail. Papa had requested a dozen pallbearers, six black and six white.

The actual number turned out to be eight, among them Lou Brock; Roy Sievers, a St. Louisan who hit more than three hundred major-league home runs, mostly for the Washington Senators in the 1950s; and Cool's collector friends, Jackson and Krizan. In the endeavor to serve as an instrument of harmony, Bell had hoped that the *guests* would be racially balanced as well. People said they were.

The venue was Central Baptist Church, where Cool Papa, uncomfortable in crowds over his later years, had not attended in quite a while. For this final visit he wore a linen suit described as "dazzling." Cool always dressed up for funerals, and he always attended them from the heart. His reverence did not go unrequited. It was an eloquent affair.

Knowing what was just ahead, Bell had asked Ed Stack, the president of the Hall of Fame, to make an appearance at the service and perhaps say something. Stack seldom went to ballplayer funerals, but this was different. His tribute succeeded scripture, "Amazing Grace," the mayor, other dignitaries, and "Nearer, My God, to Thee."

The Cooperstown emissary told the considerable crowd that, year after year, Bell's presence was the highlight of the dinner for Hall members at the Otesaga Hotel. As the evenings progressed, the immortals would stand, one at a time, to share a few heartfelt words with their baseball brethren. And when Cool's turn came around, "there would be a hushed silence," Stack said. "You could hear a pin drop. Cool Papa was the dean of living Hall of Famers. And what he said had a tremendous amount of meaning. It was the sermon of the evening, the inspiration and mood-setting for that whole weekend, when Cool Papa would rise to speak to this fraternity."

Bell's Negro League confederates were scarce, of course. Satchel Paige had died in 1982, Willie Wells and Judy Johnson in 1989, Mule Suttles back in 1966, Bullet Joe Rogan in 1967, Leroy Matlock in 1968, Willie Foster in 1978, Turkey Stearnes in 1979, Oscar Charleston long ago, and Josh Gibson, of course, even longer.

But Lester Lockett, who had so often come calling from Chicago with Double Duty Radcliffe, called on Bell once more, bearing a statement from the Negro League Baseball Players Association. "If it weren't for the demons of time," Lockett read, "you'd still be running like the wind. Now, you are the wind that freshens the spring, that cools off the dog days."

Willie Mays sent flowers.

And Lou Brock stole home.

He spoke of meeting Cool Papa that day when Brock was at Busch Stadium as a young Chicago Cub. As a rule, he pointed out, he wouldn't walk up to a fan hailing him from the fence rail, but there was something about that slender, impeccably attired ramrod gentleman asking him politely for a word. Something harmless. Something compelling.

Something special. James Bell, he knew even then, was "an invisible man who played in an invisible time.

"To his grave," said Brock, "goes a whole chapter in the black history of baseball—in black history, period.

"His dream got deferred. I just hope that, somewhere in history, his performance gets accurately recorded."

MORE THAN A QUARTER CENTURY LATER, IT appears that Lou Brock's desire for Cool Papa—that his "performance gets accurately recorded"—was probably a bit fanciful. Even if Bell's steals and bunt singles and wing-footed acts of trickery could be archaeologically disinterred and painstakingly reassembled, their authenticity would be called into question for the very accident of provenance. Standards of competition, uniformity, and all that.

Anyway, there's nowhere to dig. Cool's pal, Tweed Webb, in some ways the final word in Negro League study—SABR's Negro Leagues Research Committee now confers a lifetime achievement award in his name every year—had perhaps the final word on the credibility of blackball statistics when he lamented, in an oral history interview for the University of Missouri–St. Louis, "I hate to say it, but the records of black baseball are inadequate. In many cases, the true statistics just don't exist. It's hearsay. Anybody that's got any sense knows there's nothing to prove it."

The accurate recording of Cool Papa's *life* is a proposition nearly as futile, although its essence, much as the legend paints his baseball persona, comes through in a portfolio of kindness, sensitivity, selfless-ness, humility, merit, morality, conscience, devotion, and unflagging grace. And thereby, while Bell's career and daily particulars still defy exhaustive cataloguing, Brock's wish, in spirit, has not fallen flat. In America's tapestry, a noble black man, loosely flanneled, wheels around the bases at the speed of fluorescent light in a cheap hotel. Bell's historical standing, if not comprehensively specified, has at least been conceded.

For that, much credit goes to Connie Brooks. Whatever the agenda, Cool Papa's self-appointed daughter was devoted to the great Negro Leaguer's legacy—fierce, in fact, about its magnification—long after his passing.

She was especially relentless about seeing Bell properly recog-nized in Mississippi, which seemed scarcely cognizant of the connec-tion even though it put the state in Cooperstown. Brooks's energy was rewarded in 1994 when city officials in Jackson renamed the street approaching Smith-Wills Stadium, home to the local minor-league team, as James (Cool Papa) Bell Drive. The following year, on the same site, the native son was belatedly inducted into the Mississippi Sports Hall of Fame. Brooks, though, was not entirely mollified. In a letter to the Baseball Hall of Fame, she pointed out that the Mississippi shrine nevertheless declined—"refuses" was the word she used—to include the new street address on its stationery.

Five years after Cool Papa was put to rest, Brooks, still not rest-ful, designed and paid for a ten-foot memorial of African granite, lav-ishly inscribed, to be placed on his grave site at St. Peter's Cemetery in Normandy, a northern suburb of St. Louis. The monument was dedicated on James "Cool Papa" Bell Day in Missouri, as declared by the governor.

It was her proactivity, also, that put Bell's batting stance and smil-ing face on the front and back of a Wheaties box in 1996. On a lark one morning, with the Breakfast of Champions on the table, Effa Manley's niece had fetched a photo of Pop and pasted it onto the cardboard for a mockup. She then pitched the idea to General Mills, which added pictures of Satchel Paige and Josh Gibson beside him, stuffed the boxes with flakes, and placed them on grocery shelves.

While Brooks pressed on as Papa's volunteer publicist, his overdue commemoration in Starkville was engineered without her persuasion. Brother Rogers, a Mississippi public service professional who had his hand in various regional heritage initiatives, was with a group touring the new Negro Leagues Baseball Museum in Kansas City as they came upon the striking centerpiece display, featuring a statue of a transcendent blackballer at every position on a miniature field. When the other visitors noted Bell in the outfield and read that he hailed from Starkville, they assumed that Rogers would have much to add. He was startled and embarrassed. The local authority had no idea that his town had produced a player of Cool Papa's repute.

For Rogers, the ignorance was too close to home to go unremedied. Cool Papa Bell Day in Starkville was set for 1999, complete with the placement of a historical marker at the McKee Park ballfields—a few miles from the old Nichols home behind Ebenezer Baptist Church—and the surrender of yet another street name in deference to Cool Papa's. Special guests included the usual dignitaries, extended family members, Buck O'Neil, and Mississippi author Willie Morris, who died later that month. Rick Cleveland covered the festivities for the *Jackson Clarion-Ledger* and heard Morris say, "I just wish I could have seen Cool Papa run once."

"I wish you could have, too," O'Neil replied.

The banquet that night was held on the campus of Mississippi State University, where at the age of fourteen James Nichols had occasionally stood in for Professor Brown and taken temporary charge of the cotton and corn class. Subsequently, a Bell exhibit was installed at the Oktibbeha County Heritage Museum, where he shares the spotlight with Hall of Famers from football and basketball, Jerry Rice and Bailey Howell, respectively.

And on it went. In 2006, Bell and six other Negro League luminaries who coursed through Pittsburgh—Oscar Charleston, Satchel

Paige, Josh Gibson, Judy Johnson, Buck Leonard, and Smokey Joe Williams—were commemorated with bronze statues in the Legacy Square segment of PNC Park, home of the Pittsburgh Pirates. Nine years later, however, the monuments were controversially removed for the purported reason that Legacy Square's popularity had left other areas of the lovely stadium neglected in comparison. They were ticketed for destruction, saved at the last moment by the Josh Gibson Foundation, and sold at auction for a quarter of a million dollars. Four of them—Gibson, Charleston, Leonard, and Bell—were purchased by a Los Angeles sports museum for $132,250.

But of all his posthumous honors, it seems intuitive that the one Cool Papa would most cherish is the statue the Cardinals erected for him at Busch Stadium in 2002. The Pittsburgh memorial was collective and ultimately undone. Mississippi, while dear to him for mother and memories, is a place he purposefully vacated as a young man. The St. Louis statue, on the other hand, much like his plaque in Cooperstown, testifies to the cultural passage that Bell pursued as a player and finally caught up with as a legend. On the Busch plaza, Cool Papa keeps company with men who played in front of bigger crowds for more money and greater renown. They were men with whom he identified, nevertheless, as peers—Stan Musial, Rogers Hornsby, Dizzy Dean, Bob Gibson, Lou Brock.

Bell is captured in a running position with his right knee raised and bent, his hands pushing in that direction, his left foot pressing down on the inside corner of the base—the idiosyncratic custom of his that he called to the attention of umpires—and his weight collecting at his left hip as if he's about to turn. For this aspect, sculptor Harry Weber was informed by Jerry Vickery, curator at the St. Louis Sports Hall of Fame (a short-lived precursor to the current institution with the same name). Vickery had met Bell in the process of adding the quintessential Negro Leaguer's likeness to the wall of baseball Hall of Famers at the stadium, where the shrine was quartered.

"When I went to his house," he recalled, "I knocked on the door, he told me to come on in, and one of the first things he said was 'Don't pay attention to my wife. She curses.' Clara was in the other room and yelled back, 'Shut up, old man.' Over the next month and a half, I went there on a pretty regular basis. What I found interesting was that he talked about everything like he'd had the greatest life. None of the bad things that happened to him ever came out. He'd laugh until I'm sure he forgot what he was laughing at."

In that time Vickery came to know Bell so well, and was so confident in the perception he took away, that he was emboldened to impart some pressing advice to the accomplished sculptor. "Harry Weber had Cool Papa standing straight up going through first base. I said, 'Harry, you have to change that. Cool Papa would

On the Busch Stadium plaza, it appears that the ball has been hit down the right-field line and Cool Papa, characteristically cutting the inside corner of first base with his left foot, is thinking triple, maybe more.

almost never just run through first base. He was always thinking about second.'"

CONNIE BROOKS TOOK a keen interest in a Hollywood screenplay about Cool Papa that was written but never produced. Her last public intervention on Bell's theoretical behalf involved a legal dispute with Topps, the prominent publisher of baseball cards.

In 2001 the company issued a special Bell card that addressed the derivation of his iconic nickname, claiming that he earned it "after falling asleep right before a game." Brooks took umbrage at that characterization and sued Topps over what she described in court documents as a "bogus, painful lie." As a source of its information, Topps cited a book titled *Players of Cooperstown: Baseball's Hall of Fame* by baseball historian David Nemec and others.

"In his life, he did not smoke or drink," Brooks told the *New York Sun*, implying that the card insinuated otherwise. "But they take a Negro Leaguer and think it's okay to make him a little buffoonish, a little clownish, and suggest that he's nodding off. That's an insult to a man's legacy."

Among her demands were the destruction of all the offending cards and a short, accurate bio of Bell, accompanied by a photo, placed by Topps in six newspapers or magazines every Sunday for six years, a period matching the duration the cards were in print. Her argument, however, did not compel the district judge, and a settlement was ultimately reached. The terms were not disclosed, although Brooks had earlier declined an offer of $35,000.

If nothing else, the case manifested the mystique of one of sport's most evocative nicknames. "My name happened to stay alive," Bell once said, "because it's Cool Papa Bell. If you say James Bell, people wouldn't know who you're talking about. Like Satchel Paige. If you would say Leroy Paige, people wouldn't know who you're talking about."

The effect, in fact, has resonated far beyond the point of mere recognition. Bell was fortunate in that respect, the recipient of a copious gift. His speed and grace having been shaded on baseball's back roads, something else was needed to promulgate Cool Papa's narrative. The name itself took up the task. In time it was even set to music by Paul Simon: *"Meet Dr. Well, Well, Well, / And Cool Papa Bell / The fastest man on Earth did dwell / As Cool Papa Bell."*

James Nichols's lyrical sobriquet has also made its way into a few movies and at least one novel, not counting the fictional Cool Papa Blue character in William Brashler's book *The Bingo Long Traveling All-Stars & Motor Kings*. And on a less public level it came up time and again beginning late in 2013—the year lightning struck Bell's old house, burning down the last one still standing on that side of Cool Papa Bell Avenue—when the Cincinnati Reds called up a promising young player named Billy Hamilton.

Like Bell, Hamilton was a switch-hitting center fielder from a small town in eastern Mississippi with speed so extraordinary it could spin a game off its customary orbit. And, like Bell, Hamilton delighted in the ruckus his velocity could raise, deriving irrepressible joy in seeing how far he could push it in the interest of an extra base or possibly two if someone on the other side lost his bearings or took his precautions too lightly. The Reds were the team I watched on a regular basis, and when Hamilton outraced a fly ball to the wall, I could imagine Bell at full throttle on a fenceless field in Nebraska, where the bus had stopped on a weekday. When Hamilton tapped back to the mound, I could nearly hear the opponents screaming, as Cool Papa's often did to their pitcher, "Hurry up!" When Hamilton scored from first base on a soft single, I could appreciate the astonishment of the major leaguers when Bell did the same to them in an exhibition game. When Hamilton forced a wild pickoff throw or a misplay from a panicky infielder, I could glimpse, if only for a fleeting moment, what it must have been like to witness Cool Papa play baseball in his heyday.

But Billy Hamilton's motor didn't come with a manual, and the parallels with Papa veered off at charming Billy's batting and bunting, both of which left much to be desired. His here-to-there was so frightening that third basemen, unpersuaded by the speedster's inability to lay one down, moved in to defend against a bunt anyhow, which begged for a ball to be slapped through the infield in their general direction. But that, too, was a talent alien to Hamilton, who might not have been taught it. He certainly hadn't been inspired by the game-changing brand of bunting and slapping that was Rube Foster's prototype of tricky ball. And he hadn't seen Cool Papa Bell. He hadn't seen what it looks like to marry that outrageous speed with all that's required—the will, the technique, the gamesmanship, and of course the artful bat—to put it to full, sustainable, spectacular effect.

But then, few if any of us have. To an extent regrettably and irreversibly significant, a fair amount of imagining is still required to complete the profile of the player presumed, or at least anecdotally acknowledged, to be the national pastime's fastest ever. It's all he asks of us.

Should one choose to comply in that regard, and if, in so doing, you were to imagine him as not only a supercharged Negro Leaguer but also as a singular, consequential, game-changing *major* leaguer, you would then have something in common with the lovely man they called Cool Papa.

ACKNOWLEDGMENTS

N EGRO LEAGUE RESEARCHERS ARE A GENER-
ous lot. Devoted to the further enlightenment of the collective Cool Papa Bells, they share their work. And regarding
Cool Papa specifically—understanding that he, perhaps more than any
other figure of his standing, resonance, and compelling charms, has
been left in the dark for far too long—they tend to share beyond the call.

So it was that Larry Lester, the de facto chairman of all things
Negro League, selflessly volunteered his files, his game logs, his record-
ings, his contacts, and his personal encounters.

Gary Ashwill, a methodical researcher whose findings are published in Seamheads.com and *Agate Type,* kindly shared his uncommon knowledge of Cool Papa's family and baseball beginnings.

Marc Lancaster, a friend and former colleague at the erstwhile
Cincinnati Post—whose active interest in Bell had been unknown
to me—surprisingly shipped over his catalog of pertinent clippings.

The Baseball Hall of Fame was swift and prolific with assistance.
Jessica Perkins Smith at the Mississippi State University Libraries
was attentive and helpful, as were Bill Blackwell of the Mississippi

Sports Hall of Fame and his predecessor, Rick Cleveland, also a former sports columnist at the *Jackson Clarion-Ledger.* Brother Rogers of the Mississippi Department of Archives and History was a gracious and important source. The Missouri Historical Society was wonderful.

Thanks go out to Tom Shieber, senior curator at the National Baseball Hall of Fame, and Dr. Raymond Doswell, curator of the Negro Leagues Museum in Kansas City. Chuck Bolton, who had spent considerable time gathering biographical material on Cool Papa, didn't hesitate to help me out. Jim Overmyer and Bryan Steverson provided useful insights. In his marvelous subscription series, *Pages from Baseball's Past,* baseball writer and historian Craig Wright published a perceptive Cool Papa profile that rekindled my fascination with the noble outfielder, then followed it with sound advice as usual.

I'm beholden, also, to such friends of Bell's as Barry Krizan, Dave Jackson, Jerry Vickery, and Martin Matthews, all from greater St. Louis, and broadcaster George Grande, like Cool a longtime fixture in Cooperstown. Norman Seay, Cool Papa's nephew in St. Louis, and Lisa Bell Hart, his niece in Starkville, assisted me in sorting through family matters. Ken Webb, another nephew, contributed in that way as well, and also with his professional perspective. Roger Webb is no relation to Bell or Ken Webb but is the son of the eminent blackball historian Tweed Webb, Cool's best friend and greatest advocate. Roger's support was much appreciated.

Dennis Tuttle, my friend and sounding board, played a role in guiding this project. And the esteemed John Baskin, my friend and champion—who knows little about the Negro Leagues but quite a lot about bookmanship—did me the considerable honor of assessing every last sentence along the way.

My astute and longtime agent, David Black, came through in the clutch, hooking me up with Jamison Stoltz of Abrams Press. Every writer should be so fortunate as to find an editor like Jamison who, in addition to being engaged and almost always right, simply gets it.

And, of course, there's my matchless wife, Martie, who never once questioned me about spending well over a year on a book with no commercial prospects yet in sight.

Books

Bak, Richard. *Turkey Stearnes and the Detroit Stars.* Detroit: Wayne State University Press, 1994.

Baker, Jean-Claude, and Chris Chase. *Josephine: The Hungry Heart.* New York: Cooper Square Press, 2001.

Bankes, James. *The Pittsburgh Crawfords.* Dubuque, Iowa: William C. Brown, 1991.

Banks, Ernie, and Jim Enright. *Mr. Cub.* Chicago: Follett Publishing, 1971.

Beer, Jeremy. *Oscar Charleston.* Lincoln: University of Nebraska Press, 2019.

Biddle, Dennis. *Secrets of the Negro Baseball League.* Charleston, South Carolina: BookSurge, 2005.

Brashler, William. *The Bingo Long Traveling All-Stars & Motor Kings.* New York: Harper & Row, 1973.

Brock, Lou, and Franz Schulze. *Stealing Is My Game.* Englewood Cliffs, New Jersey: Prentice-Hall, 1976.

Dixon, Phil, with Patrick J. Hannigan. *The Negro Baseball Leagues: A Photographic History.* Mattituck, New York: Amereon House, 1992.

Fields, Wilmer. *My Life in the Negro Leagues.* McLean, Virginia: Miniver Press, 2013.

Freedman, Lew. *African American Pioneers of Baseball.* Westport, Connecticut: Greenwood Press, 2007.

Gay, Timothy. *Satch, Dizzy & Rapid Robert.* New York: Simon & Schuster, 2010.

Hauser, Christopher. *The Negro Leagues Chronology.* Jefferson, North Carolina: McFarland, 2006.

Hogan, Lawrence. *Shades of Glory.* Washington, D.C.: National Geographic, 2006.

Holley, Joe. *Slingin' Sam.* Austin: University of Texas Press, 2012.

Holway, John. *Blackball Stars.* Westport, Connecticut: Meckler Books, 1988.

——. *The Complete Book of Baseball's Negro Leagues.* Fern Park, Florida: Hastings House Publishers, 2001.

——. *Josh and Satch.* New York: Carroll & Graf, 1991.

——. *Voices from the Great Black Baseball Leagues.* New York: Dodd, Mead, 1975.

Honig, Donald. *Baseball When the Grass Was Real.* Lincoln: University of Nebraska Press, 1975.

Kelley, Brent. *The Negro Leagues Revisited.* Jefferson, North Carolina: McFarland, 2000.

——. *Voices from the Negro Leagues.* Jefferson, North Carolina: McFarland, 1998.

Klein, Alan M. *Baseball on the Border.* Princeton, New Jersey: Princeton University Press, 1997.

Lanctot, Neil. *Campy.* New York: Simon & Schuster, 2011.

——. *Negro League Baseball.* Philadelphia: University of Pennsylvania Press, 2004.

Lester, Larry. *Black Baseball's National Showcase.* Lincoln: University of Nebraska Press, 2001.

——. *Rube Foster in His Time.* Jefferson, North Carolina: McFarland, 2012.

Luke, Bob. *Willie Wells.* Austin: University of Texas Press, 2007.

McBride, James. *The Good Lord Bird.* New York: Riverhead Books, 2013.

McCormack, Shaun. *Cool Papa Bell.* New York: Rosen Publishing, 2002.

McNeil, William F. *The California Winter League.* Jefferson, North Carolina: McFarland, 2002.

——. *Cool Papas and Double Duties.* Jefferson, North Carolina: McFarland, 2001.

Overmyer, James. *Queen of the Negro Leagues: Effa Manley and the Newark Eagles.* Lanham, Maryland: Scarecrow Press, 1998.

Peterson, Robert. *Only the Ball Was White.* New York: McGraw-Hill, 1970.

Reisler, Jim. *Black Writers/Black Baseball.* Jefferson, North Carolina: McFarland, 1994.

Ribowsky, Mark. *Don't Look Back.* New York: Simon & Schuster, 1994.

——. *The Power and the Darkness.* New York: Simon & Schuster, 1996.

Riley, James A. *The Biographical Encyclopedia of the Negro Baseball Leagues.* New York: Carroll & Graf, 1994.

——. "Bell, James Thomas (Cool Papa)," *The Biographical Encyclopedia of the Negro Baseball Leagues,* 72–74. New York: Carroll & Graf, 1994.

——. *Dandy, Day, and the Devil.* Cocoa, Florida: TK Publishers, 1987.

Rogosin, Donn. *Invisible Men.* Lincoln: University of Nebraska Press, 1983.

Rust, Art. *Get That Nigger off the Field.* Los Angeles: Shadow Lawn Press, 1992.

Sanford, Jay. *The Denver Post Tournament.* Cleveland: Society for American Baseball Research, 2003.

Schilling, Peter, Jr. *The End of Baseball.* Chicago: Ivan R. Dee, 2008.

Smith, Averell. *The Pitcher and the Dictator.* Lincoln: University of Nebraska Press, 2018.

Smith, Curt. *America's Dizzy Dean*. St. Louis: Bethany Press, 1978.

Snyder, Brad. *Beyond the Shadow of the Senators*. New York: McGraw-Hill, 2003.

Trouppe, Quincy. *20 Years Too Soon*. Los Angeles: S and S Enterprises, 1977.

Tye, Larry. *Satchel*. New York: Random House, 2009.

Veeck, Bill, with Ed Linn. *Veeck—As in Wreck*. New York: Ballantine Books, 1962.

Virtue, John. *South of the Color Barrier*. Jefferson, North Carolina: McFarland, 2008.

White, Sol. *Sol White's History of Colored Base Ball*. Lincoln: University of Nebraska Press, 1995.

Winegardner, Mark. *The Veracruz Blues*. New York: Viking, 1996.

Wolf, Gregory, editor. *Sportsman's Park in St. Louis*. Phoenix: Society for American Baseball Research, 2017.

Woodward, C. Vann. *The Strange Career of Jim Crow*. London: Oxford University Press, 1974.

Newspapers and Periodicals

Abrams, Al. "10,350 See Grays Defeat Monarchs in Night Game," *Pittsburgh Post-Gazette*, June 24, 1943.

———. "Conversation Pieces," *Pittsburgh Post-Gazette*, January 26, 1976.

Anderson, Dave. "An Honor, Not a Thrill, for Cool Papa," *New York Times*, February 14, 1974.

Baker, Lee. "Cool Papa, 5 Others Sprint into State Shrine," *Jackson Clarion-Ledger*, August 20, 1994.

Baltimore Afro-American, 1933–1943.

Baltimore Afro-American. "Big League Scouts May Watch East-West Classic," August 8, 1942.

———. "NNL Clubs Must Return Nine Players," June 12, 1943.

Bankes, Jim, and Mary Sue Zeeck. "Travelin' Man," *St. Louis Magazine*, August 1982.

Belson, Ken. "Apples for a Nickel, and Plenty of Empty Seats," *New York Times*, January 6, 2009.

Black Sports Magazine. "Aaron's the Coolest," June 1974.

Bogage, Jacob. "Washington's Last World Series Team Was Not the Senators. It Was a Negro League Dynasty," *Washington Post,* October 25, 2019.

Brandon, Karen. "The Value of Cool Papa's Legend," *Kansas City Star,* July 22, 1990.

Branham, Leo. "Moberly Shoe Shiner Shines on the Baseball Diamond as One of Negro League Best Pitchers," *Moberly (MO) Monitor-Index,* December 9, 1931.

Broeg, Bob. "Cool Papa—A Genuine Speed Merchant," *Sporting News,* May 26, 1973.

———. "Fast? Cool Papa Could Score from First on a Bunt," *St. Louis Post-Dispatch,* February 13, 1974.

———. "Cool Papa Bell—A Living Legend," *Sporting News,* February 23, 1974.

———. "Cool Papa Steams Up for Hall of Fame Induction," *St. Louis Post-Dispatch,* August 9, 1974.

———. "A Day in Yankee Country," *St. Louis Post-Dispatch,* August 13, 1974.

———. "Slide Secret to Brock's Climb," *Sporting News,* August 24, 1974.

———. "Switch-Hitter Charleston Without Peer in His Day," *St. Louis Post-Dispatch,* August 9, 1976.

———. "Cool Papa to Swell with Pride as Ernie Enters Shrine," *St. Louis Post-Dispatch,* August 7, 1977.

———. " 'Cool Papa' Bell Asks Hall to Give 'Devil' His Due," *St. Louis Post-Dispatch,* January 25, 1989.

———. "Above It All: 'Cool Papa' a Rare Presence," *St. Louis Post-Dispatch,* March 9, 1991.

———. " 'Cool Papa' Bell Big Man on Field and in Granite," *St. Louis Post-Dispatch,* July 28, 1996.

Brown, Dave. "Just How Good Are Race Ball Players?," *Chicago Defender,* September 12, 1936.

Bryant, Tim. " 'Cool Papa' Case Jury Hears Tape," *St. Louis Post-Dispatch,* July 26, 1990.

——. "U.S. Drops 'Cool Papa' Case," *St. Louis Post-Dispatch*, November 22, 1990.

Callahan, Tom. "Cool Papa Bell Was So Fast That Only Time Ever Caught Him," *Washington Post*, March 11, 1991.

Cavanaugh, Jack. "Placing Ballparks in the Sweep of History," *New York Times*, October 3, 1993.

Chass, Murray. "Campanella Recalls Negro League Days," *New York Times*, August 3, 1969.

Chicago Defender. "Giants' Recruits Work Hard," April 5, 1919.

Chicago Defender. "St. Louis Stars Win, 9–1," May 6, 1922.

Chicago Defender. "20,000 See West Beat East in Baseball 'Game of Games,'" September 16, 1933.

Chicago Defender. "Expect 30,000 at All-Star Game Sunday," August 10, 1935.

Chicago Defender. "American Giants and Baltimore Grays Split," July 18, 1942.

Chicago Defender. "Posey to Demand Baseball Commissioner," June 12, 1943.

Chicago Defender. "B. B. Martin Wants Bell as Manager," February 3, 1945.

Chicago Defender. "'Duo' Honored by Old Pros," June 19, 1975.

Clark, John L. "Baseball Commissioner Would Balance Payroll, Protect Owners, Players, Says," *Pittsburgh Courier*, December 24, 1932.

——. "Wylie Avenue," *Pittsburgh Courier*, May 13, 1933.

Clark, William E. "Dizzy Dean's Major Leaguers Take Double-Header from the Colored All-Stars at Stadium," *New York Age*, October 19, 1935.

Clay, William. "Normal 'Tweed' Webb," *Congressional Record*, July 9, 1975.

Cleveland, Rick. "Cool Papa's Roots: Starkville Honors Its Native Legend," *Jackson Clarion-Ledger*, May 11, 1999.

Cole, Haskell. "Grays Beat Philly and Tie Cubans," *Pittsburgh Courier*, September 28, 1946.

Cordaro, Tony. "Major League Stars Beaten," *Des Moines Register*, October 3, 1936.

Detroit Free Press. "Stars Lose in Tenth," June 27, 1922.

Dial, Lewis. "The Sport Dial," *New York Age,* October 19, 1935.

Dine, Philip. "Two Charged in Theft Here from 'Legend,'" *St. Louis Post-Dispatch,* April 7, 1990.

Dismukes, Dizzy. "Dismukes Names His 9 Best Outfielders," *Pittsburgh Courier,* March 8, 1930.

———. "Dizzy's Dope on Baseball," *Pittsburgh Courier,* March 19, 1932.

Donovan, Dan. "At 80, Papa Bell Has Cool Outlook," *Pittsburgh Press,* July 3, 1983.

Down, Fred. "Cool Papa's Road to Hall of Fame Perhaps Was Hardest of All," *Baltimore Afro-American* (United Press International), August 24, 1974.

Durso, Joseph. "Baseball to Admit Negro Stars of Pre-Integration Era into Hall of Fame," *New York Times,* February 4, 1971.

———. "Mick, Slick, and Cool Papa," *New York Times,* August 13, 1974.

Ebony. "Whatever Happened to . . . 'Cool Papa' Bell?," March 1974.

Eisenbath, Mike. "St. Louis Was a City of Champions for Negro National Leaguers, Too," *St. Louis Post-Dispatch,* July 4, 1997.

Evans, E. S. "Street Names Come and Go Briskly," *St. Louis Post-Dispatch,* October 8, 1984.

Evans, Howie. "The Militant Side of Cool Papa Bell," *New York Amsterdam News,* June 3, 1984.

Fallstrom, R. B. "James 'Cool Papa' Bell Takes Things as They Come," Associated Press, February 10, 1990.

Feldman, Jay. "Tweed Webb: 'He's Seen 'Em All,'" *Baseball Research Journal,* 1989.

Fink, David. "Cool Papa: He Rings a Bell for Nostalgia," *Pittsburgh Post-Gazette,* January 26, 1976.

Fort Wayne Journal-Gazette. "Local Giants Lose to St. Louis Stars," May 13, 1922.

Gallas, Bob. "Old and New All-Stars Meet at Comiskey," *Daily Herald* (Arlington Heights, IL), July 6, 1983.

Gilmore, Richard, Jr. "A Historical Look at the Pittsburgh Crawfords and the Impact of Black Baseball on American Society," *Sloping*

Halls Review Journals, Carnegie Mellon University Research Showcase, 1996.

Goldstein, Joseph. "What's in a Name? For James Bell, It's a Baseball Lawsuit," *New York Sun,* October 24, 2006.

Gregorian, Vahe. "Belated Respect," *St. Louis Post-Dispatch,* March 17, 1991.

Gurley, Earl. "My Pitching Experience," *California Eagle,* February 13, 20, and 27, 1925.

Haraway, Frank. "Garver Junketeers Find Colorado Cool," *Sporting News,* October 20, 1954.

Hardwick, Leon. "Here Are 20 Who Could Make Big League Grade," *Baltimore Afro-American,* February 12, 1938.

Harris, Peter. "Sportsoul Attends Black Baseball Reunion," *Baltimore Afro-American,* July 4, 1981.

Helena Independent Record. "Smelterites Will Play Monarchs at East Helena," July 31, 1949.

———. "Kansas City Monarchs Will Play Mountaineers at East Helena Park," July 11, 1950.

Henderson, Morris. "Efforts Underway to Organize Caravan to Cheer 'Cool Papa' into Hall of Fame," *St. Louis Argus,* February 21, 1974.

Holway, John. "How to Score from First on a Sacrifice," *American Heritage,* August 1970.

———. "Shutting the Door on Negro League Stars," *New York Times,* July 31, 1977.

Hughey, Robert, "'Candy Jim' Taylor, New Pilot of Grays, One of Baseball's Greats," *Pittsburgh Courier,* April 24, 1943.

Hummel, Rick. "Wide-Eyed Willie Meets Heroes," *St. Louis Post-Dispatch,* July 6, 1983.

Indianapolis Star. "A.B.C.s Win Again, 11–5," May 10, 1922.

Jackson, H. J. "200 Well-Wishers Honor Bell on His Home Street," *St. Louis Post-Dispatch,* September 27, 1987.

Jackson, Harold. "On the Sports Front," *Baltimore Afro-American,* August 7, 1943.

———. "Gibson and Suttles Hit Long Home Runs," *Baltimore Afro-American,* August 14, 1943.

Jet. "Jackson, MS, Names Street for (Cool Papa) Bell, 'Fastest Man Ever to Play Baseball,'" July 25, 1994.

Jones, Landon. "Another St. Louis Summer," *New Yorker*, August 22, 2014.

Jordan, David M., Larry R. Gerlach, and John P. Rossi. "A Baseball Myth Exploded," *National Pastime*, 1998.

Kaegel, Dick. "He's a Real Thief: Lou! Lou! Lou!" *St. Louis Post-Dispatch*, September 11, 1974.

Kee, Lorraine. "Final Tribute: Woman Works to Get Headstone for Cool Papa," *St. Louis Post-Dispatch*, April 27, 1994.

——. "'Tweed' Webb Helped Make Negro Leagues Fashionable," *St. Louis Post-Dispatch*, April 29, 1995.

Kirkland, Kevin. "Greenlee Field Site Earns Place in History," *Pittsburgh Post-Gazette*, July 17, 2009.

Kram, Mark. "No Place in the Shade," *Sports Illustrated*, August 20, 1973.

Kurtz, Paul. "Grays Sign Veteran Star Outfielder," *Pittsburgh Press*, April 24, 1943.

Lacy, Sam. "I Just Couldn't Do the Job, Friends," *Baltimore Afro-American*, February 16, 1974.

——. "'Cool Papa' Excellent Hall of Fame Choice," *Baltimore Afro-American*, February 23, 1974.

Lamb, Richard J. "Gus 'Whereas-es' Diplomats into Action over Foreign Raid on Negro Ball Team," *Pittsburgh Press*, June 20, 1937.

Lardner, Rex. "A League with Two Strikes on It," *New York Times*, July 12, 1970.

Lattman, Peter. "Cool Papa's Daughter Sues Topps over Daddy's Baseball Card," *Wall Street Journal*, October 25, 2006.

Leonard, Buck, with John Holway. "Lost Stars in Baseball's Firmament," *Washington Star*, August 30, 1970.

Lethbridge (Alberta) Herald, 1945–1950.

Lipman, Dave. "This Was Cool Papa: Better Paid Than Satch, Faster Than Owens," *St. Louis Post-Dispatch*, March 3, 1963.

Los Angeles Times. "Royal Giants to Open Winter Loop Saturday," October 11, 1934.

Lundy, Dick. "Dick's Diamond Dope," *Baltimore Afro-American*, March 26, 1932.

McSkimming, Dent. "St. Louis Negro Pitcher a 'Big Leaguer' in Mexico," *St. Louis Post-Dispatch*, February 16, 1941.

Medlin, Jarrett. "North Side Story: A Brief History of the Near North Side," *St. Louis Magazine*, October 27, 2009.

Moberly (MO) Monitor-Index. "Negro Stars Play Moberly Tonight," August 4, 1931.

Morrison, Robert. "The Chocolate Rube Waddell," *St. Louis Post-Dispatch*, June 30, 1941.

Murray, Jim. "Move Over, Satchel," *Los Angeles Times*, August 12, 1971.

New York Age, 1933–1935.

New York Times. "U.S. Negro League Is Launched with Brown Dodgers in Brooklyn," May 8, 1945.

Nunn, William. "And the Color Will Be Black," *Pittsburgh Courier*, February 25, 1933.

———. "West's Satellites Eclipse Stars of the East in Classic," *Pittsburgh Courier*, September 16, 1933.

———. "Plucky Nashville Team Loses Three Thrillers to Craws," *Pittsburgh Courier*, October 7, 1933.

———. "Sport Talks," *Pittsburgh Courier*, September 22, 1934.

———. "Satchell Paige Is Magnet at E-W Game; Players of Big League Calibre Perform," *Pittsburgh Courier*, August 29, 1936.

O'Neill, Brian. "Statues Honoring Negro Leagues Gone from PNC Park Entrance," *Pittsburgh Post-Gazette*, July 30, 2015.

Paige, Satchel. "Paige Says He Prefers Jungles to N.N.L. Play," *Baltimore Afro-American*, July 31, 1937.

Parish, Norm. "Neighbors Hope New High School Spurs Redevelopment," *St. Louis Post-Dispatch*, November 12, 1999.

Pearson, Richard. "James 'Cool Papa' Bell, Baseball Legend, Dies," *Washington Post*, March 9, 1991.

Pedulla, Tom. "Negro League Stars Grace Wheaties Box," *USA Today*, February 21, 1996.

Pierce, Charles. "Thieves of Time," *National Sports Daily*, May 10, 1990.

Pittsburgh Courier, 1929–1949.

——. "Bright Hair Wins Says Popular Star," November 23, 1929.

——. "Vic Harris Helps Phila. Giants Win," December 5, 1931.

——. "Team Hits Stride on Invasion of Dixie," April 15, 1933.

——. "Crawfords Cop Hot Series from Detroit Stars," June 24, 1933.

——. "Babe Ruth Lauds Negro Players," August 19, 1933.

——. "Bell Bats .342 to Lead Coast Winter League," February 24, 1934.

——. "'Cool Papa' Speaks," August 11, 1934.

——. "Hunter Hurls 1-Hit Game, 'Cool Papa' Gets 6 Hits as Craws Win," April 20, 1935.

——. "Craws Win 4, Lose 2, Tie 1 in Gray Feud," July 13, 1935.

——. "Grays to Lose Josh to Island Ball Club," June 12, 1937.

——. "Barons Shutout in Game at Chi," October 2, 1943.

——. "Bell's .515 Tops Hitters," June 3, 1944.

——. "Eagles Are Topped Twice," September 8, 1945.

Pittsburgh Post-Gazette. "Four Crawfords Desert," May 20, 1937.

Pittsburgh Press, 1937–1944.

Posey, Cum. "Posey's Points," *Pittsburgh Courier*, May 29, 1943.

Povich, Shirley. "Clowning Delayed Negroes' Start in Majors," *Washington Post*, May 11, 1953.

Renfroe, Chico. "Chicago Old Timers to Honor 'Cool Papa,'" *Atlanta Daily World*, June 12, 1975.

——. "The Game of Life Is Never Over Until the Final Whistle Has Blown," *Atlanta Daily World*, August 25, 1991.

Rhoden, William C. "Cool Papa's Stolen Moments," *New York Times*, August 7, 1990.

——. "Out of the Hot, Into the Cool: A Tribute to James Bell," *New York Times*, July 4, 1994.

——. "Cool Papa Is Anointed by Wheaties," *New York Times*, February 17, 1996.

Rivas, Rebecca. "Norman Seay Is White House–bound," *St. Louis American*, December 12, 2013.

Russo, Neal. "Cool Papa Bell Ranks Among Baseball Greats," *Southeast Missourian* (originally in *Midwest Motorist*), September 21, 1974.

——. "Larcenous Lou Plotted Record Heist in '73," *Sporting News*, September 28, 1974.

Rust, Art. "James Bell: Cool Papa," *New York Amsterdam News*, June 9, 1979.

Simmons, R. S. "Speaking in General," *Atlanta Daily World*, May 6, 1942.

——. "Speaking in General," *Atlanta Daily World*, May 19, 1942.

Simmons, Grace. "Street Named for Negro League Baseball Great," *Jackson Clarion-Ledger*, May 20, 1994.

Smith, Wendell. "Brooklyn Dodgers Admit Negro Players Rate Place in Majors," *Pittsburgh Courier*, August 5, 1939.

——. "'Would Be a Mad Scramble for Negro Players if Okayed'—Hartnett," *Pittsburgh Courier*, August 12, 1939.

——. "'No Need for Color Ban in Big Leagues'—Pie Traynor," *Pittsburgh Courier*, September 2, 1939.

——. "Introducing 'El Diablo' Wells of Mexico," *Pittsburgh Courier*, May 6, 1944.

——. "Hail to the New Champions!," *Pittsburgh Courier*, September 29, 1945.

——. "The Sports Town Express!," *Pittsburgh Courier*, February 26, 1949.

Sporting News. "Satch to Hurl 'Paige Day' Kansas City Game Oct. 11," October 7, 1953.

——. "Satchel Paige to Barnstorm Against Ned Garver All-Stars," September 1, 1954.

——. "There's Been Changes—for Barnstormers," November 3, 1954.

——. "Former Stars of Negro Ball Recall Old Days at Reunion," August 5, 1959.

——. "Baseball's 100 Greatest Players," April 26, 1999.

Sports Illustrated. "A Loss for Baseball," March 18, 1991.

St. Louis American, 1974–2011.

——. "'Cool Papa' Bell Memorial," July 25, 1996.

St. Louis Argus, 1919–1926.

——. "Union Electrics to Play the Cubs Next Sunday," June 18, 1920.

——. "Cubs Win Again," October 15, 1920.

——. "Compton Hill Cubs Win Double Header," May 6, 1921.

——. "Stars Win at East St. Louis," May 5, 1922.

St. Louis Globe-Democrat. "St. Louis Stars Win from Kansas City, 3-0," June 1, 1922.

——. "Local Negroes Beat Tiger Barnstormers," October 3, 1922.

——. "Negro Team Again Beats Tigers, 11 to 7," October 4, 1922.

——. "Tigers Capture Final Game from Negroes, 10 to 3," October 5, 1922.

——. "Stars Run Winning Streak to Seven by Downing Memphis," August 30, 1927.

——. "The St. Louis Stars Are the World's Champion Negro Baseball Team," July 26, 1931.

St. Louis Post-Dispatch, 1922–2006.

——. "St. Louis Stars Open New Baseball Park," July 10, 1922.

——. "St. Louis Stars Win Final from Memphis," July 8, 1924.

——. "Negro Umpire Loses Job to White, Sues," September 20, 1925.

——. "St. Louis Stars Win from Chicago Giants," September 25, 1928.

——. "St. Louis Negro Nine Tied for World Championship," October 1, 1928.

——. "Negro World Championship Won by St. Louis Stars," October 6, 1928.

——. "Negro Pitcher So Mad He Shoots Teammate," May 31, 1929.

——. "Night Baseball Game Slated Here Tonight Between Negro Teams," May 19, 1930.

——. "St. Louis Stars Take Fourth Straight Game from Chicago, 17–3," July 1, 1930.

——. "St. Louis Stars Hope to Have Lights by End of Week," July 20, 1930.

——. "St. Louis Stars Break Even in Doubleheader," September 8, 1931.

——. "Bell's Homer Gives Stars Victory over Cardinal Farm Nine," September 25, 1931.

——. "'Old Pete' Alexander Still Draws Crowds," September 28, 1931.

——. "'Cool Papa' Bell Avenue Passed by Aldermen," January 29, 1983.

——. "Man Faces 3 Charges in Fatal Shooting," June 13, 1983.

——. "Clara Bell, 82; Wife of Baseball Great," January 22, 1991.

——. "Baseball's 'Cool Papa' Bell Dies," March 8, 1991.

St. Louis Star & Times, 1928–1942.

——. "St. Louis Stars Beat Chicago for U.S. Negro Baseball Title," October 6, 1928.

——. "Negro Stars, So Powerful They Broke Up League, May Return," May 4, 1933.

Stewart, Ollie. "San Domingo Club Pays $30,000 for Americans," *Baltimore Afro-American*, July 24, 1937.

——. "Senor Paige Is the Rage in San Domingo," *Baltimore Afro-American*, July 24, 1937.

——. "Santo Domingo Imports a Sport," *Baltimore Sun*, September 19, 1937.

Strauss, Joe. "Cardinals Report," *St. Louis Post-Dispatch*, May 19, 2002.

Thomas, Robert McG, Jr. "James (Cool Papa) Bell, 87, Dies; Legendary Star of Negro Leagues," *New York Times*, March 9, 1991.

Tygiel, Jules. "Revisiting Bill Veeck and the 1943 Phillies," *Baseball Research Journal*, 2006.

Uniontown (PA) Morning Herald. "Dizzy Dean Hurls Against Negro Team," September 1, 1943.

Vorel, Lauren. "The Great Depression: Catalyst for Change in America's Game," *Constructing the Past*, Illinois Wesleyan University, 2010.

Wartzman, Rick. "Negro League Ball Players Feted," *Wall Street Journal*, September 14, 1988.

Washington, Chester. "Suttles' Bat, Foster's Arm Help West Win," *Pittsburgh Courier*, September 16, 1933.

Washington, Chester. "Sez Ches," *Pittsburgh Courier*, September 29, 1934.

——. "Watching the Cleveland Rout," *Pittsburgh Courier*, July 7, 1935.

——. "This Wire May Give Pirate Manager Some 'Food for Thought,'" *Pittsburgh Courier*, December 11, 1937.

——. "Challenge Hurled at Pittsburgh Pirates on Sepia Players Issue," *Pittsburgh Courier*, December 11, 1937.

——. "Reflections from Wylie," December 31, 1938.

Washington Post. "Crawfords and Elite Giants Tie, 8–8," August 16, 1936.

——. "18,000 Watch Grays Blast Satch Paige," June 25, 1945.

Webb, Ken. "Cool Papa and Satchel Tell It Like It Is," *St. Louis American*, February 2, 2011.

Wheatley, Tom. "Cool Papa Lives with No Regrets," *St. Louis Post-Dispatch*, September 1, 1985.

Wheeler, Lonnie. "Memories: Foster Recalls Good Ole Days," *Jackson Clarion-Ledger*, August 14, 1977.

Wilson, W. Rollo. "Sport Shots," *Pittsburgh Courier*, July 15, 1933.

Wolf, Al. "Paige Attracts Throng of 10,800," *Los Angeles Times*, October 25, 1943.

Wray, John. "Wray's Column," *St. Louis Post-Dispatch*, October 4, 1931.

Young, Doc. "How Negro Players Saved Organized Baseball," *Chicago Defender*, April 28, 1965.

——. "An Open Letter," *Chicago Defender*, February 21, 1967.

——. "Here We Go Again," *Chicago Defender*, February 21, 1974.

——. "Rube and Others . . . ," *Chicago Defender*, May 14, 1974.

Young, Fay. "ODT Refuses Negro Clubs Use of Buses," *Chicago Defender*, April 3, 1943.

——. "Bell's Single in Eleventh Beats Barons," *Chicago Defender*, October 2, 1943.

Websites and Blogs

Ancestry.com.

Ashwill, Gary. "How Cool Papa Got His Name," *Agate Type*, July 27, 2006.

——. "The Cool Papa Conundrum," *Agate Type*, December 24, 2009.

——. "Giants Park, St. Louis 1919–1922," *Agate Type*, September 15, 2010.

——. "Cool Papa's Rookie Season," *Agate Type*, July 15, 2016.

——. "Negro League Wages," *Agate Type*, September 4, 2017.

Baseball-Reference.com.

Bell, Cool Papa, with John Holway, Frank Ceresi, and Carol McMains. "A Journey Through the Negro Leagues with Cool Papa Bell," *National Pastime Museum.*

Encyclopedia.com. "James 'Cool Papa' Bell."

Exploring St. Louis. "James 'Cool Papa' Bell and St. Louis Stars' Park," July 29, 2010.

Howard, Josh. "Disappointment in Pittsburgh: How the Pirates Ditched Pittsburgh's Negro Leagues Past," Sport in American History, USSportHistory.com, October 12, 2015.

Hoyt, Ed. "Donn Clendenon," Society for American Baseball Research, SABR.com.

Keyes, Allison. "The East St. Louis Race Riot Left Dozens Dead, Devastating a Community on the Rise," Smithsonian.com, June 30, 2017.

Lester, Larry, and Dick Clark. Game Logs, Cool Papa Bell. Negro Leagues Researchers and Authors Group, 2004.

Mandel, Ken. "Speed to Burn," MLB.com.

Mead, William B. "The Day I Rooted Against Jackie Robinson," *About Editing and Writing*, JackLimpert.com, August 6, 2014.

Missouri History Museum. "A Rare Baseball Find: Stars Park," *History Happens Here*, MOHistory.org, October 26, 2016.

Newspapers.com.

Posnanski, Joe. "Cool Papa Bell," *JoeBlogs*, JoePosnanski.com, December 3, 2013.

Revel, Dr. Layton, and Luis Munoz. "Forgotten Heroes: James Allen 'Candy Jim' Taylor," Center for Negro League Baseball Research, 2013.

Rogers, Brother. "Buck O'Neil Helps Celebrate Cool Papa Bell," BrotherRogers.com.

Rogers, Brother. "Cool Papa Bell," *Mississippi History Now*, Mississippi Historical Society, January 2008.

Seamheads.com. Negro Leagues Database.

Seamheads.com. "History of a St. Louis Baseball Franchise: The St. Louis Stars," February 27, 2018.

Society for American Baseball Research. "SABR Salute: Tweed Webb," Sabr.org.

Wartts, Adrienne, "The Ville (St. Louis, Mo.)," BlackPast.org, September 5, 2008.

Wikipedia. "Cool Papa Bell."

Wright, Craig R. "Cool Papa Bell," *Pages from Baseball's Past*, BaseballsPast.com, March 7, 2016.

Recordings, Videos, and Transcripts

Banker, Stephen, with Newt Allen, Ernie Banks, Cool Papa Bell, Roy Campanella, Judy Johnson, Dave Malarcher, and Double Duty Radcliffe. *Black Diamonds: An Oral History of Negro Baseball*. Washington, D.C.: Tapes for Readers, 1978.

Davidson, Craig (director). *There Was Always Sun Shining Someplace*. Refocus Productions, 1989.

Harville, Charles, with Cool Papa Bell. Oral history interview. Oral History Collection, Society for American Baseball Research.

Kachline, Cliff. Baseball panel discussion including Cool Papa Bell and Buddy Blattner. Recorded by Eugene Murdock. St. Louis: June 29, 1979.

Lester, Larry. Recording of Cool Papa Bell funeral service. St. Louis: March 16, 1991.

——. Recorded interview with Richard Berg. 1995.

Morgan, Chester, with James "Cool Papa" Bell. Oral history interview. Starkville, Mississippi: Mississippi Oral History Program, University of Southern Mississippi, 1974.

Morrison, Bill, with Normal "Tweed" Webb. Negro League Baseball Project. Oral History Collection, State Historical Society of Missouri, 1971.

——. Oral history interview. St. Louis: University of Missouri–St. Louis, Archive & Manuscript Division, 1974.

Roberts, Rod. Cool Papa Bell oral history interview (five segments). St. Louis: National Baseball Hall of Fame Digital Collection, September 26–27, 1981.

Shaffer, Dr. Arthur, and Dr. Charles Korr, with James "Cool Papa" Bell. Oral history interview. St. Louis: Western Historical Manuscript Collection, University of Missouri–St. Louis, 1970.

Simon, Paul. "Cool Papa Bell," *Stranger to Stranger* (album), 2016.

Tuttle, Dennis. Interview with Sammy Baugh. Rotan, Texas: November 17, 1995.

page 96: Charles L. Blockson Afro-American Collection, Temple University Libraries

page 98: National Baseball Hall of Fame Library

page 106: Photograph by Charles "Teenie" Harris, 1908–1998. © 2020 Carnegie Museum of Art, Pittsburgh

page 109: Restoration by Robert A. Flischel Photography, Cincinnati

page 115: Photograph courtesy of Negro Leagues Baseball Museum

page 119: NoirTech Research, Kansas City

page 126: Charles L. Blockson Afro-American Collection, Temple University Libraries

page 129: Photograph by Charles "Teenie" Harris, 1908–1998. © 2020 Carnegie Museum of Art, Pittsburgh

page 135: Photograph by Charles "Teenie" Harris, 1908–1998. © 2020 Carnegie Museum of Art, Pittsburgh

page 139: NoirTech Research, Kansas City

page 146: National Baseball Hall of Fame Library

page 149: National Baseball Hall of Fame Library

page 154: National Baseball Hall of Fame Library

page 173: NoirTech Research, Kansas City

page 177: NoirTech Research, Kansas City

page 184: Charles L. Blockson Afro-American Collection, Temple University Libraries

page 193: NoirTech Research, Kansas City

page 196: NoirTech Research, Kansas City

page 202: National Baseball Hall of Fame Library

page 204: NoirTech Research, Kansas City

page 214: Photograph by Charles "Teenie" Harris, 1908–1998. © 2020 Carnegie Museum of Art, Pittsburgh

page 217: NoirTech Research, Kansas City

page 226: NoirTech Research, Kansas City

page 232: NoirTech Research, Kansas City

page 245: National Baseball Hall of Fame Library

page 254: NoirTech Research, Kansas City

page 259: NoirTech Research, Kansas City

INDEX